QUAKER MILITANT
JOHN GREENLEAF WHITTIER

JOHN GREENLEAF WHITTIER
At Twenty-Two
From a miniature painted by J. S. Porter

QUAKER MILITANT
JOHN GREENLEAF WHITTIER

BY

ALBERT MORDELL

WITH ILLUSTRATIONS

BOSTON AND NEW YORK
HOUGHTON MIFFLIN COMPANY
The Riverside Press Cambridge
1933

The Riverside Press
CAMBRIDGE · MASSACHUSETTS
PRINTED IN THE U.S.A.

DEDICATED
TO
MY PARENTS

'You know my estimate of Whittier. He is my favorite among all the living poets of the age. His inspirational effusions during the Anti-Slavery Conflict, in defence of the weak against the strong, of the enslaved against the enslaver, had much to do in effecting that revolution in public sentiment which has secured to the millions in bondage freedom and citizenship.'

WILLIAM LLOYD GARRISON *to* CHARLES H. BRAINARD

(From an unpublished letter quoted in part in *The Stephen H. Wakeman Collection.*)

WHITTIER

A poem written for the unveiling of the bust of Whittier at the Hall of Fame. John G. Whittier ascended into his glory in 1892.

By Edwin Markham

He knew the nesting birds and bees,
  The long call of the whippoorwill,
The spiders busy in their trees
  On rocky pine-sweet Haverhill.

He knew the loon's call on the lake,
  The rattle of the barnyard bars,
The creek of well-poles as they break
  The quiet of the evening stars.

Yet Whittier, beauty-lover, bred
  To sow the field, to note the flower,
Turned from the paths of peace, to tread
  The darkness, mount the battle-tower.

He turned from friends and beckoning fame,
  Turned at the call of the Inner Voice:
He risked Posterity's acclaim:
  He dared the venture, dared the choice.

He flung aside his silver flute,
  Snatched up Isaiah's stormy lyre;
Loosened old angers, pent and mute;
  Startled the iron strings with fire.

The Quaker's voice grew hoarse with rage,
  His tranquil face grew strangely grave,
He towered a flame upon the age,
  The God-touched laureate of the slave.

Earth heard in him a prophet-king,
  Crying of judgment and award,
Loud-crying from the whirlwind's wing, —
  The wrath and challenge of the Lord.

He made his song a sword for truth:
  He dared to lose the world's applause.
Now hark to his ringing cry to youth:
  'Join, join, some high unfriended cause!'

CONTENTS

CONTENTS

ILLUSTRATIONS

INTRODUCTION

PROFESSOR GEORGE RICE CARPENTER, the author of the last biography of Whittier, published nearly thirty years ago, hazarded the surmise that there must 'somewhere exist very considerable bodies of letters and reminiscences that would aid us in tracing further the development of his genius.'

If Professor Carpenter were still alive, he would be amazed at the amount of available material in print and manuscript about the poet that has accumulated in the last generation. In the present volume I have endeavored to utilize and co-ordinate some of the hitherto ungathered spoils. As a result of having uncovered in my researches many important un-collected editorials and unknown poems by Whittier, I have been led to interpret him and his work in a new light. The finished portrait that evolved gives an entirely different con-ception of him from the conventional one which previous biographers have drawn. I have forced no conclusions but have let the documents speak for themselves. They revealed a strikingly new figure; the familiar Whittier we know, the modest, mild, and passionless saint, gave way to a militant and radical agitator who was charged on a number of occa-sions with blasphemy and sedition. The victim of a long-drawn-out and painful love tragedy evolved, becoming a frustrated celibate and vain philanderer. The reactionary and religionist, and the harmless genial poet of the people, finally emerged.

A complete re-examination of all his works from every angle, together with an application of literary theories, not excluding psychoanalytic and economic interpretations now accepted by various schools of modern criticism, has led me to a different appraisal of his work from that which many former literary critics have given.

Whittier, being one of the first American poets to avail himself of the vast stores of New England lore for poetic purposes, was a pioneer in the production of regional literature. Furthermore, this favorite poet of juvenile readers and composer of hymns for the elderly, was for the greater and more important period of his poetic life a stormy prophet. He was the author of poems which on account of their bold stand on free speech and their violent attacks upon the clergy are really still too dangerous to be introduced into the public schools. As a matter of fact he should be accepted by advanced critics today as a fellow spirit whose songs in the cause of freedom are still timely.

The legend of his utter innocuousness, based upon undue prominence given to some of his later poems and elaborated in academic circles and in the schoolroom, has prevented his acceptance as an important writer by our sophisticated age. One of the truly heroic radical American writers in the cause of human freedom, the first of our great poets to sacrifice a glorious future by casting in his lot with the hated abolitionists, has become the favorite only of sentimentalists, schoolchildren, and the respectable middle class. A thirty-year-old reputation which he acquired as one of the few social propagandists of American literature disappeared in the doubtful glory that finally surrounded him because of his later and more popular poems of farm life and ballads of New England history. The agitator and radical abolitionist, the trumpeter of humanitarian causes, was effaced in the aged invalid who sought rest and ultimately became resigned to the tacit acceptance of the established order. When the slaves were freed, there spread a misleading critical judgment that his antislavery poems were no longer significant and could be permitted to pass into oblivion.

Though some of Whittier's rural and legendary poems are superior in literary merit to many of his poems of freedom, the latter as a whole, in the opinion of some critics, represent his chief and most permanent contribution to American literature. These poems are no less valid than when they were first issued. For as long as men like the abolitionists of old are persecuted for freedom of speech because they agitate a course harmful to some vested interests, the battle for liberty goes on. As a matter of fact a body of poetry that, to use Whittier's own words, sets honor above profits and man above cotton can never become outdated.

If we constantly harp on the close resemblance between Whittier and the British poets Burns and Cowper, as we do, we tend to lose sight of his real significance. Whittier struck notes that Cowper and Burns never did. His earlier admirers compared him to poets like Tyrtæus, Béranger, Körner, Ebenezer Elliot, and Shelley, because by his songs he awoke the public conscience against a great injustice. The chief influence upon him was that of the great champion of English liberty, John Milton. Again and again he quoted Milton's plea in prose for the liberty of the press. How numerous and revelatory are the references to Milton in the editorials that Whittier wrote but never collected! In short, while not epic in his grandeur, Whittier was the Milton of America rather than its Burns. The failure of most critics to realize this has led to the prevailing misconceptions about him. As Whittier himself once said, Milton approached his conception of the true hero more than his Quaker favorites.

In our consideration of Whittier as a truly great American poet who was primarily a prophet and champion of liberty, we need not underestimate his ballads nor his poems depicting rural pictures and domestic scenes. I have endeavored to analyze him in his various phases. If I have dwelt upon his songs blazing with indignation at an iniquitous system, I have not failed to consider the lyrics in which he indulged in tender memories of the past. If I have shown him as the inveterate foe of a slavery-defending clergy, I have not forgotten him in his capacity as exhorter for faith and resignation. If I have detailed his various political activities as a radical, I have also emphasized the circumstances of the intellectual ossification that came with old age and made him countenance social abuses of the day, and rendered him indifferent to reforms demanded by evils arising from industrial changes.

I have devoted considerable space in this volume to an aspect of the poet's life which his fame as a poet has obliterated, namely, his political activities. As a matter of fact, politics interested him as much as poetry. He was one of the ablest and shrewdest politicians we have ever had, and he shaped the careers of several of our most important statesmen. He often exerted a powerful influence by engineering party coalitions in which he urged antislavery voters holding the balance of power to vote only for candidates favoring abolition. He really launched Caleb Cushing upon his diplomatic career, by first sending him to Congress; he gave John P. Hale of New Hampshire advice that helped send him to the Senate; he first selected Charles Sumner for Senator from Massachusetts; he sought to make Robert C. Winthrop leader of the new Republican Party, by urging him — alas, in vain — to go over altogether to the antislavery cause. Whittier wielded a trenchant pen against Edward Everett because of his sympathetic attitude towards the Southern slaveholder. On numerous occasions he violently attacked those conciliatory statesmen Henry Clay and Daniel Webster. He never sought public office for himself, except for a term in the Massachusetts legislature which he served as a young man. Only as a matter of policy, certain that he would not be elected, did he consent at different times to run for Congress and the legislature on the Liberty Party ticket.

I have, however, treated him primarily as a poet. I have endeavored to appraise his work not only from an æsthetic point of view, but from a psychological and sociological one. One should not censure Whittier, as critics often do, by overemphasizing his minor faults such as his misuse of rhymes, his limitation to few meters, and his habit of introducing a moral; nor should one panegyrize him by over-stressing such undoubted virtues as his adroitness in the portrayal of rural life, his excellence as a balladist, and his merit as a composer of consoling hymns. As a matter of fact he had more serious faults than using bad rhymes, for he not only wrote poems untrue to life, but soulless effusions in verse, some directed against scientific progress and some countenancing social abuses or suggesting feeble remedies for their cure; and he had greater virtues than being merely a rural bard, since he was a prophet whom the 'strain' 'of a higher mood' lifted into the position of a universal poet of freedom. He was an accomplished lyricist who made his own noble personality enhance the value of his poetry. He really deserves a place with Walt Whitman among our great American poets.

II

Whittier also offers a very interesting and baffling problem in sex psychology. Yet his biographers have in the main ignored this phase of his life. I have dealt at length with his love life, which was so influential upon his career and his work, and I have allowed him to speak for himself, especially in some unknown poems and letters that have come to light. In this volume I have brought together for the first time some new facts in his life. I have been able especially to disclose the most important love tragedy in his life — his relations with Mary Emerson Smith. I found that the philosophy he advanced in 'Maud Muller' and other poems, that wealth or class difference should never be a barrier to love, was an outgrowth of the circumstance that he had been discarded by her on account of his poverty.

It was his fortune or misfortune to be handsome and attractive to women; yet he refused to marry and always remained a celibate. He developed into a male coquet; and rejected several woman writers who, succumbing to his blandishments, determined to capture him as a husband. He early recognized his power over women and his own failings in his inability to respond to them. As Burns wrote against seduction but continued to practice it, so Whittier early in life wrote against male coquets, but continued to act like one for the rest of his life. Yet he was not to blame altogether for his philanderings. The woman writers of America, young and old, kept making a trail to his home — 'the pilgrims,' as he called them. They wrote letters to him, sought consolation, confided in him, and lingered on encouragement that promised nothing. Many of the letters that he received from admiring women he chivalrously destroyed. When Samuel T. Pickard published the authorized biography, some of these women were living; he therefore never even hinted that many of these so-called Platonic friendships were one-sided love affairs. But if Whittier wounded the women, he also injured himself. I refer not to the moral twinges he may also have experienced at times, but to the physical effect his abstinence and celibacy had upon him, for he suffered from headaches, nervousness, and sleeplessness. In fact, he was an invalid all his life — undoubtedly a victim of repression. Further, he hated exploiters of sensuality in literature and he railed at Walt Whitman in particular. His own poetic work, however, suffered because of the very 'purity' for which critics like Edwin Whipple commended it.

Here, then, is a problem for the psychoanalyst as baffling as that which biographers have found in Herman Melville and Emily Dickinson. How should we account for the fact that a man whose 'passions strove in chains,' as he wrote, 'beneath his aspect grave' philandered all his life with beautiful women writers, almost any one of whom he could have married and never did? It is also interesting to note that, though in two or three poems he even condoned illicit love, he retained his chastity until he died at the age of eighty-five.

III

I am grateful to Mr. Donald K. Campbell, Librarian of the Haverhill Public Library, who placed before me its collec-

tion of books, articles, and letters by Whittier, and the files
of the Essex *Gazette* and Haverhill *Iris* for which the poet
wrote. I am indebted to Miss Harriet S. Tapley, of the
Essex Institute of Salem, who allowed me to examine the
Oak Knoll Collection of letters by and to Whittier, to which
no previous biographer of Whittier has had access. I have
been helped, I am pleased to record, by the officers of the
Whittier Home Association of Amesbury. I profited by the
kindness of Mr. Sawyer, President of the Lowell Historical
Society, and of the Rev. Wilson Waters, its librarian, for
permitting copies to be made for me of editorials in the
Lowell *Middlesex Standard*, of which the only file in existence
is in that institution. A personal interview with Mrs. Phœbe
Grantham, the adopted daughter of one of the poet's cousins,
who was his constant companion at Oak Knoll during the
last fifteen years of his life, gave me important information
that I never could have obtained in books or letters. Mrs.
Grantham also furnished me copies of the manuscripts of
two unpublished poems written by Whittier in the years he
was at Oak Knoll.

I have received photostats or typewritten copies of letters
by Whittier from the libraries of Harvard University, Yale
University, Cornell University, Duke University, Haverford
College, Wellesley College, Brown University, from the
Huntington Library, the Massachusetts Historical Society,
the New Hampshire Historical Society, the New York Public
Library, the Library of Congress, the American Academy of
Arts and Letters, and the Congregational Library of Boston,
and I have personally copied documents in the Pierpont
Morgan Library in New York, the Pennsylvania Historical
Society in Philadelphia, the Boston Public Library, and the
Longfellow House in Cambridge. For such services and
privileges I wish to thank the librarians or curators of those
institutions.

I have examined most of the newspapers Whittier edited
or for which he wrote and some which extensively reprinted

his work. I have gathered data from the Boston *Statesman*, Providence *Patriot*, and *National Era* in the Library of Congress, from the *American Manufacturer* in the American Antiquarian Society in Worcester, from the New England *Review* in the Connecticut Historical Society, from the Philadelphia *Album* in the Pennsylvania Historical Society, from the *Liberator*, *Emancipator*, Pennsylvania *Freeman*, and *National Anti-Slavery Standard* in the Ridgway Branch of the Philadelphia Library Company, and from the *Harbinger* and the *Independent* in the New York Library. Passages from the two issues of the *American and Foreign Anti-Slavery Reporter*, of which there is only one file in existence, in the Cornell University Library, were copied for me by Mr. Irvin F. Elber, a student of Cornell.

A number of private collectors like Charles Francis Jenkins, of Philadelphia, and especially Carroll A. Wilson, Esq., of New York, have been of assistance to me. Mr. T. Franklin Currier, of the Harvard Library, who has been working on a Whittier bibliography which will be published in the near future, Mr. John Albree, editor of *Whittier Correspondence*, of Boston, and the Hon. Albert L. Bartlett, of Haverhill, an old friend of the poet, have given me some information. And I should not fail to record delightful visits to the different places of residence occupied by Whittier at various periods of his life — Haverhill, Amesbury, and Danvers.

I am very grateful to Dr. Charles I. Glicksberg, author of *Walt Whitman and the Civil War*, for reading the manuscript and offering many fruitful suggestions. My friend Judge James Gay Gordon has greatly encouraged me during the process of writing this work. Edwin Markham has been kind enough to allow me to use his unpublished poem on Whittier, read in 1905 at the time Whittier was admitted to the Hall of Fame. The late Mrs. Allinson, widow of Professor Francis Greenleaf Allinson ('My Namesake'), son of William J. Allinson, Whittier's bosom friend, generously supplied me with copies of correspondence between the poet and members of the Allinson family. The late Profesor Roland Thaxter, son of Celia Thaxter, sent me copies of letters exchanged between Whittier and Mrs. Thaxter. Mr. Stanley V. Henkel permitted me to copy a Whittier letter before it was sold at auction. Miss Mildred Howells has allowed me to use an extract from an unpublished letter of her father, William Dean Howells, that I found in the Essex Institute; Mrs. Annie Longfellow Thorp has permitted me to publish the letters of Whittier to her father, Henry Wadsworth Longfellow, in the old home in Cambridge. I have quoted from documents in the Pierpont Morgan Library and the Henry E. Huntington Library with the permission of those authorized to give it. In behalf of my publishers I am exceedingly grateful to Mr. Greenleaf Whittier Pickard, of Boston, grandnephew of Whittier, for offering no objections to the use of any manuscript material in this book. I have profited by communications from several women who knew Whittier personally, among them Miss Annie C. Pettengill and Miss Elizabeth F. Hurne of Amesbury, and Miss Caroline Carter of Boston. Mr. Lewis Chase of Washington supplied a few bibliographical items. The names of a number of men and women who sent me copies of Whittier's letters are mentioned in the notes.

Other authorities besides the poet's own collected prose and poetical writings, have been the biographies, memoirs, and articles mentioned in the bibliography.

ALBERT MORDELL

PHILADELPHIA
November, 1932

QUAKER MILITANT

.·.

CHAPTER I

THE DREAMING FARMER BOY

THE strains in Whittier's ancestry differ from those of other New England poets such as Longfellow, Holmes, Emerson, and Lowell, who were of Brahmin caste. Though the son of a farmer, he was not, however, of mere plebeian descent. Some of his direct ancestors and others to whom he was collaterally related occupied positions of considerable importance, having distinguished themselves both as military officers and as scholars. What was most noteworthy and determinative in his blood-stream was, that it was a mingled one, coursing through Huguenot, Puritan, and Quaker tributaries — a fact that largely accounts for the contradictory forces in his nature.

He was proud of his heritage from the Puritans, because their descendants struck the blow against England at Concord. The Quaker and Huguenot strains in him, with their love of religious independence and liberty of speech, were, however, resentful of the Puritan stock. In turn the peaceful, non-resistant Quaker and the armed, fighting Huguenot, who were both allied against the Puritan, could never come to terms of truce with each other. Hence, when the poet enlisted in any cause, he really took up arms, as it were, against members of his own family; he cast stones upon the tombs of men whose blood was now flowing in his veins.

Thomas Whittier, the founder of the family, and great-great-grandfather of the poet, came from England with some relatives to America in 1638, and eventually settled in Haverhill, where he built the homestead, the scene of 'Snow-Bound.' Though a Puritan, he practiced, in his pacific dealings with the Indians, and in his defiance of the General Court in behalf of liberty of speech, some principles of the Quaker creed. By the marriage of his youngest son to a Quakeress, one branch of the family, of which the poet was a descendant, became members of the Society of Friends.

He derived one of his chief characteristics — his martial temperament — from the Greenleaf side of the family. He often referred to the warlike proclivities and firebrand elements in his nature, and he was in fact very proud, if the truth were told, that these could be traced to the Greenleaf Indian-fighters of early Puritan days. In his antislavery poems the wrath of the old Greenleaf warriors was transformed into a blaze of prophetic indignation. The military propensities of those ancestors which found an outlet in bloodshed were in him unconsciously sublimated into ballads of an inflammatory character directed against the upholders of slavery. He was ever ready to enlist in a cause for freedom. In the Quaker and Huguenot traits he inherited were sown the seeds of his abolitionism.

Whittier also believed himself descended from the famous Puritan clergyman, Stephen Bachelir, who in spite of his unsavory reputation was a striking and engaging figure. Since Bachelir has had numerous distinguished descendants, particularly among statesmen in American history, an attempt has been made to give him a thoroughly clean bill of moral health. The man whose blood flowed in the veins of John Greenleaf Whittier, as well as in those of Daniel Webster and Caleb Cushing, has been "proved" by a descendant innocent of the ancient charge of having allowed his attention to stray to a neighbor's wife; in Whittier's behalf a further attempt by a relative of his was made to relieve him even from any blood relationship to Stephen Bachelir.

Whittier never doubted his ancestor's guilt, and availed

himself of it to apologize for any conduct he disapproved of in his own relatives. 'We are weak on the Hussey side,' he used to say, alluding to his descent on his mother's side from Bachelir, whose daughter had married Christopher Hussey. He even flaunted Bachelir's guilt in his poem 'The Wreck of Rivermouth.'

Coming to the poet's parents, we find that his father, John, was a man of rectitude, not learned, though shrewd and intelligent. He was quick in arriving at decisions, uncouth, stern yet generous, strict but kindly towards his children. An old-fashioned Democrat, a religious and orthodox Quaker, he was the least likely person to become the father of a poet. Possessing good common sense, he was often called upon to act as arbitrator in disputes among the members of the village. Though he was several times chosen as a selectman of Haverhill, he was not gifted with profound insight, as is apparent from a remark of his about public charities: 'There are the Lord's poor and the Devil's poor; there ought to be a distinction made between them by the Overseer of the Poor.' He was, however, hardy and adventurous, having in his early youth made trips through the wilds of New Hampshire to Canada, where he often encountered Indians, who, knowing him to be utterly fearless, never molested him.

Whittier's mother, Abigail Hussey Whittier, who came of a long line of Quakers of the Hussey family, was saintly, kindly, and refined. Though she probably did not understand her son's æsthetic yearnings, she sympathized with his tastes and interests. In 'Snow-Bound' he has painted his parents, with such colorful strokes, as to make them forever known to readers of American literature. In the poem we hear the tales of his father recalling the days when he sat down eating moose meat in the Indian camp. More impressive still is the picture of the mother at the spinning-wheel, telling how the Indians had tomahawked and almost killed her great-uncle, or recounting the hardships and martyrdoms of the Friends. Quakers though the parents were, they had the ebullient spirits of youth, and found a keen zest in life.

On December 17, 1807, John Greenleaf Whittier was born in the homestead three miles distant from the town of Haverhill, Essex County, Massachusetts. He was the second child and the first boy in the family. Two other children were born later — a brother, Matthew Franklin, and a sister, Elizabeth Hussey.

The farmhouse, surrounded by beeches, poplars, and oaks, was so situated that no other house could be seen from it. The famous brook, celebrated in 'Snow-Bound,' purled and rippled in front of the dwelling, as it still does; it was then spanned, where it crosses the road, by a 'crazy' wooden bridge. Except for a newly built adjoining L and for some repairs made after a fire in the early part of the present century, the homestead looks very much as it did in the poet's early days.

Whittier attended two schools before he enrolled in the Haverhill Academy. Joshua Coffin, to whom he later addressed his poem 'To My Old Schoolmaster,' undertook his instruction. For a while the boy studied in an unfinished L of a farmhouse, a smoked and dingy room, where he could hear the bickerings between the farmer and his tipsy wife, as well as the rocking of their baby's cradle. Instead of flogging his pupils, Coffin, being an antiquary and gifted with a rare sense of humor, entertained them with stories. Whittier also attended a school kept by a Newburyport woman, about a half-mile away on the north road. This is the school, no longer in existence, made famous in the poem 'In School Days.' Here he met his schoolmate Lydia Ayer, celebrated in the same poem, though the episode of her purposely misspelling a word, so as not to go above her boy love in the class, is fictitious.

Whittier did the chores and performed such light duties of the farm as driving the cows to and from the pasture, rid-

VIEW OF HAVERHILL, MASS, IN 1820

HAVERHILL IN WHITTIER'S BOYHOOD

ing to the mill, fetching wood for the kitchen fire, and aiding
in the lighter work of the haying and harvesting. When the
family went to Amesbury to meeting, he often stayed at home,
since there was not enough room in the chaise to take them
all. On such occasions he would wander about and give vent
to his dreams, coming early into communion with Nature.
To this contact with her by daily toil and through day-
dreams, he attributed the picturesque truth in his poetry,
and especially the fidelity to Nature shown in 'Snow-Bound.'
When he became a little older, he did the usual farm work,
such as milking the cows — a task for which he had an
aversion — · and threshing grain with the heavy flail, with
which he once injured himself from over-exertion.

Though his duties often secluded him from the outside
world, he became acquainted with the different types in the
village. Here he would come with his father or Uncle Moses
to bring the produce of the farm in exchange for various
household supplies, and he would observe keenly what was
going on. The tavern-proprietor, the country storekeeper,
the blacksmith, the man who sold combs and cigars, the widow
who made his homespun trousers and coats — these characters became stamped indelibly on his mind.

Whittier's life as a farm-boy then was the typical one of
those old New England days. Though the farm was not
large, he always had to help, for labor was expensive.
The ground was rocky, and neither well manured nor ever
thoroughly cleared, and there was always a want of good
rotation of crops. Only the maize, or Indian corn, required
careful cultivation, usually with oxen and a few hoeings.
Whittier attended to the breaking of the ground with the
plough, and the levelling with the harrow. He had to see
that the corn was planted in hills about three feet apart,
and as it grew he had to keep it hoed. The oxen he drove,
'Buck' and 'Old Butler,' responded to their own names, and
guided their movements by different tones of his voice.

Following the common practice, the Whittier family also

raised potatoes on a border of the cornfield, and small grains like rye and oats in the open field, which at times they turned into grass-land.

While the boy was a faithful worker, he liked to loaf and invite his soul, since a lad of his temperament could not be expected to love drudgery; in fact, he was not a proficient farmer. A poet's spirit was incarnated in the farm-boy's body. A thirst for knowledge burned within him, ambition already gnawed at his heart, and he really led a dual life — of fancy on the one hand and hard reality on the other. The high ideals of the characters in the Bible at the same time impressed themselves deeply upon him. The variety and beauty of nature helped break the monotony of the daily round of his toils. He had his diversions, too. In spite of the hardships of rising early to milk the cows and keep the oxen from the corn, he enjoyed merry times at huskings, when he would help break the ears from the stalks, and strip the husks. He participated in quilting parties and joined in games of blind-man's-buff. In later years, he told in a poem, 'The Pumpkin,' how the children sat on uncut pumpkins round the corn-heap and listened to stories.

Of all the American poets Whittier was the one who could draw most faithfully on memory to describe the rural scenes in which he had taken part. The farm made him familiar with wild life, with birds, flowers, and trees. In the famous poem of 'The Barefoot Boy' he has recorded that he acquired much knowledge that it would have been impossible to learn in schools. No course in zoölogy could ever have imparted to him such acquaintance with the habits of squirrels and moles, woodchucks and orioles, bees and pickerel, wasps and hornets, as he gathered on the farm. He walked hand in hand with Nature, and she answered his questions.

Soon an event occurred which moulded his life anew — his discovery of the poems of Robert Burns. He first heard them sung by a wandering Scotch minstrel; but he was shortly afterwards able to read them himself from a volume that his old schoolmaster brought to the house. He mastered the glossary at the end of the book and became familiar with the Scotch dialect. Though only fourteen at the time, he felt a spiritual awakening; a new star had swum into his ken.

He soon began writing verses himself, though obviously he had as yet nothing to say and was simply indulging in a pastime. Meanwhile his practical father, aware that one who makes rhymes does not as a rule grow up to be a successful farmer, became alarmed about the boy's future, and tried, but without success, to discourage his son's efforts. Young Whittier continued writing his poems in secrecy, aided and abetted by his mother and older sister, Mary. A pretty girl cousin, Mary Emerson Smith, also encouraged him, and he promptly fell in love with her.

Besides Burns's poems, his chief reading was in two famous school readers — Lindley Murray's 'English Reader' and Caleb Bingham's 'American Perceptor.' He read these books so often that he used to turn with relief for fresh reading-matter to the poems in the 'Poet's Corner' of the weakly village newspaper.

Caleb Bingham's 'American Perceptor' especially formed his mind, for it awoke his first sympathies for the slaves. He has recorded his indebtedness to one poem in particular in this school reader — 'The African Chief.' In 'Snow-Bound' he has recalled how as a boy he used to stammer the lines from that poem:

> 'Does not the voice of reason cry,
>   Claim the first right which Nature gave.
> From the red scourge of bondage fly,
>   Nor deign to live a burdened slave!'

Elsewhere he has told how as a grown man, when he saw slavery spreading over the land, he used to quote to himself stanzas from the poem.

He soon resorted to the shelf in his father's library, which held about thirty books. After reading 'Pilgrim's Progress' he would at night in his sleep portray in imagination on the walls of his room the terrifying scenes in the book, and by contrast would also picture himself being welcomed into the House Beautiful. The dreams were so vivid that he recalled them years later when writing about Bunyan. The illustration of Apollyon, with his horns, hoofs, scales, and breath of fire, in combat with Christian, particularly made a frightful and unforgettable impression upon him.

Among other books on the shelf were a number dealing with Quaker doctrines, but the books of travel and biography fascinated him most. Tales of shipwreck, as well as stories of adventure in the Sahara and on the Nile, and a sprinkling of such narratives as that of the rogue Stephen Burroughs and that of the pious Quaker sea-captain Thomas Chalkley, whom he mentions in 'Snow-Bound,' added spice to the collection. Even more delightful than these were the biographical accounts of some of the English poets, the volumes being no doubt Johnson's 'Lives of the Poets.' The only volume of poetry in the library was 'Davideis,' by Thomas Ellwood, the Quaker poet and friend of Milton — a poem which Whittier soon imitated, as he had Burns's lyrics. He also somehow obtained Scott's 'The Pirate' and devoured it stealthily at night. Here was a new life, much pleasanter than toiling in the sun. He was so proud of the number of books he read that he made a list of some of them in rhymed doggerel together with critical comments.

Stimulated by his mother's tales of the sufferings of the Quakers, he soon read their histories for himself; and he naturally admired the Colonial Quakers more than he did their Puritan persecutors.

Since the Bible was read at home on First Day afternoons, he became deeply steeped in its spirit. He came to know it so well that at the age of seven he could repeat many passages and even chapters from it by heart. His father, proud of his son's feats of memory, would have him recite passages to wondering members of the Society of Friends. He would ask visitors at the Quarterly Meeting to begin some Biblical passage in the middle of a chapter and then he would tell young John to recite the rest of the verses.

The boy developed a passion for reading that included books of magic, farmers' almanacs, theological tracts, Cotton Mather's ponderous but fascinating 'Magnalia Christi Americana' and the poems of Mrs. Hemans and Thomas Moore. He was soon familiar with Milton, Thomson, Chatterton, Ossian, and the English poets of the Romantic School — Byron and Coleridge. He became so absorbed in thinking about his books that often while at work he had to be rudely awakened out of his day-dreams by his father or uncle.

His earliest known poems, written when he was fifteen were 'The Willows,' an imitation of 'The Old Oaken Bucket,' and 'The Emerald Isle,' in which he showed his concern for the struggles of the Irish for liberty. The latter poem, in the rhythmic swing of Thomas Moore, already foreshadowed at an early age his interest in people who fight for freedom. He thought well enough of some of the poems he wrote between the ages of fifteen and eighteen to publish them shortly afterwards in the newspapers. Even sixty years later he sent a poem on William Penn, composed when he was sixteen, to be read at a celebration of the bicentennial of William Penn's landing.

Among the unpublished specimens of his poetry [1] written when he was seventeen, and typical of his characteristic vein, was a poem called 'The Martyr' about William Leddra, the Quaker, who was executed in Boston in 1659 for returning from banishment.

The following two stanzas from the poem indicate that Whittier himself, like his hero, felt no animosity against the misguided persecutors:

'Bright through the thick mists of the morning
　　The sunbeams had darted dispersing the gloom.
Hark, the rude clash of arms! 'tis the ominous warning
　　That Leddra receives as the voice of his doom.

---

[1] In the Essex Institute, Salem, Massachusetts.

'Serene was his look, for the strictest observer
  No symptoms of fear on his aspect could see
As he prayed for his foes, and his pure holy fervor
  Evinced that his heart from resentment was free.'

Another typical poem, unpublished, was 'New Year's
Address' written at the end of 1824 — the year in which
Byron died — showing young Whittier's interest in struggles
for liberty as well as his preoccupations with the famous
English poet. Whittier's address to Greece in the poem contains the first of his several judgments on Byron, whom he
admired so intensely, but accepted with reservations because
of his skeptical beliefs and scandalous morals. Greece, the
subjugated nation fighting for independence, engaged his
attention to an even greater degree than ever because Byron
had died in her behalf. The following passage, also never
published, shows that the youthful Whittier was willing to
overlook Byron's frailties, because of his death in the cause
of freedom:

'One bright, bold star has fallen on thy coast,
  Byron, renowned on Albion's classic page,
A master spirit of the times — the boast,
  The pride, the shame, the wonder of his age.
But peace to him; let deep oblivion shade
  The memory of his wanderings, for there was
A spirit in him which has oft display'd
  Its pure devotion to the sacred cause
Of freedom; let this serve to palliate
  His numerous errors, for the generous mind
That mourns the loss of genius, mourns the fate
  Of him, whose haughty form is now reclined
Where Pindus lifts itself.'

Whittier's emergence from rustic obscurity and introduction to the public form an interesting chapter in literary
history. In the early summer of 1826, his elder sister, Mary,
without his knowledge sent a poem called 'The Exile's Departure' to the office of the Newburyport 'Free Press,' a
paper edited by William Lloyd Garrison, to which the elder

Whittier was a subscriber. The postrider left the poem lying on the floor near the door. With some misgivings the young editor began reading the manuscript; he had no doubt that the poem was one of the usual vapid outpourings of country rhymesters. Discovering merit in the poem he decided to print it. This was how William Lloyd Garrison chanced to discover John Greenleaf Whittier.

When the postrider delivered the paper, he threw it to the young poet, who was at the time engaged in mending a stone wall by the roadside. When he paused in his work to glance through the paper he caught sight in the 'Poet's Corner' of the title of his own poem. His heart came into his mouth with surprise and joy, the blood tingling in his veins. His father reproving him for neglect of his duties, he resumed his labors. Again he paused to reread the poem, but he merely looked at it vacantly, without seeing a word. He now secretly rejoiced that Mary had sent the poem; he only regretted that she had not sent a better specimen of his verses.

Soon the postrider told Garrison the name of the author. Accompanied by a woman, the editor went down to the farm, fourteen miles from Newburyport, to see his contributor. The young poet in working-day clothes, besmeared with dirt, was crawling at the moment under the barn in search of a hen that had stolen her nest. His sister came running up to him, shouting excitedly as she told him of his visitors. He stopped hunting the eggs, crept stealthily into the house, and changed his clothes, in his haste putting on a pair of trousers much too short for him. He then came into the room abashed and tremulous, but eager with anticipation. Neither he nor Garrison then realized what a turning-point in the annals of both American poetry and American politics this meeting in the humble kitchen would some day prove to be. Garrison, finding after a few words with the poet that his education was limited, assured him that he would have a career before him if this defect was remedied. When Whittier's father came in, the young editor tried to convince him of the need and value of scholastic training for his gifted son. But the old farmer, though proud of the boy's achievements, was obdurate; in fact he was altogether opposed to sending to school one so necessary to him on the farm. He explained to Garrison that he could not see any practical advantage in the boy's becoming a poet. Garrison could not answer the elder man's objections and politely took his departure.

Whittier soon sent Garrison a second poem, 'The Deity.' It appeared with a brief note by Garrison who, comparing him to Bernard Barton, the English Quaker poet, prophesied that he would achieve high rank in American letters. Garrison designated the poem itself as a graphic sketch, manifesting true poetic genius. Before retiring as editor of the 'Free Press' at the end of the summer, Garrison published all together about a dozen poems by Whittier.

Meanwhile Whittier was storing his mind with local lore. He heard numerous stories, not only from members of his family, but from neighbors and wandering gypsies and minstrels. A rich store of legends had gathered around the vicinity. There were accounts of witches and ghosts, of phantom ships, and haunted houses; tales of mysterious events that could not be accounted for; episodes connected with massacres and battles; numerous traditions about Indians and Puritans and Quakers. He heard at home how his own Aunt Mary, his mother's unmarried sister, one evening imagined she saw her absent lover go by on horseback, and how shortly afterwards she learned that he had died the very moment she had that vision. Then he became familiar with the current gossip about a red-nosed farmer, the husband of an Ohio witch, who followed him to New England, whither he had fled and married again, and who compelled him to return with her. Whittier himself met this farmer, who had, after the witch's death, again taken up his abode in Haverhill and resumed cohabitation with his second wife. The young poet was impressed by the tales of men married to beautiful women, who, being really evil demons, resumed their original form and destroyed their husbands; several of his poems centered around this Christabel theme. In the neighborhood were women who still had the reputation of being witches, and men to whom people resorted for aid as conjurers. Who did not know the story of Aunt Morse, the witch, returning from her grave to see that the squire properly executed her will? Who ever doubted the authenticity of the tale of a certain general's compact with the devil, whom he tried to cheat by cutting out the soles of a boot that was being filled with gold and silver in exchange for his soul?

Whittier soon made an important literary connection. While staying with his relative Mrs. Greene, a descendant of Bachelir, he made a marked impression upon her husband, Nathaniel Greene, who was editing at the time a paper called the 'Statesman' and later introduced Whittier to a Boston public. He never forgot his Boston visit, for he met an actress while there, whose endeavors to persuade him to visit the theater compelled him to flee home in consternation.

Abijah W. Thayer, editor of the Haverhill 'Gazette' (later called the 'Essex Gazette'), assisted him most in the steep pathway of a literary career, for he published a poem by him every week. He also wrote eulogistic notices of Whittier. In one issue he marveled over the fact that the young poet was writing such excellent poems without any preparation but a common-school education, and he stated with assurance that the youth's genius would be greatly assisted by a classical education. Chanting the praises of Whittier — or Adrian, as he signed his poems — Thayer said in another issue that his genius was unparalleled among American poets, and asserted that even the most celebrated modern poets did not display so early such richness of language, brilliancy of imagery, and delicacy of sentiment.

Poems suggestive in theme and sentiment of Whittier's mature work were appearing very frequently in the 'Essex Gazette.' In these juvenile efforts he was using his pen in the cause of peace, or was courageously attacking religious doctrines that laid emphasis on ceremony rather than on the inner light. In an early poem, 'The Song of Peace,' he was already dedicating his career to the cause of pacifism.

Other early poems of Whittier written for the 'Gazette' were often weak imitations of Thomas Moore, Felicia Hemans, Mrs. L. E. Landon, and other poets of the day. Though Whittier believed even then that the poet should describe the scenes about him and the emotions that the common people feel, he often deviated from his theories, and wrote on subjects suggested by books. He followed too often the practice of the poets of his day in writing poems on Biblical texts. Needless to say, such secondary inspiration was not conducive to originality or poetry of a high order.

Now that he was a regular contributor to the newspapers, his father decided to take the advice of Garrison and permit his son to go to an academy. Being himself in only moderate circumstances, he was not able to pay his son's tuition and board. Since Whittier received no remuneration for his poems, he was compelled to turn to shoemaking as a means of earning his expenses. Except for some few experiments at home in making ladies' slippers and shoes, he never worked as a regular shoemaker. But some people who reported that they had found him at these tasks spread the story that he was a cobbler, and Thayer capitalized it. In later years several books on the lives of eminent shoemakers included Whittier among them — a distinction that he did not relish. Whittier has denied that he ever was a shoemaker. 'I did not work at shoe-making except some experiments in the winter between 16 and 18,'[1] he wrote. He did once admit that he learned how to make ladies' shoes and slippers from a young man working on his father's farm, and that he thus earned enough to carry him through the first term at the Haverhill Academy. He was only following the custom of

[1] Manuscript letter dated Feb. 28, 1871, in possession of Mr. P. J. Tomanoczy, Civic Center Book Shop, San Francisco.

many farmers in those early days of making shoes to increase their earnings.

Having accumulated sufficient funds to defray his expenses at the Haverhill Academy, just being opened, he moved into the village, where he boarded with Thayer. Before becoming a pupil, he received a singular honor as the local poet — a request to write an ode for the dedication to take place April 30, 1827. An aged Scotch poet, whom he knew and admired, Robert Dinsmore, was also asked to be one of the poets of the occasion. The additional honor of leading the procession that marched to the academy was bestowed upon them. The erect, dignified figure of the sober, somewhat frightened young Quaker, presented a marked contrast in the procession to that of the aged Scotch poet, a little hilarious from liquor. Whittier's poem was sung to the air of 'Pillar of Glory,' and an address was delivered by a distinguished lawyer, Leverett Saltonstall, of Salem. Whittier, in his poem, welcomed the spirit of science to an educational institution, which, he said, would put no check or trammel upon knowledge.

At Haverhill Academy he had as classmate his cousin Mary Emerson Smith, with whom he was still in love, but he met a new fancy, Evelina Bray, who helped to divert him, and with whose affections he was soon to trifle.

Whittier was rather reserved for a school-boy; he was too dignified and aloof. He was respected by his fellow-pupils, but was never too familiar with them. He defended the rights of wronged pupils, as Shelley used to do.

At the end of the term in November he returned home. In order to get tuition and expenses for the coming year, he taught a district school in Birch Meadow, about four miles away from his father's house. He had difficulties with some badly behaved boys, and found it tedious teaching dull children not interested in study. 'I killed a schoolmaster that winter,' he once said. It is not surprising that though his superiors commended him highly for his work, he never returned to teaching.

CHAPTER II

NEWSPAPER POET

DURING the two years that Whittier spent at the Haverhill Academy he published about one hundred and fifty poems. He gives us more information in them about himself from a psychological point of view than a biographer could furnish. A study of some of them from the files of the newspapers where they originally appeared will help us understand the development of his mind and spirit.

His first contribution to Garrison's 'Free Press' marked the beginning of his career as newspaper poet. Though he soon had *entrée* into a few periodicals, he made newspapers his chief poetical vehicle. The editors were glad to get his work, since they were not required to pay for it, and he, on his side, was satisfied to have his poems printed in newspapers, for publication there made him the poet of the local community.

Leaving the love poems aside for future consideration, in connection with the events that inspired them, let us glance at the nature of his poetical work for the years 1827 and 1828, as it anticipates the subjects he dealt with later in life. The 'Essex Gazette' published the largest number of his poems of those formative years — indeed nearly a hundred. It also had a few prose pieces by him on war and temperance and on such subjects as spectral illusions and Robert Burns, his favorite poet.

A number of poems published in the first summer he was at the Academy are imbued with one of his deep-seated characteristics, antipathy to militarism. In reply to a warrior's song that had appeared in an annual, 'The Memorial,' he wrote a poem, 'Lines,' expressing the sentiment that the blood spilt by heroes who have monuments erected to them would eternally send forth a cry from the earth, while the men who won glory in peaceful pursuits would have a noble influence upon posterity. In another poem, 'The Ruin,' he contemplated a desolate castle where warriors and oppressors of a former day once dwelt. He was not prompted to mourn the splendors of its past; on the contrary, he reflected on the blessings of peace. Yet he did not shun writing martial poems.

He was also developing a poetical creed which he never abandoned, namely, that one of the duties of the poet was to record the legends of his own soil instead of going to other climes for sources of inspiration. He thus became the first of our exponents of regionalism in literature. His early efforts in this direction are chiefly important because they foreshadow many of his masterly poems on New England. An early poem about an Indian who ascended the White Mountains — the reputed residence of supernatural beings — where he was trapped by his own daring, was inspired by reading Josselyn's 'New England's Rarities' and is an example of Whittier's autochthonous material.

We get hints and gleams of the later antislavery poems in one of the most famous of his early poems, 'The Song of the Vermonters,' a poem which had a curious history. It was written in his school days but later anonymously published in a magazine, and it acquired renown as the composition of Vermont's well-known hero Ethan Allen. Only very late in life did Whittier admit its authorship. It was really a war poem and scarcely the kind that a Quaker would write. It dealt chiefly with Vermont's difficulties during the Revolution with adjoining colonies, who wanted to divide her among them. Vermont attracted Whittier for another reason — she was the first of the Northern States to abolish slavery. In its passionate protest and spirit of independence the poem is a forerunner of his antislavery poems.

Whittier's nature was complex. As a Quaker he believed in peace, but he nevertheless enjoyed writing tales of military valor and bloodshed. He devoted many early stories and poems to massacres, combats, and shocking cruelties, and he was in a sense a predecessor of Poe. He never outgrew his admiration for military heroes.

His newspaper poems gave him a growing reputation, and Greene, following Garrison and Thayer, prefaced one of the lyrics he copied in the 'Statesman' from the 'Gazette' with a glowing eulogy on the poet, in which he said that training alone would make Whittier's gift shine as one of the brightest lights in our poetical firmament. Like Garrison he compared him with the English Quaker poet Bernard Barton, but he added a few patronizing touches and preached to him that skill and toil were synonymous.

In 1827 Greene copied some of Whittier's poems from the 'Gazette,' but in the beginning of the next year, he not only copied a poem but published an original one by him 'To the Memory of Chatterton.' These two poems he prefixed by a brief article headed 'John G. Whittier,' comparing him to Bloomfield and Hogg because like them he followed a manual occupation. Greene expressed surprise that a Quaker should write with such fervor, animation, and intensity of thought. He saw in him an exception to the rule that only those learned in books could be true poets. Greene continued publishing poems for several months thereafter.[1]

---

[1] Owing to an error made by Pickard, who assumed that 'Ichabod' was one of Whittier's pen names, Miss Pray reprinted in her thesis as by Whittier nine poems from the Boston *Statesman* for 1827 and 'The Jersey Prison Ship' from the Boston *Spectator*, 1827, all originally signed 'Ichabod.' Patrick K. Foley has seen copies of the annual *The Memorial*, 1827, in which the name John W. Whitman was written in pencil under the pseudonym 'Ichabod' signed to the tale 'The Light in the Pinnacle.' I have, however, found more convincing evidence than this that 'Ichabod' was John W. Whitman from noting that in the *Specimens of American Poetry*, 1829, the editor, Samuel Kettell, assigns to Whitman the poem 'The Jersey Prison Ship' which Miss Pray includes as Whittier's. Miss Pray reprints, altogether, eleven poems from the Boston *Statesman* of 1827, of which only one, 'Life's Pleasures,' is by Whittier. (The first one she reprints, 'Charles Edward After the Battle of Culloden,' though not signed originally by 'Ichabod' but W., and copied by the *Statesman* from a New Hampshire paper, also seems not to be Whittier's.) 'Ichabod' had been contributing to the *Statesman* since the summer of 1826. He married Sarah Helen Whitman, to whom he wrote the poems addressed to Sarah published by Miss Pray as love poems of Whittier's. My friend Carroll A. Wilson who first told me of Mr. Foley's discovery, has followed up the career of Whitman after I gave him the definite proof that 'Ichabod' was Whitman.

Shortly after Whittier reached his twenty-first birthday, Mr. Thayer issued in the 'Essex Gazette' the prospectus of a book of poems to be published by subscription. It was to consist of over two hundred poems, including not only the fifty or more poems Whittier had thus far published in the 'Gazette,' but also the poems he had written for Garrison and Greene. Since he had most frequently adopted the pseudonym 'Adrian,' Thayer decided to issue the poems under that *nom de plume*. Thayer stated that the purpose of the publication was to give him a classical education, also mentioning that the poems had been copied in the most respectable papers in the country; he ventured his own opinion that the compositions indicated a genius of a high order.

Nothing came of the project, even though twenty-odd subscriptions had been obtained in Philadelphia. The most plausible explanation for abandoning the venture is that a sufficient number of subscribers could not be obtained to make it profitable. Since Whittier thought little of his first volume, 'The Legends of New England,' issued three years later, which contained more mature poems than those in the contemplated first book, he would undoubtedly have regretted the publication of the Adrian poems.

If he did not succeed in appearing as the author of a book, he at least became the editor of one — the poems of his old friend Robert Dinsmore, the Rustic Bard of Windham, New Hampshire, whose 'Incidental Poems' Thayer published in January or February, 1828. Its chief interest today is that it is the first book to contain both a poem and a prose essay by Whittier. The poem 'J. G. Whittier to the Rustic Bard,' which had already appeared in the 'Essex Gazette,' was the best of his experiments in Scotch dialect.

The six-page preface [1] Whittier wrote contains his earliest views on his own art. He particularly commended Dinsmore because he was the poet of domestic life in New England who described the incidents of the farmer's house and sang

[1] I follow Miss Pray in assuming that Whittier wrote this unsigned preface.

of the bobolink instead of the nightingale. Especially interesting is a discourse on poetry in which Whittier shows his dislike for both crude realism or naturalism and excessive idealism in art. He never changed these early views.

Garrison helped widen Whittier's reading public by accepting poems from him for the two other publications he edited after the 'Free Press' and before he founded the 'Liberator.' He published an editorial article about the poet in Boston in his temperance paper, the 'National Philanthropist,' in which he told the story of his first visit to Whittier. Praising the purity of sentiment and finish of execution of the poems, he called for subscriptions to the new book of poems by Adrian at the time under way. He spoke also of their negative virtues, of their freedom from ornament and melancholy madness, and commentated on their remarkable metrical qualities.

Garrison continued to publish poems by Whittier in the 'Philanthropist' and, a few months later, in another paper he edited, the 'Bennington Journal of the Times.' As the poet's financial condition was then extremely precarious, Garrison offered him some cheering counsel and told him not to despair, for fortune would soon come to his aid. One of the poems published by Garrison in the fall of 1828, 'A Dream,' was copied by Robert Morris, the editor of the 'Philadelphia Album,' with the enthusiastic comment that it had exquisite merits and was the best specimen that had yet appeared from the poet's pen. It did not really merit much praise, for it was an incongruous medley of medieval chivalry in a Byronic setting with Quaker sentiments directed against militarism.

At the same time Whittier took an interest in the young American poets of the day, especially in a young poet on the 'Statesman,' James Otis Rockwell, with whom he became acquainted. He was deeply moved by the fate of two poets, Edward C. Pinkney and John G. C. Brainard, who both died in 1828, and he celebrated their deaths in elegies. Pink-

ney who had served several years in the navy and had engaged in duels was a curious foil to Whittier. It will be recalled in this connection how highly Poe thought of Pinkney's
celebrated toast 'A Health,' beginning 'I drink this cup to
one made up of loveliness alone.'

Whittier, at this time meeting with some rebuffs, and seeing in the poverty and sad misfortunes of these young poets
portents of his own fate, became discouraged and desperate,
and he poured out his embittered feelings to his friend John
Neal, editor of the 'Portland Yankee':

'I have just written something for your consideration.
You dislike — I believe you do at least — the blank verse of
the modern poets and poetesses. Nevertheless I send you a
long string of it. If you don't like it, say so privately; and I
will *quit poetry, and everything else of a literary nature*, for I am
sick at heart of the business. Insult has maddened me. The
friendless boy has been mocked at; and years ago he vowed
to triumph over the scorners of his boyish endeavors. With
the unescapable sense of wrong burning like a volcano in the
recesses of his spirit, he has striven to accomplish this vow,
until his heart has grown weary of the struggle.'

Like many young men at the age of twenty-one, he was
uncertain about his future career. But Garrison bestirred
himself in his behalf, for, having discovered his poet and
awakened his ambitions, he thought that he should assist
him in a practical way. He now suggested to the Reverend
William Collier, the owner of the 'Philanthropist,' that he
employ Whittier in his stead as editor. Collier soon made
Whittier an offer, which, after some hesitation, was accepted.
He was too poor to go to college, and too independent to accept financial help; and he did not want to become a teacher.
Besides, as an editor, he could earn his living and serve humanity at the same time.

'The situation of editor of the "Philanthropist,"' he wrote
to Thayer, 'is not only respectable, but it is peculiarly pleasant to one who takes so deep an interest, as I really do,

in the great cause it is laboring to promote. I would enter upon my task with a heart free from misanthropy, and glowing with that feeling that wishes well to all. I would rather have the memory of a Howard, a Wilberforce, and a Clarkson, than the undying fame of Byron.'

He realized this wish a few years later when he became an abolitionist.

CHAPTER III

THE YOUNG NEWSPAPER EDITOR

ARRIVING in Boston, December, 1828, at the age of twenty-one and making his home with his employer, the Reverend William Collier, at No. 30 Federal Street, Whittier assumed editorship not of the 'Philanthropist,' but of the 'American Manufacturer,' another paper owned by Collier, a Henry Clay organ, pledged to the cause of the protective tariff and the furtherance of the development of American industries.

The young fighting Quaker poet stamped his personality upon the newspaper in the eight months during which he edited it. In an early issue he vented his Quaker dislike for music, thereby calling forth some mirthful reproaches from George D. Prentice, the editor of the 'New England Review,' who had recently accepted some poems from him. Prentice took him to task for saying that he preferred the music of a high-pressure steam-engine, and especially the music of thought, to instrumental music, but he charitably attributed such singular views to the poet's Quaker blood. Whittier, resolutely defending himself against the onslaughts of the most vitriolic editor in New England, threw down the gantlet to him thus: 'He will yet have to learn, that although far from being pugnacious in our general deportment, we can for his special benefit divest ourselves of Quakerism in our paper at least.'

Whittier continued to expound his favorite doctrines with great animation. He was captious in book reviews, and he attacked Kettell's 'Specimens of American Poets,' the first important anthology of American verse, even though it contained his 'Sicilian Vespers.' Finding the collection disappointing, he predicted oblivion for most of the poets represented, except Bryant, Halleck, Sigourney, and Percival.

Setting forth his own views on contemporary letters in the editorial 'American Literature,' he accounted for the imbecility of most of our poetry by the dangerous encouragement given to 'bright flashes of fancy, to the tinsel and drapery of poetry, rather than its substance.' He was annoyed to find that the poems of the time evinced 'no interest to chain down our sympathies and work upon our sterner passions.' In another editorial, 'Aristocracy,' he defended the aristocracy of mind against that of wealth. 'Mind — that transcendent gift of the Eternal Spirit,' he wrote, 'the Godlike Intellect, which holds communion with the past, that searches out the hidden things of earth, and extends its broad vision to the very confines of eternity — is debased and humbled by the influence of wealth into moral slavery, a mental bondage by far more terrible than physical incarceration.'

He wrote editorials against infidelity — he always did — that sound rather amusing today, for he was apprehensive that the country was then becoming atheistic. As usual he declaimed against war; in fact the very first editorial he contributed was a bold and manly utterance that is still timely.

For some reason or other Whittier became dissatisfied with his employer, and resigned his position in August. Besides, his father was ill, and he thought it best to return to Haverhill.

During the year another American poet, Edgar Allan Poe, received his first public encouragement in the pages of 'The Yankee.' No stranger bedfellows ever appeared together in the same pages of a magazine. To the December issue Poe sent a letter, which he interlarded with extracts from his forthcoming second book 'Al Aaraaf, Tamerlane, and Other Poems,' and Whittier contributed 'The Minstrel Girl,' a long poem much admired at the time. Neal, the Quaker editor, who early recognized the ability of these two young poets, lived to witness the great poetic reputation attained by them both.

It is singular that Whittier celebrated the raven as a bird

of evil omen many years before Poe. The reprinting of this
unknown poem is therefore, of some interest:

THE RAVEN

Thou of the evil eye,
And the dark pinion, given to the wind,
When the storm cometh, like a host behind,
Sweeping the sunless sky! —
Evil and lonely bird!
In the dark places of the desert earth,
Where the strange monsters of the wild have birth,
Thy fearful voice is heard, —
A hoarse, unwelcome scream,
Making unearthly echoes by the rude
Fall of the cataract — in the groaning wood,
And where the sluggard stream
Creeps through the ghostly fen,
Veiled from the sunlight and uncheered by mirth,
Whence the damp vapours of disease steal forth,
Poisoning the hearts of men;
Or on the lifeless bough
Lifted above the crags, by thunder shorn,
Watching the pilgrim, faint and travelworn,
Toiling his way below, —
Thou sittest, evil one,
Screaming above thy victim's dangerous path
Till his brain dizzies at the thought of death;
And he hath headlong gone
Down the far precipice,
Down to the rocks — the ragged rocks that lift
Their grim forms upward to the mountain rift,
Guarding the black abyss;
Or, in the battle plain
Where the red angel in his pride hath been,
Thou bendest o'er the unseemly forms of men, —
The foul uncharnelled slain;
Holding thy banquet there
With the dark feasters upon human blood,
Marring the awful, workmanship of God —
The Jaguar of the air.[1]

---

[1] 'The Raven,' American *Manufacturer*, Oct. 15, 1829.

While on the 'Manufacturer,' he attracted the attention of many Eastern editors — especially Robert Morris of the Philadelphia 'Album,' who copied and used original poems by him.

'We think highly of this young person, both as a man and as a writer,' Morris wrote eulogistically a second time. 'If we rightly understand his character, he is full of high-spirited independence and noble generosity. Without even the ordinary advantages of classical acquirements, he has, through his industry and genius, attained a station not unworthy the most intellectual and respected. He is a Quaker neither bigoted in his opinions, nor contracted in his doctrines, yet firm in the faith of his forefathers and energetic in the advocacy of his peculiar creed. As a poet, Whittier has for the short time he has been before the public attained a distinguished station among American writers. His style, although not so polished and classical as that of some other of our writers, is highly imaginative and nervous, and is replete with many of the best characteristics of poetry.' [1]

Whittier spent the fall of 1829 at Haverhill, attending to the farm and nursing his sick father. He continued his devotion to the muse, and found an additional stimulus in life in encouraging the poetic talent budding forth in his youngest sister, Elizabeth, now a girl of fourteen.

His respite from journalism was brief. For in January, 1830, his old editor, Thayer, offered him the editorship of the 'Essex Gazette' — a position which he immediately accepted. In his exordium he assured his readers that he was under no party banner, but would advocate social or political reforms when he thought them essential; that he would avoid theological subjects, but in matters of morality he would speak boldly and vehemently. He was not long connected with the paper before he engaged in his favorite diversion of strangling infidelity, using the occasion for an attack upon Shelley, referring to his 'depraved heart, and of his dying

[1] Philadelphia *Album*, May 20, 1829.

with a cloud upon his soul and infamy upon his memory.'
As Shelley had admirers even at that time, they were soon
belaboring Whittier for his narrow prejudices. One of the
editors who defended Shelley was the friendly Robert Morris
of the Philadelphia 'Album.' Whittier, standing his ground,
renewed his assaults upon Shelley as an infidel, though he
admitted that he admired the poet's intellect. In his condemnation this time he included Shelley's mother-in-law, Mary
Wollstonecraft, speaking of her as 'licentious, profligate, and
shameless.' He also took up arms against Byron, by whom
he was alternately attracted and repelled, but he thus again
exhibited his own critical limitations.

Much as he detested Byron at times, he found himself
stimulated by the English poet's success. We are so ac-
customed to think of Whittier as modest and idealistic that
we forget that as a young man he was devoured by desire for
worldly success. That he was passing through a struggle is
clearly evident to us, if we read between the lines of a brief
essay, 'Life,' written at the time.

In the early summer of 1830 Whittier suffered his first
grievous domestic loss in the death of his father. The burden
of the family henceforth falling chiefly upon him, he decided
to resume his labors as a farmer, and he bade his readers
farewell.

Contrary to his expectations, he almost immediately
afterwards returned to editorial work. Through the good
offices of George D. Prentice, who in spite of attacking
Whittier considered him a 'man-giant' and continued publishing his work, he received the offer of a position on the
'New England Review' in Hartford. For Prentice was called
in the summer of 1830 to Kentucky to write a life of Henry
Clay, who was a presidential candidate. The proprietors of
the 'Review' asked him to recommend an editor, and he
suggested Whittier.

On receiving the call to Hartford, Whittier was much surprised. So were the proprietors when they met the boyish-

looking youth in his Quaker garments. He impressed them, however, by appearing taciturn in their presence, and they offered him the position at five hundred dollars a year. He accepted it and moved to Hartford, where he soon established himself in the home of Jonathan Law, a former postmaster.

His singular piece of good fortune in becoming editor of the 'Review' — the most important position that he had thus far held — gave him great prestige. From the start he tried to make life unbearable for Jackson, and he also attacked the Secretary of State, Van Buren, whom he charged with having done nothing for the country. He had controversies with Lincoln's future Secretary of the Navy, Gideon Welles, the Democratic editor of the Hartford 'Times,' because Welles made personal attacks upon Prentice, then in Kentucky. He approved the New Working Men's Party, showing that he was then more interested in labor problems than he was in later life. When he left the paper, he administered a final thrust at the Jackson administration 'because of its incompetency, its violence, its proscription, its bribery, its corruption, its disregard of the constitution of our fathers, and its turning of the necessary machine of government into a vast machine of party.'

He found a literary outlet in the 'Review' for short stories, sketches, and book-reviews. In the year and a half that he was in charge of this paper, he contributed a sufficient number of tales and poems to make a permanent reputation for himself. Most of this work, however, except for a few poems which he collected, is now forgotten.

The personality of the young Quaker, as on previous occasions of his editorship, permeated the paper. He wrote against infidelity as usual, especially in two tales, 'The Sceptic' and 'Henry St. Clair,' reprinting the latter from the New York 'Amulet,' where it obtained a prize. He generally showed poor literary judgment, as when he condemned the publishing of Moore's 'Life of Byron.' But he deserves our gratitude for having been one of the first to recognize Hawthorne's greatness, for he welcomed the unsigned sketch 'Sights from a Steeple,' one of the very first of the 'Twice-Told Tales,' published in Goodrich's annual 'The Token.' He commented on the versatility of the author's powers and quoted from the sketch at length.

He wrote excellent prose-poem sketches on various features of New England, consistently carrying out his theory of using local color in his writings. He praised her scenery and customs; he pictured a beautiful hanging hill; he described husking and quilting parties.

He was always interesting when he introduced a personal note. He projected his own private views so frankly that he practically gave the reader the raw material of an auto-biography. He wrote a short article on dreams, where he vividly described the terrors of a nightmare in which he was to be executed — a remorse dream resulting from a feeling of guilt for having committed some wrong. It arose from a consciousness of having trifled with the affections of a girl. Gideon Welles thought so well of this essay on dreams that he copied it without mentioning its source. This gave Whittier an opportunity of exercising the rare wit that never failed him. 'If the editor of the *Times*,' he wrote, 'would hereafter do us the *honor* of copying an original article from this paper, will he be so good as to give us credit therefor? *Dreams* are not always in the market, but we should think the said editor sufficiently a dreamer, and his faculties sufficient somniferous to manufacture his own night visions.'

Because he harped too persistently upon his love affairs in his poems, he provoked an adverse comment from Joseph Buckingham, editor of the Boston 'Courier.' In reply, Whittier said that he had written similar poems for Buckingham's own paper, and, in a mirthful spirit of daring and defiance, he reprinted a poem 'To Mary' that he had contributed to the 'Courier.'

Part of January, 1831, Whittier spent in New York doing some exhaustive research work in the libraries, looking up old newspapers, getting data for Prentice's book on Henry Clay, and even writing many pages for it. In New York, Whittier met Mordecai M. Noah, who was surprised at his youth. Whittier refused to partake of the convivialities of the town with the literati.

In June, 1831, Whittier's friend James Otis Rockwell, who had been editing the Providence 'Patriot' since November, 1829, died, in his twenty-fourth year. He had suffered from blighted feeling — a misfortune with which Whittier was in a position to sympathize. They had hobnobbed in Boston in 1829, when Whittier was on the 'Manufacturer' and Rockwell on the 'Statesman.' The two poets had had much in common; they both did editorial work; both advocated temperance; both were, according to their critics, guilty of the crimes of obscure birth and deficient scholarship. Rockwell, however, was a Democrat. When he became editor of the Providence 'Patriot,' he occasionally twitted Whittier about his political views. Nevertheless he reprinted stories and poems by Whittier. On Rockwell's death, Whittier wrote an elegy,[1] as he had done on the occasions of the deaths of Brainard and Pinkney.

Whittier's most celebrated poem in the 'Review' was 'New England,' a poem which smacks richly of the soil and is one of the earliest regional poems of a high order in our literature. He took great pride in New England even though he at times attacked the intolerance of her early settlers. Whittier soon incorporated the poem in a longer one, 'Moll Pitcher,' but showed poor judgment in never afterwards reprinting this deservedly popular lyric, in which, while praising his native soil, he also expressed his early ambition to become its bard — an ambition which he realized.

Another uncollected poem of those days, 'The Pharisee,' [2] in which he retold the story of Paul's conversion from soldier

---

[1] The elegy on Rockwell was in the *Review*, June 20, 1831. Whittier reprinted it in the 1838 edition of his poems and then dropped it.

[2] 'The Pharisee' appeared in the *Review*, Nov. 15, 1830.

to apostle, showed that even then his heart was with the cause of the oppressed. The following lines already exemplify the mind and spirit that characterized him in his antislavery days:

> 'Man may raise
> His arm against his brother, and the axe
> Fall heavily and frequent, and the cord
> Be prodigal of life — the dungeon stone
> Be worn by prayerful knees — the dagger grow
> Dark red with midnight murder, in the vain
> And idle hope to fetter human thought
> And cross the will of Heaven; — and every blow
> In persecution dealt shall be returned
> Back on the giver — every instrument
> Of foul oppression changed unto an aid
> Of that which it had threatened. Wo to those,
> Who trample down the sacred rights of man
> And o'er the God-like mysteries of mind
> Usurp dominion. There will come a time
> Of awful retribution. Not a groan
> Bursts upward from the persecuted heart
> But reaches unto Heaven? No martyr's blood
> Reeks up unheeded to the circling sky.'

The poet apparently was thinking at the time of the French Revolution of 1830, and, of course, his heart was with the revolutionists.

While on the 'Review' he achieved the distinction of being satirized in a book, 'Truth, a Gift for Scribblers,' by W. J. Snelling. The satire opened with a 'Prologue' in dialogue between the author and a friend who warned him that some of the writers attacked might assail his life, particularly Whittier with his paring knife. Snelling praised only Bryant and Brainard.

Whittier's social life in Hartford was more diversified than ever before, for he associated with doctors, lawyers, writers, editors, office-holders, and politicians. Here he began his friendship with F. A. P. Barnard, who later became President of Columbia. He became intimate with Charles M.

Emerson, a young lawyer, to whom he confided the story of his love affairs, his conquests and defeats. For Whittier had numerous feminine admirers, though they did not console him for his disappointment with Mary Emerson Smith. He became temporarily interested in another girl, also called Mary, and he succumbed to a passion for the daughter of one of his friends, Judge Russ, Miss Cornelia Russ, who rejected him and helped precipitate his nervous prostration.

In the spring of 1831, he returned to Haverhill, to help settle his father's estate, worth about six thousand dollars, of which he was one of the residuary heirs. He left Hartford in the fall on account of illness, intending to return after his recovery. Unfortunately he was not able to do so, for the breakdown in his health then began. Meanwhile he had been appointed a delegate to the National Republican Party Convention, which was to meet in Baltimore in December and nominate Clay, for President. He made an effort to go, but, being taken sick while on his way to Baltimore from Boston, he had to return to Haverhill. Compelled to give up his editorship, unable to travel to Baltimore, rejected by Miss Russ, and harassed by his affair with Miss Smith, he was seized with a terrible despondency.

CHAPTER IV

THE PIONEER OF REGIONAL LITERATURE

IN THE early winter of 1831, Whittier's first book, 'Legends of New England,' was published in Hartford. This slender volume is a pioneer work in regional literature and the earliest collection of poetry issued by any writer of the so-called New England school. Although he disowned the work in later years — even buying stray copies in order to destroy them — he could not remove the landmark that the volume fixed. Because of the novelty of its subject-matter, it still remains a significant book. In it he made his first convincing popular and academic appeal. In these legends, originally published in the Essex 'Gazette' and other periodicals, he introduced a new note into American literature. Brainard anticipated him, but Whittier made more effective and artistic use of his material. Whittier was the earliest of our great poets to draw his inspiration from the native soil of New England, and to avail himself of its early legends.[1]

The eleven poems and seven prose tales constituting the volume dealt with subjects taken from Colonial history. They were in the vein that both Longfellow and Hawthorne subsequently followed. We may dismiss the few experiments on Indian lore Whittier made in this book as the least

[1] Whittier reprinted in *Poems*, in the Appendix, only two of the poems from *Legends of New England*, 'Metacom' (original appearance *Ladies Magazine*, Feb., 1830) and 'Mount Agiochook' (original title 'The White Mountains').

George B. Cheever, in his *Commonplace Book of American Poetry*, 1831, included two of the poems, 'The Unquiet Sleeper' and 'The Indian's Tale.'

There has been no bibliographical record of any contemporary review of *Legends of New England*. I have been fortunate in discovering a two-page review by George P. Morris in the *New York Mirror*, March 19, 1831. It cites 'The Weird Gathering,' and of the prose quotes 'A Night Among the Wolves.' It recognizes that Whittier opened a mine, says that he presents his material 'clothed in the language of a practised and able writer,' and calls the book 'decidedly the most agreeable work of the kind we have read since the "Sketch Book."'

interesting of the legends recorded. In fact he was never successful with tales on this subject; he never wrote a poem so good as even 'Hiawatha.' In versifying Indian legends he was naturally constrained to stalk through sanguinary scenes, but, being a Quaker, he could not portray these with historic detachment or poetic sympathy. He sought in vain to emulate Scott in his bloody stories of the Scotch border. Since he could not identify himself with the Indians either in spirit or in temperament, he was incapable of enchanting the American public with Indian folk-lore.

He was more successful when harking back to Puritan traditions, as when he elaborated some tales from Cotton Mather's 'Magnalia Christi Americana.' One of these 'The Weird Gathering' is a tale of revenge taken by a girl at a gathering of witches in Salem, against a young man who had wronged her. A priest, learning from him of her share in casting the spell of enchantment upon him, was instrumental in hanging her. The poet unconsciously interwove in the tale his own regrets for having trifled, as we shall see later, with the affections of a young girl. He thus stood in judgment upon his own tendencies as a male coquet. He was, however, more incensed at the community and the priest for their unjust accusation and conviction of the alleged witch than he was at the youth for whatever wrong he did her; nor was he in sympathy with the girl for the ruthless vengeance she wreaked for her injuries.

Stories about reputed witches fascinated Whittier all his life. Since a witch is the central figure in his second book, 'Moll Pitcher,' this poem also belongs to the category of regional literature. He began it while he was in Hartford, but finished it after his return to Haverhill. He composed the verses to help while away the time when suffering from both physical indisposition and love disappointment. He gave the manuscript to a friend who published it anonymously as an octavo pamphlet in the early part of the year 1832. Whittier in his introduction modestly disclaimed any literary merit for the poem on the ground that it had been written under circumstances of illness. On the other hand, he stated that he did not publish the book to earn money, since he never dreamed of converting, 'by an alchemy more potent than that of the old philosophers, a limping couplet into a brace of doubloons; or a rickety stanza into a note of hand.'

The poem itself — over eight hundred lines in length — was not based on Moll Pitcher of Revolutionary fame, but on a handsome woman fortune-teller who had the same name — a resident of Nahant while Whittier was still a boy. Reading the account of her in Upham's 'Lectures on Witchcraft,' he decided to re-create it in a poem. He drew Moll Pitcher as an old hag, and the heroine, Adela, as a beautiful young woman, whom he had consult Moll Pitcher as to the whereabouts of her absent lover on the high seas, and he portrayed her as going insane as a result of the portentous answers she received. Eventually the lover returned safely, thereby restoring her to her senses, and married her. A daughter born of the union later ministered to the witch in her last moments, thus requiting her cruel conduct to Adela with kindness.

The outstanding artistic blemishes of this poem were the numerous long digressions. Whittier has preserved one of them, which he calls 'Extract from "A New England Legend,"' in his collected poems. Passages from an uncollected poem called 'The Exile' were also interwoven in the story — a fact which has escaped Whittier students. 'The Exile' is a tale of a man in love going away in search of gold in order to win over his sweetheart's parents, who objected to him because of his poverty. The poem, somewhat imitative of Scott, has occasional swift action and easy flow of narrative. It is replete with excellent descriptive passages, but it is most interesting for some lines of self-revelation.

Besides composing original poetry, Whittier also edited, during this year, a volume of poems — those of John G. C. Brainard. This volume is of interest because of Whittier's preface, in which he expounded his views of regional literature. He wrote:

'New England is full of Romance; and her writers would do well to follow the example of Brainard. The great forest which our fathers penetrated — the red men — their struggle and their disappearance — the Powwow and the War-dance — the savage inroad and the English sally — the tale of superstition, and the scenes of Witchcraft — all these are rich materials of poetry.'

He enlivened his preface by personal touches, particularly in a passage (to be cited later) where, speaking of a love disappointment of Brainard's he unconsciously voiced his own sufferings under a similar misfortune. His critical views, while speaking his familiarity with the recent and contemporary poets of England — Wordsworth, Coleridge, Byron, Shelley, and Keats — showed his limitations. He commended the moral tone of Brainard, especially because the age was poisoned by the licentiousness of Byron and Shelley! He quoted the endorsement of a pastor that Brainard had died a Christian as if that were a critical encomium upon his verse.

Unfortunately Whittier, in his desire to display his learning, was guilty of plagiarism. In dwelling upon the unpractical bent of Brainard's genius, he enumerated a number of men of genius — among them Locke, Akenside, Blackmore, Lord Mansfield, Erasmus Darwin, and Home — who had also been unfitted for worldly pursuits. The reviewer for the 'New England Magazine' said that this identical list, together with Whittier's comments upon them had appeared ten years previously in an article 'On Vulgar Prejudices Against Literature' in 'Blackwood's Magazine.' He pretended to make light of the unhappy coincidence but added that one could now readily understand why Whittier's writings abounded so frequently in literary illustrations. The charge of literary dishonesty against a man of Whittier's integrity must have been very galling to him.

Whittier never reprinted the Brainard book, nor the introductory essay. When another edition of Brainard's poems appeared later, Edgar Allan Poe wrote one of his famous castigating reviews and permanently shattered Brainard's reputation.[1]

The next of Whittier's important experiments in regional literature, 'Mogg Megone,' his third book of poetry, may be considered here because he wrote most of it during this period. Although he published it in 1836, after he had joined the antislavery ranks, he returned in it to his stock theme of the betrayed maiden taking vengeance on a false lover. The main plot, however, revolves around Ruth Bonython's murder of Mogg Megone, the Indian chief, who had killed her seducer and to whom her father had promised her in marriage. By this murder she defeated the plans of the Jesuit Ralle to convert him and his tribe to Catholicism. Her confession to the priest of her slaying of Mogg Megone is not altogether without literary merit. But the absurd story with its murders was not a theme in which a Quaker poet could be at ease. He justly called it later 'a big Indian in war paint, strutting in Walter Scott's plaid.' The poem has, however, several characteristic passages, especially one in which he expounded his views of the worship of nature. His own objection to the poem was that it had no moral; as a matter of fact it was one scene of horrors after another. It is the least known of his collected poems, though for years it was placed at the beginning of all editions.

Whittier was the first American writer who did not seek his themes or his background abroad. Anticipating many writers who have received credit for fostering a national liter-

---

[1] Whittier wrote an elegy 'To the Memory of J. G. C. Brainard' for the *New England Review*, April 30, 1830. In Pray, pp. 226–227. Though Griswold says Whittier knew Brainard intimately, he probably never met him, for Brainard died in Connecticut, Sept. 26, 1828, while Whittier, who had never been out of Massachusetts, was finishing school at Haverhill. Whittier was not then twenty-one, and Brainard had been ill for the year previous. Whittier in his Introduction does not say he knew Brainard.

ature, he urged American poets to break away from English literary influences. He has received little credit for his originality, because he helped efface the memory of his pioneer work by refusing to reprint it. Whittier's first three books, as well as the prefaces he wrote for the Dinsmore and Brainard volumes have been ignored ever since. His reputation, originally founded on them, is no longer connected with them.[1]

[1] I am enabled to clear up the question of his alleged coauthorship with B. L. Mirick in *The History of Haverhill*, published in March, 1832, for the publication of which Whittier issued proposals in the *Essex Gazette*, on March 27, 1830. Pickard thought that Whittier had been unjustly deprived of the credit of being the author of this book, and believed that the fact that the title-page was missing from Whittier's copy was proof that he had torn it out as an expression of his indignation. In an unpublished letter in the Yale University Library, Whittier practically disclaimed authorship of the book. Writing from Danvers, December 21, 1887, to someone inquiring for information on the subject, he said:

'I remember assisting Mr. Mirick somewhat in the preparation of his *History of Haverhill*, but the work is substantially his own.'

CHAPTER V

THE DISCLOSURE OF HIS LOVE FOR
MARY EMERSON SMITH

READERS of two of Whittier's famous love poems, 'Memories' and 'My Playmate,' used to be curious to know whom they commemorated. At least four different women have each received the distinction of being the heroine of these poems. Although a knowledge of the actual person who inspired them is by no means necessary to an appreciation of their literary merit, yet we do find a greater human interest in the poems on learning the true story of their origin.

In these poems, as well as in others, Whittier enshrined a distant relative, Mary Emerson Smith, a granddaughter of Mary Whittier, a second cousin of his father, and the wife of Captain Nehemiah Emerson, a veteran of the Revolution. The two children often met when they were guests at the captain's house in Haverhill, roaming the countryside and loitering on the banks of the Merrimac on moonlight nights. He would recite his poems to her, and she would listen to him encouragingly.

Although we are not acquainted with all the details of this love affair, we know that Mary, after trifling with him for seven or eight years, finally rejected him because of his poverty. We have records of the vicissitudes of the affair and the capriciousness of the sweetheart in numerous uncollected poems, and descriptions of his grief and despair in prose sketches and letters.

From the very first time he met her he was impressed by her Grecian features, her wavy brown hair, and her hazel eyes. He frequently portrayed heroines with Mary's features — Adela in 'Moll Pitcher,' for example.

But Mary's character was not ideal, for she was vain, even

selfish, and too fond of dancing. He often heaped reproaches
upon her for her worldly ways. Not being a Quaker, she paid
little attention to his admonitions. Her foibles gave him food
for thought; he has thus recorded his mental struggles:

'I saw her, and could not forget her; I sought her society,
and was gratified with it. It is true, I sometimes (in the first
stages of my attachment) had my misgivings in relation to
her character. I sometimes feared that her ideas were too
much limited to the perishing beauty of her person. But to
look upon her graceful figure yielding to the dance, or reclin-
ing in its indolent symmetry; to watch the beautiful play of
coloring upon her cheek, and the moonlight transit of her
smile; to study her faultless features in their delicate and
even thoughtful repose, or when lighted up into conversa-
tional vivacity, was to forget everything, save the exceeding
and bewildering fascination before me. Like the silver veil of
Khorassan it shut out from my view the mental deformity
beneath it. I could not reason with myself about her; I had
no power of ratiocination which could overcome the blinding
dazzle of her beauty. The master-passion, which had wres-
tled down all others, gave to every sentiment of the mind
something of its own peculiar character.' [1]

Nevertheless his love for her deepened and by the time he
was nineteen years old he was helplessly in her toils. He now
used to write out of the bitterness of his own heart, like
Keats when he saw that he was in the thrall of *la Belle Dame
sans Merci*. Such being his emotions even before he entered
the Haverhill Academy, they were intensified by constant

[1] 'The Opium Eater,' *New England Magazine*, March, 1833. *Prose* v. I, pp. 278–
304.

I had from the very beginning of my researches become convinced that Whittier
in his sketch 'The Opium Eater' was telling the true story of his love-affair with
Mary Emerson Smith. When I later went to Hartford to look up the *New England
Review*, to my surprise I found that the most important section of the opium-eater
sketch, that dealing with a love affair, had appeared there under the title 'Confessions of a Suicide' in 1830, and had thus been written at a time when the affair was
still going on; proving conclusively that the opium-eating motive was an afterthought, and that the penning of his love woes was the true reason for writing the
early sketch later incorporated.

association with Mary there. It is only too evident that he was not feigning grief for literary purposes. Alas, it was too genuine! He had fallen under the spell of a girl whom in his gloomy moments he was compelled to regard as a Lorelei. She encouraged him and discarded him, trifled with him and again enfolded him in her embraces. But she would not marry him; he was only a poor farmer boy; he merely 'fed her father's kine.' He began to feel that his growing fame, his handsome figure and face, his integrity of character were futile, since they did not help him win the girl he loved. What though the other village girls idolized him and sought his attentions! That good fortune could not allay the fiery tempest which swept over him. His poverty and lowly position in life were a barrier between him and his sweetheart. He had even been willing to sacrifice his religious principles for her. Though she was not a member of the Society of Friends, he was ready to 'marry out of meeting,' for he did not care that hers was 'the Genevan's sternest creed' and his the 'Derby dalesman's simple truth.'

Nevertheless, he proceeded more arduously than ever with his courtship. He tried to arouse her jealousy by paying attention to other girls. At times she would resent such flirtatiousness and persuade him to return to her, but, finding that he still yielded to her wiles, she gave him to understand that he was but a friend and a cousin. She continued attending dances and giving herself up to earthly vanities. He again preached to her but in vain about the serious things in life and about the future world. He often tried to convince himself that her character was defective; but the sight of her brown hair would always make him forget her faults. He vented his feelings in poems addressed to her under fictitious names as well under her own. But he could not improve her; nor could he make her fall in love with him.

Shortly after he went to Boston to edit the 'Manufacturer,' she definitely rejected him. He knew that she did so because of his straitened finances; yet he could not reconcile himself to losing her. Meanwhile Mary had moved to Kennebunk, Maine, where she was attending a seminary. He decided to continue the friendship; he still might miraculously guide it into the path of love. Possibly he would later be earning more than five hundred dollars a year; he would persevere as long as he felt that he might receive an encouraging response in the future. He knew that the affair might be prolonged for years, but he would wait patiently; there might be a favorable outcome to it. So the young poet and political editor, idolized by women, decided to act the part of the page in the days of chivalry, and dance attendance upon his lady. One day, hearing that she was betrothed to another his despair reached such a state as to compel him to write to her in abject humility.[1]

He began by addressing her formally as 'Miss Smith,' deliberately and rudely omitting even the 'Dear' as if to give convincing proof to her of his future intentions to maintain their relations on the strict basis of friendship. He realized that it was absurd to cherish his hopeless love and resolutely declared he had now done with sentimentality. He had killed his love for her and merely pleaded as a favor for her friendship. But when he reminded himself that she was probably engaged, as he heard, to another, he burst out pathetically and poignantly into declaring for her that very love he so bravely affected to have buried. 'Mary! I have loved you passionately; deeply; and you, if there is faith in woman's words, you have not *hated* me.' He reminded her of the many walks they had taken on the banks of the Merrimack — walks which were still living in his memory. Then he recovered himself and told her that he loved her as only a brother should love a sister, and then again he reverted to his passion and impressed her with the fact that she was the beau ideal of his imagination. 'You have known my devo-

[1] Whittier's letter to Miss Smith, dated May 23, 1829, was first published in Miss Swett's book *John Ruskin's Letters to Francesca* (1931), pp. 417-421. Miss Laurin Martin, a niece of Mary Emerson Smith, gave the letter to Mrs. C. H. Vinton, a sister of the author of the book, Miss Lucia G. Swett.

tion and such, too, as none other will ever exact from me,'
he added. The purpose of his letter, however, he insisted
was to ask for friendship, nothing more. Surely she could
not be so unreasonable as to deny him such a request. Mary
had put a quietus on their friendship as something that had
given him illusive hope, and for his own good had been seeking to effect his recovery by withdrawing herself completely
from him. He now even descended to a white lie by saying
he admired her disposition, when as a matter of fact he was
very critical of it and had written so in a number of poems.
He awaited anxiously a letter, his heart throbbing at the
mere prospect of again seeing her well-known handwriting.
For he is anxious soon to say a thousand things to her, about
his literary friends and even the fashions, in fact anything
and everything — if she would only write and grant his
request.

At the same time he relieved his feelings by writing the
editorial 'Aristocracy' previously quoted, in which he defended a form of aristocracy based on the qualities of the
mind rather than on rank and wealth.

As Mary's answer — if there was any — was undoubtedly
unfavorable, Whittier now decided that he must forget the
painful humiliation he had suffered, and root out the passion
that was festering in him like a sore. Assuming an air of independence, he sought to convince himself, as is evident from
a poem 'To My Cousin,' that he was no longer in love with
her. He defiantly told her that it was futile for either of
them to linger upon past memories. But apparently she was
not disturbed, for he heard reports that she was happy, and
that the steps of her dance on the ballroom floor were higher
than those of any of the other dancers. He tried to persuade
himself that this 'gay coquette' was unfitted for him in the
serious path of life. Yet he recalled their moonlight walks
and again saw her dark eyes turned towards the blue sky.
Nevertheless he now assured her that she could, if she
wished, kindle in another heart the flame that no longer

burned in his, and he concluded the poem on a note of derisive defiance, telling her, to send him, if she married, a piece of bridal cake, for him to write a sonnet upon; — so little did he care for her now.

He published his poem in the 'Manufacturer.' But scarcely before the printer's ink on the poem was dry, a sudden revulsion of emotion stirred him to the depths. No, he could not lose her so lightly! He felt a recrudescence of his old passion, and in his despair he wrote 'Stanzas,' [1] a poignant poem for the next issue of the paper. I quote part of it:

'Forgive thee — ay — I do forgive thee,
    And bless thee as we part,
And pray that years may never leave thee
    My agony of heart.
I call no shadowy malison
    Upon thy fair young brow,
But would thy life might ever run
    As sunwardly as now.

I know that I have knelt too lowly
    For smiles so oft withdrawn, —
That trusting love received too slowly
    The lesson of thy scorn, —
That thou hast had thy triumph hour,
    Unquestioned and complete,
When, prompted by a spell of power,
    I knelt me at thy feet.

'Tis over now — the spell is broken —
    The lingering charm hath fled,
And pass away like thought unspoken,
    The vows which thou hast said;
I give thee back thy plighted word —
    Its tones of love shall be
Like music by the slumbrous heard —
    A dreamer's melody...

.   .   .   .

Thy pleasant path may yet be shaded, —
    A shadow cross thy sun —

---

[1] 'Stanzas,' *American Manufacturer*, July 23, 1829.

The rosy wreath that Love has braided
  Fall from thee one by one.
The flatterer's tones may pass away —
  The lyres of love be broken —
And manhood's evil scorn repay
  The fondness thou has spoken.

Go, heartless girl! thou'll smile to-morrow,
  As I had never been —
And spurn thy lover's words of sorrow,
  For those of happier men.
A darker destiny thy page
  Of coming years may tell!
God keep thee, on thy pilgrimage,
  Loved being! fare thee well.'

During the summer of 1829, he wrote a number of love poems depicting the emotions he was experiencing in the wake of his final rejection by Mary. In 'Memory' he recalled the sadness of their parting; in 'The Dream of the Misanthrope' he reproached all women because their love was 'a changeful gem,' and concluded that every hope of the human heart, except that of heaven, was vain. But he still could not pluck out of his heart the love that had become so deeply rooted there. As he watched the sunrise one morning, he addressed to her the following poem, 'To S. E. M.,'[1] and published it in the 'New England Review':

TO S. E. M.[2]

The morning is a blessed one — the distant trees are shaking
Their tall plumes up against the sky, like warriors awaking;
The clouds are slowly stealing off — the vapour-folds are thin,
And a path is opening beautiful, for the sun to journey in.

And gloriously he cometh up — the streams have caught his eye,
They have given all their robes of mist to the breeze that passeth by,
They are hurrying from their forest-paths, where the shade is long and
    cold,
To dance before his pleasant beam, and flout their robes of gold.

---

[1] These letters are an anagram, forming the initials of Mary Emerson Smith's name, reversed.

[2] 'To S. E. M.,' *New England Review*, Sept. 14, 1829.

Dost thou watch this opening glory? Do thy fairy footsteps pass
Like the wing of some elastic breeze among the stirring grass?
Does the light wind freshen up thy cheek, and toss the rich, dark curl
With a playful hand around thy brow — thou loved and loving girl?

I have stood beside thee often times, at such an hour as this,
When nature seemed to image back thy passing loveliness;
And have knelt in that idolatry, by hearts of passion given
To woman's shrine of priceless love — the purest out of Heaven!

Thou hast answered that idolatry with a lip and with an eye
Uplighted with a love as wild, as passionately high.
Thou hast given me thy confidence — thou hast given me thy vow,
And their memory is as sunlight on my spirit's darkness now.

Thou art far away, fair creature! — do thy tho'ts come back to me,
Like the sunny waves that wander from a very distant sea?
Does the spirit of the dreamy past bend sweetly o'er thy pillow,
To shape its sleeping visions, as the night-wind shapes the billow?

God keep thy sun unclouded — thou art very dear to me,
Even as a green spot 'islanded' in a dull and shoreless sea.
In the spirit's high communion, I greet thee from afar
As Nature's untaught worshippers would hail a distant star.

The gusts of furious blasts of inhibited sex passion now swept over his poetic work. In 'The Vestal' he wrote of love madness in the manner of the Latin nations.[1] This poem is an assumedly impersonal retelling of an old Roman legend about a crime of violence instigated by baffled love. Strange, is it not? that a Quaker should select a tale with such a conclusion for treatment! It is apparent that a personal bias made him do so. He never returned in late years to this species of poetry.

As Mary again encouraged Whittier, they both resumed their friendship. There were soon other poems of farewell, of reconciliation, of reproach, of anger, of tenderness, and of self-pity. In short, it was the typical case of a passionate

---

[1] 'The Vestal,' *The Yankee*, Nov. 1829. Reprinted in *The New England Magazine*, Feb. 1904.

youth in the toils of a coquette. Mary did not want to marry him; but she was human and she submitted to his ardent love making. He was still hopeful enough to think she might accept him.

The best of the farewell poems was the one he published in the 'Boston Courier.' This is the poem he reprinted in the 'New England Review,' in a spirit of mirthful challenge to Buckingham, the editor of the 'Courier,' who reproached him for printing too much love poetry in the 'Review.' Addressed to Mary in her own name, it is one of the most personal and autobiographical poems he ever wrote. It records the story of his griefs and the difficulties of his love quite fully.

TO MARY [1]

Yes, I am changed — and really, Mary,
　　I marvel thou hast yet to learn
How strangely human hearts will vary
　　Amid this dark and cold sojourn.
The world would be a happy one —
　　If grown up men could ape the boy,
And ripened intellect bow down,
　　To trifle with its childhood toy; —
If manhood's spirit never knew
　　The promptings of that loftier feeling
Which bids us stand erect and view
　　The shrine at which our youth was kneeling;
And curl the lip and bend the brow
　　At lisping tones and pensive beauty
And reconcile the broken vow
　　With notions of a sterner duty.
But, the world changes sadly, Mary —
　　Its early love, its deeper passion —
Its sympathies and friendships vary;
　　As often as thy bonnets' fashion!
And we may love a little while
　　Ere yet the heartless world begin
To write upon affection's smile
　　The passages of shame and sin:

---

[1] 'To Mary,' reprinted from the *New England Review*, Aug. 30, 1830.

Yet, what avails the feverish beam
　　That, dimmed with tears, must shortly fade? —
Vain as the desert-sleeper's dream
　　Of fountains gushing in the shade,
When broadly to his waking eye
　　The parched and arid sands are spread —
The poison Siroc creeping by —
　　The hot sun glaring over head!

Mary! — I leave thee to the joy
　　Which youth and love and wealth may cherish —
Oh — how unlike the wayward boy
　　The memory of whose love must perish!
Yet thou hast praised his idle rhymes,
　　And words of very fondness spoken,
Whose memory rests on evil times
　　Like moon-light on a wave that's broken!
Yet what of this? — Thy heart may bear
　　At times the traces of emotion,
But none will linger longer there
　　Than keel-tracks on the level Ocean;
And thou wilt dress thee for the ball —
　　And part thy dark locks from thy brow
And let their shadowy richness fall
　　In beauty on thy neck of snow: —
And other eyes will follow thee
　　As fondly as mine own have done;
And other forms will bend the knee
　　Like Persians to their idol Sun:
And thou wilt lay thy Euclid by
　　To talk of marriage, love and laces
Lest study dim the laughing eye
　　And intellect eclipse the graces!
Friend of my boyhood! — Fare thee well!
　　The light of song is waning now
And inspiration scorns to dwell
　　Upon my broken fiddle-bow.
And I am as 'another man' —
　　The freshness of whose hope is dead —
An idler in Life's caravan —
　　A scribbler for my daily bread!

But he could not keep up this mood of pathetic resignation very long. He wrote another farewell poem, very Byronic, in which he imagined her dead; for he again heard that she was being married, and her marriage meant her death so far as he was concerned.

The most important contribution growing out of his love for Mary was a sketch in prose called 'The Confessions of a Suicide,' in which he told the poignant tragedy of his love.[1] He afterwards incorporated the sketch in a longer one, 'The Opium Eater' from which I have previously quoted. The piece of mystification he indulged in prevented biographers from recognizing the truth of the facts in the earlier confessions imbedded in the later-written essay. In these confessions, we see how much he suffered from the woman upon whom in later life he looked back with tenderness and to whom he wrote sentimental poetry. In those early days, however, he was so fired with the injustice done him that in despair he had thoughts of suicide. Mary, however, did not marry at the time, and he continued dangling again at her beck and call until he finally had a nervous breakdown.

While we do not know whether Whittier himself ever attempted suicide, we need have no doubt that he personally experienced the emotions he described in 'Confessions of a Suicide,' and that Mary was responsible for his perturbations.

He now resolved to recover his spirits and render himself independent of her; he would no longer even bear any malice toward her. He rewrote the concluding part of 'Stanzas,' the poignant poem that he had contributed to the 'Manufacturer,' and published it in its altered form in the 'New England Review' with the following substituted lines:[2]

> 'And yet thou hast my earnest prayer
> For blessings on thy way,

---

[1] 'Confessions of a Suicide,' *op. cit.*, Oct. 18, 1830.

[2] 'Stanzas' with the new conclusion, *New England Review*, Dec. 27, 1830. This version is in Pray, pp. 241–242 (from a later reprint in the Haverhill *Iris*).

> That flowers may spring and blossom there
> Which know not of decay.
>
> The oak whereon the falling thunder
> Hath passed, may yet remain,
> The cliff by lightning torn asunder,
> May dare the storm again; —
> And I can bear myself so well,
> In manhood's sterner part
> That neither brow nor lip shall tell
> The ruin of the heart.'

During the entire year of 1831 he tried to forget his griefs in his exacting labors on the 'Review.' He wrote poems of parting and unhappy maidens, and tales of men marrying witches who throttled or suffocated them. He made love to girls at Hartford, and he even developed temporary passions for two of them.

When Whittier left Hartford, he was almost a nervous wreck. We get an inkling of the state of his mind from a passage in a letter to Jonathan Law:

'I have been at home — that is to say, in this vicinity — all the time, — half sick, half mad. For the last fortnight I have been kept close.'

Mary Emerson Smith departed for Cincinnati about this time, to take up her permanent residence in the Middle West. In spite of her rejection of Whittier's advances, she continued to correspond with him.

Whittier's own feelings at the time when he was writing 'Moll Pitcher' and brooding over Mary even entered into the 'Introduction' he wrote to the poetical works of J. G. C. Brainard. For while describing in it, vividly and at great length, a love disappointment of Brainard, he drew on his own painful memories:

'This great passion of the heart,' he wrote,' when connected with disappointed feeling, is not easily forgotten. Mirth, wine, the excitement of convivial intercourse, — the gaities of fashion, — the struggles of ambition, may produce a

temporary release from its presence, but a word carelessly uttered — a flower — a tone of music — a strain of poetry —
"Striking the electric chain wherewith we are darkly bound,"
may recall it again before the eye of the mind, — and the memory of the past — the glow and ardor of passion — the hope — the fear — the disappointment — will crowd in upon the heart.'

A little later, in a sketch, 'The Nervous Man,' [1] published in the 'New England Magazine,' he again dilated on his own love woes. *He* was the nervous man and, like his fictitious hero, was reading Byron extensively — 'Conrad,' 'Lara,' 'The Giaour,' and 'Manfred.' He himself wrote the two Byronic verse compositions in the sketch whose authorship he assigned to the nervous man.[2]

Influenced by Coleridge's 'Christabel,' Whittier took an imaginary revenge against Mary by writing a poem, 'The Demon Lady,' in which he drew her as the siren he now conceived her to be. He represented the woman as murdering her noble warrior husband on the bridal night. The poem contains a covert attack upon Mary for having trifled with him. Though in later life he wrote tenderly about her, we see how bitter he was against her in those days.

> 'The wildest demon ever wrought,
> In fancy's wizard web of thought,
> Is powerless to the *human fiend*,
> Wearing an angel's loveliest form,
> Hiding with rainbow hues the storm,
> Lovely without, but dark within
> As the recorded pages of sin —
> A veiled monster who can smile
> Witchingly for a little while,
> Until some noble heart hath given
> Its all on earth, perhaps in Heaven,
> A free and fearless sacrifice,

---

[1] 'The Nervous Man,' *New England Magazine*, Aug., 1832.
[2] One of these was a reprint from a farewell poem he had published two years previously.

Then wake the victim from his dreaming,
Cast off her false and lovely seeming —
A demon to his waking eye.' [1]

Unfortunate Whittier! His was the noble heart that had given its all and been ill rewarded.

I have given only a few examples of the many ungarnered love poems Whittier wrote in his youth. It is apparent that he had other reasons for refusing to collect his early poems than their lack of literary merit. He did not want to reprint his early poems, because they told the world the story of the course and defeat of his chief love passion. As he was a very proud man, he never wanted the true story disclosed. He kept everybody in the dark as to why he never married, and he always gave evasive answers on the subject. He tried to screen from the world the tragedy of his life and the identity of the girl who had held him captive.[2]

The subsequent life of Mary after she rejected him was not eventful. She married Judge Thomas of Covington, Kentucky, and became the mother of a large family. She watched the poet's abolition activities, but did not approve of them. During the Civil War, though Kentucky did not secede, she showed her sympathies with the Secessionists.

After she had become a widow, she and the poet renewed their friendship, meeting at times in the mountains in New Hampshire, where she came for her summer vacations. They corresponded towards the end of their lives. She gave him a photograph of herself in 'widow's weeds,' which he treasured in an old album. She survived him by several years.

Though he kept the story of his love for Mary secret from the world, he revealed his tale at times to intimate friends. When Mrs. Elizabeth Cady Stanton and her husband,

---

[1] 'The Demon Lady,' copied from the Philadelphia *Album*, March 24, 1832, where it was reprinted from the *Albany Literary Gazette*.

[2] There are two early 'love' poems in the Appendix of Whittier's collected poems 'Isabel' and 'Stanzas: Bind up thy tresses.' I found that though the former poem is assigned to the year 1832 in the Cambridge Edition, it is quoted in *The Providence Patriot*, December 12, 1829, as copied from the *Essex Gazette*.

Henry B. Stanton, the poet's close abolitionist friend, on their return from England visited him in the summer of 1841, the year in which 'Memories' was published, he told her the tale of his love.   In her autobiography she wrote of the circumstances that prompted this disclosure of confidence:

'Sitting on the piazza one moonlight night, admiring the outlines of Bunker Hill Monument and the weird effect of the sails and masts of the vessels lying in the harbor, we naturally passed from the romance of our surrounding to those of our lives. I have often noticed that the most reserved people are apt to grow confidential at such an hour. It was under such circumstances that Whittier opened to me a deeply interesting page of his life, a sad romance of love and disappointment, that may not yet be told, as some who were interested in the events are still among the living.'

Mrs. Lucia Gray Alexander, wife of the famous artist, and friend of Whittier, also knew of his love affair. We find her writing in 1870 to a cousin: 'He [Whittier] was really attached to a very beautiful woman of Dover when he was young, but his father died poor. The care of the family came on him. He could not propose at the time. She married a Southerner. She is now a widow with ten children, and they are good friends.'

Mrs. Alexander once in a letter to the poet asked him if a story in a newspaper just published about his love for Mary Emerson Smith was true. The poet in his reply wrote, 'Yes, it did rather squint that way.'

Whittier's placing 'Memories' at the head of the division of poems that he called 'Subjective and Reminiscent,' made shortly before he died, is sufficient comment as to the importance he assigned to Mary in his life.

Speaking of the poem to someone who said it was a favorite of his own, he replied; 'I love it too; but I hardly know whether to publish it, it was so personal, and near my heart.'

CHAPTER VI

LOVE INTERLUDES

MARY, however, was not the only girl with whom Whittier was infatuated in those trying years, for he was frequently attracted to other paragons of feminine beauty — especially if they had brown hair. Love cast its spell upon him, surprising him, the Quaker and Puritan, by the strength of the power with which it held him.

For a brief period he paid attention to Evelina Bray, whom he met at the Academy. She was a tall brunette of seventeen, with brown hair, and a face of good color. She boarded on Water Street, opposite Thayer's house, where Whittier lived. They took walks together, and she entertained him with tales of people in foreign lands, which she had heard from her father, an East Indian sea-captain. She soon thought she had reason to believe herself engaged to him. But Whittier, discovering that he loved Mary, decided to sever his relations with Evelina. It was a delicate task, for he did not want to appear a trifler with woman's affections or a man without honor. He explained to her that marriage with her would cause great anxiety to his parents, as he was too poor to marry. The truth of the matter was that he was not sufficiently in love with her. He was even swayed by public opinion, for his Quaker friends had censured her for her worldly ways, and above all because she loved music and owned a piano. He did not tell her that he was ready to overlook similar faults in Mary. Evelina became grief-stricken, but resolved to bear her misfortune as stoically as possible. She vowed to herself that she would marry the first man who proposed to her. She was not bitter against Whittier, for he presented his side in such a plausible way.

A year or two later he visited her again in Marblehead,

and they took the walk to which he referred in his beautiful love lyric, 'A Sea Dream.' Whittier wrote this poem late in life, when he revisited the scenes of the early walk.

He soothed his conscience at the time he abandoned Evelina, by writing many poems about the cruelties of faithless lovers and the grief of rejected maidens. In the early spring of 1829 he contributed to the 'Manufacturer' a poem entitled 'The Church-Yard,' in which he represented a lover, stricken by remorse, visiting the grave of a girl who had died for love of him: [1]

> 'Contrition, mighty as the wrong
> Came o'er his haunted mind at last,
> And phrensied feelings smothered long
> O'er heart and brain in lightning passed.
> Well might he mourn — a fairer flower
> Ne'er bloomed to fend the spoiler's pride,
> To be the idol of an hour,
> Then flung, a worthless weed, aside.'

Since he also knew how painful it was to be deserted, he drew upon his own emotions in his affair with Mary. What a state of mind he was in that spring! Contrition was mingled with humiliation, for this was the time when he penned that long, pathetic letter to Mary.

In 'The Forsaken,' published a year after he had parted with Evelina, he gave a description of her grief, and indirectly and covertly launched an attack upon himself for his own fickleness. He vicariously imagined her brutally revenging herself upon him — in fact, murdering him.[2]

> 'Oh! ye may make a demon of the best
> And loveliest of God's creatures. Seek her when
> The careless air of lightsome childhood blends
> With maiden bashfulness — when first the dreams
> Of love and romance lend their pensive shade
> To the young brow, and passion flushes high
> The unstable beauty of the varying cheek;

---

[1] 'The Churchyard,' in the *Manufacturer*, March 26, 1829. Pray, pp. 198-199.
[2] 'The Forsaken,' Philadelphia *Album*, July 3, 1830.

> Bend a proud knee before her, and sit down
> Beside her when she fingereth the harp —
> And whisper in the pauses of her song;
> Or walk with her by moonlight, and compare
> The snowy whiteness of a sleeping cloud,
> With the clear beauty of her lifted brow —
> Or, tell her that the glory of the stars
> Is fainter than the lustre of her eye —
> And when her heart beats wildly, and her cheek
> Is eloquent with the most delirious thought —
> Betray her tender confidence, and turn
> Her heart's blood into tears — yes, darken all
> Her innocent being with pollution's stain.'

Since Whittier in this poem almost defended murder as a retaliatory punishment for seduction, it is apparent that he wrote out of the great remorse he suffered for forsaking a girl he had encouraged.

In the poem 'Destiny' he put the following words into the mouth of a girl whom her lover had deserted:

> 'Go now — the lingering course is given
> The spell is laid on thee...
> That spectral form shall follow thee
> The broken hearted one.' [1]

He also wrote at the same time for the 'New England Review' the poem 'The Farewell,' a parting rebuke of a girl to a lover who had left her to marry another.

As a defence mechanism to withstand the darts of his accusing conscience for instilling poisonous grief into Evelina's life, Whittier cultivated an aversion to philanderers and often wrote against them. Like Burns, who himself practiced seduction but delivered tirades in 'The Cotter's Saturday Night' and other poems against those who betray women, Whittier, who trifled with woman's affections, declaimed against insincerity in love. We, with our new psychology, can understand the mental processes of writers who make an outcry against persons for committing the very sins of which

---

[1] 'The Destiny,' *New England Review*, Aug. 23, 1830. Pray, pp. 225–226.

they themselves are guilty. They resort thus to nature's kindly healing powers in preserving them from too great agony. They purge themselves of remorse for wrongdoing by discharging their indignation at those who are similarly guilty.

Whittier wrote a short story, 'The Forsaken Girl,' beginning with this sentence: 'If there is any act which deserves deep and bitter condemnation, it is that of trifling with the inestimable gift of woman's affections.' [1]

He sought to allay his feeling of guilt for his conduct toward Evelina by writing an editorial against male coquets as he called philanderers.

'The male coquet is of all beings the most despicable. He is an anomaly in the human character, — a monster in the moral world — playing a part for which nature never designed him, — the Joan d'Arc of civil life.... His coquetry is a cold and selfish purpose; a hollow-hearted love of triumph — a morbid desire of interesting in himself hearts, of whose pangs and struggles he recks not — whose affections he would call forth, that the multitude may envy him its possessions, not to meet its full flow of confiding tenderness by the sympathy of his own cold and indurated bosom. It is an unprofitable attempt to monopolize the attention from the other sex, which he scorns to repay with honorable love.' [2]

Evelina's subsequent life is worth recording. About ten years after Whittier abandoned her, he presented her with a book of his poems. A year later, when he was very ill, she wrote to him apologetically as follows: 'I hesitate, as I place this sheet before me. I know, some would hold that I am about to do something improper. Yet, under the present circumstances, I have a strong desire to be indulged. If I do err, I trust, you will forgive me.

'I have watched your pathway, and have read, with unfeigned satisfaction, the declarations of esteem which differ-

[1] 'The Forsaken Girl,' *op. cit.*, July 26, 1830.
[2] 'The Male Coquet,' *op. cit.*, Oct. 10, 1831.

ent occasions have called forth, towards you, from the good, and the benevolent.

'But, recently, I have learned, that He, who has given you so much respect among men, has laid His hand upon you, and withdrawn you from the field of usefulness, in which you were endeavoring faithfully to labor.

'It is this knowledge, which makes me feel a strong desire to send this to you, before we meet, where time shall be no more.' [1]

In 1849, at the age of forty, Evelina married William Downey, an Englishman. Since he was neither kind nor affectionate to her, the marriage was unfortunate. He was a fanatic in his hatred of Catholics and eventually met his death — in the eighties — from wounds inflicted by a New York mob hostile to his crusades.

Whittier, later in life, met Evelina and corresponded with her. She survived him, and as she spoke for publication often, she became the best known of Whittier's loves.

Of his next experience in love we know little. After he came to Hartford he became temporarily interested in another girl named Mary, even though he was then brooding over Mary Emerson Smith. The record of a momentary jealousy that he displayed, at least, indicates this. When he was in New York City in January, 1831, doing research work to help Prentice in his life of Henry Clay, he wrote to Jonathan Law of Hartford, manifesting fear of losing the affections of this other Mary, of Hartford, and showing himself rather resentful of a rival: 'How does Mary get along with that fragment of a Frenchman — that kneely [sic] Adonis of hers — Professor Per — no — De Morris?' he asked. 'Tell Ann to take charge of her during my absence, and see that she take no other lesson from the Monsieur than his French. These foreign gentlemen are the devil and all at winning the

[1] Manuscript letter of Evelina Bray to Whittier, dated Marblehead, 1st of the 5th mo., 1840, in Essex Institute.

"smile of de *fair lady*." Elizabeth Trumbull and her Italian is a case in point.' [1]

There is another reference to a girl named Mary — apparently the same girl — in a letter Whittier received from his lawyer friend Charles M. Emerson, of Hartford, towards the end of 1832, a year after Whittier had left the city. As his publisher Hammer owed him more than a hundred dollars, Whittier asked Emerson to begin an action at law against him. Whittier may also have gone to Hartford in an effort to collect the money, for we find Emerson inquiring, after dwelling on his own love troubles: 'How did you find your old friend Mary? Any billing and cooing? She is engaged to Parker and expects to husband it next spring. Much good may it do her!' [2]

The question 'Any billing and cooing?' in this unpublished extract makes us suspect that Whittier had billed and cooed with Mary before, and that Emerson was in his confidence. Emerson was curious to know if Mary had allowed him to resume the privilege she had previously extended him. We see that young Whittier in spite of his Puritan training was not averse to caressing a girl for whom he cared.

As we shall learn later, he had several other girl friends named Mary, with whom he was half infatuated and to whom he wrote poems.

The other Hartford girl, who made a deeper impression upon him than the unknown Mary, was Cornelia Russ, the daughter of his friend Judge Russ. She was seventeen, with blue eyes and most exquisitely colored dark hair such as Whittier admired. She came from a brilliant family, one of her brothers later becoming a prominent Hartford lawyer. Whittier met her only on a few occasions; indeed, as she had many admirers, she could not devote much of her time to

---

[1] From a letter to Jonathan Law, dated January 2, 1832. Pickard omitted the passage quoted in his part production of the letter in Vol. I, p. 88. The quotation was taken from a complete typewritten copy of the letter in the library of Yale University.

[2] From the manuscript letter dated Dec. 30, 1832, in the Essex Institute.

him. In the summer of 1831 he published in the 'Review' a
poem, 'The Declaration,' addressed to a girl he did not know
well.[1]

Some of the sentiments in it resemble those in a letter he
wrote to Miss Russ a few months later, when he sought an
interview with her, apparently for the purpose of proposing
to her. It is evident that he was not on familiar terms with
her. He was contemplating a visit to the West, where he
had prospects of a position and where Mary Emerson Smith
had moved, but he wanted to sound Cornelia on her attitude to him. Since Mary had never consented to marry
him, he felt he had a right to court Miss Russ. His letter
to Miss Russ was as follows:[2]

Thursday afternoon

Miss Russ, — I could not leave town without asking an
interview with you. I know that my proposal is abrupt —
and I cannot but fear that it will be unwelcome. But you
will pardon me. About to leave Hartford for a distant part
of the country, I have ventured to make a demand for which,
under any other circumstances, I should be justly censurable.
I feel that I have indeed no claims on your regard. But I
would hope, almost against any evidence to the contrary,
that you might not altogether discourage a feeling which has
long been to me as a new existence. I would hope that in my
absence from my own New England, whether in the sunny
South or the 'Far West,' one heart would respond with my
own — one bright eye grow brighter at the mention of a —
name, which has never been, and I trust will never be, connected with dishonor, — and which, if the Ambition which
now urges onward shall continue in vigorous exercise, shall
yet be known widely and well — and whose influence shall
be lastingly felt.

[1] Reprinted in Pray, pp. 232–233.
[2] First printed by Professor William Lyon Phelps in the *Century Magazine*, May,
1902.

Thursday Afternoon.

My Dear,

I could not leave town without asking permission an interview with you. I know that my proposal is abrupt — and I cannot but fear that it will be unwelcome. But you will pardon me. About to leave Hartford for a distant part of the country, I have ventured to make a demand, for which under any other circumstances I should be pretty censurable. I feel that I have indeed no claims on your regard. But I would hope, almost against any evidence to the contrary, that you might not altogether discourage a feeling which has long been to me as a new existence. I would hope that in my absence from my own New England, whether in the sunny South or the "Far West", that one heart would respond with my own — one bright eye grow brighter at the mention of a

—name, which has never been, and I trust never will be, connected with dishonor,—and which, if the ambition which now urges onward shall continue in coming career, shall yet be known widely and well—and whose influence shall be lastingly felt. ————

- But this is dreaming,—and it may only call forth a smile. If so—I have too high an opinion of your honorable feelings to suppose even for a moment that you would make any use of your advantages derogatory to the character of a high-minded and ingenuous girl. ———— ————

———— I leave town on Saturday. Can you allow of an interview this evening or on that of Friday? If however you cannot consistently offer me the pleasure of seeing you—I have only to resign hopes dear to me as life itself, and carry with me hereafter the curse of disappointed feeling.

A note in answer will be waited for impatiently. At least you will not deny me this.

Yrs. most truly,
J. G. Whittier

But this is dreaming, — and it may only call forth a smile. If so — I have too high an opinion of your honorable feelings to suppose even for a moment that you would make any use of your advantage derogatory to the character of a high-minded, and ingenuous girl ——

I leave town on Saturday. Can you allow an interview this evening or on that of Friday? If however you cannot consistently afford me the pleasure of seeing you — I have only to resign hopes dear to me as life itself, and carry with me hereafter the curse of disappointed feeling.

A note in answer will be waited for impatiently. At least you will not deny me this.

Yrs. most truly —
J. G. WHITTIER

We do not know whether Miss Russ replied to this note, but if she did her answer must have been discouraging. The episode hastened his nervous breakdown. He had been ready again to defy the Quakers by marrying her, but Cornelia was not moved by his compromising spirit, any more than was Mary Emerson Smith. He knew what again was the obstacle — his poverty. He was also socially below her — her father was a Judge and a former member of Congress, and he was a farmer turned editor. Cornelia was proud and snobbish like Mary. Meanwhile his high passions, clogged again, brought suffering upon him. He brooded and brooded, till physical agony and mental torture wrecked him. Recoiling against the mercenary instincts and selfishness of Cornelia, he condemned the entire sex for the frailties of one or two. The rejection by Cornelia could not have come to him at a worse time than now, for he was still suffering because of Mary's coquetry.

Of Miss Russ we know nothing further than that she died unmarried in 1842, at the age of thirty-eight while nursing a sick sister. For a time she too figured as the heroine of

'Memories,' but as a matter of fact she inspired none of Whittier's later poems.[1]

[1] The history of the letter to Miss Russ is supplied to me by her grandnephew, Mr. Charles C. Russ, of Hartford, the present owner of it. His grandfather, brother of Miss Russ, settled her estate when she died about 1860, and received possession of the letter. Dying himself shortly, he left the letter to his wife, who retained it till her own death in 1901, when she left it to her grandson Mr. Charles C. Russ.

Professor Phelps furnished me the history of the controversy that arose as to the genuineness of the letter. After he had published the letter, Mr. Pickard published a statement that the letter was a forgery. Professor Phelps took the original to him, and then Pickard admitted its genuineness. Meanwhile Thomas Wentworth Higginson published his biography of Whittier and quoted from Pickard's article, accepting its conclusions. Professor Phelps then told Higginson that Pickard now admitted the genuineness of the letter, and asked him to change his statement in the next edition. Colonel Higginson replied that it would be too expensive to change the plates.

CHAPTER VII

THE BIRTH OF AN ABOLITIONIST

EVEN while suffering from nervous indisposition Whittier was thinking of his future. For a year and a half, till June, 1833, Whittier's career alternated between periods of idealism and political ambition, when his nobler strain finally triumphed. The effect of being twice rejected because of his poverty by girls whom he loved was to awaken in him a deep sense of the importance of material possessions. His writing had brought him glory but no immediate financial remuneration nor prospects of any for the future. He therefore looked askance at any fame with which posterity might crown him. He wanted his reward now.

'I would have fame with me *now*,' he wrote to Mrs. Lydia H. Sigourney a month after he left Hartford, 'or not at all. I would not choose between a nettle or a rose to grow over my grave. If I am worthy of fame, I would ask it now, — now in the spring-time of my years; when I might share its smile with the friends whom I love, and by whom I am loved in return. But who would ask a niche in that temple where the *dead* alone are crowned; where the green and living garland waves in ghastly contrast over the pale, cold brow and the visionless eye; and where the chant of praise and voice of adulation fall only on the deafened ear of Death?'

Ultimately he put his veto on poetry, and, as he said, 'knocked Pegasus on the head, as a tanner does his bark-mill donkey, when he is past service.' When he recalled that the lives of two of his fellow poets, Rockwell and Brainard, had been tragically cut off in their prime, he saw no glamour in Bohemia. Although he had realized his poetic ambition, he found the rewards ashes in his mouth. He also lost confidence in his literary ability, because he believed that other poets were writing poetry more beautiful than his. He did not altogether disdain the muse. 'The truth is,' he admitted to Mrs. Sigourney, 'I love poetry with a love as warm, as fervent, as sincere, as any of the more gifted worshippers at the temple of the Muses.'

He saw that the little political reputation he had acquired as editor was more powerful than his poetical one. Men older than he had looked to him for the assistance that he could render them by political editorials or through his influence with dominant officials and leaders. Whittier, therefore, first had a selfish reason for abandoning poetry, since he expected to acquire wealth by his political activities. Believing that his poetical reputation would interfere with the success of his career, he definitely resolved to cease writing poetry, and, as a matter of fact, during these years he wrote little verse.

His first political activities were directed towards helping elect his friend Caleb Cushing to Congress. Cushing was a young writer and lawyer from Newburyport who had been trying to enter Congress on the anti-Jackson platform since 1826. By editorials and letters to the press Whittier had tried to influence voters to give their support to Cushing, but to no purpose. After ten trials Cushing, discouraged by repeated deadlocks, gave up the fight in the spring of 1832. A third candidate, of Cushing's own political party, who had been constantly put into the field against him, was the obstacle to his election. Whittier, realizing that Cushing could not break the deadlock, thought that he himself might do so if he became a candidate. Like other politicians he also succeeded in convincing himself that his friends were persuading him to run for Congress. There was, however, one barrier; he was not eligible, since he would not reach the age of twenty-five till December, a month after election day. He wrote a letter to his friend, Edwin Harriman, editor of the Haverhill 'Iris,' a Cushing paper, boldly outlining a plan by which he

could get himself elected. He urged Harriman to induce
Cushing to remain in the fight another month, so that, he
himself, then becoming of age, could seek the nomination!
Then he would get Thayer of the 'Gazette,' as well as Cushing himself, to support him; for Whittier would run on the
ticket approved of by Cushing. In short Whittier wanted to
deceive Cushing, by having Harriman make false representa-
tions to him that he might be elected if he now returned to
the fight. This was the only time Whittier ever tried to do
anything unscrupulous. He even sought to make Harriman
think that he was not selfish in his ambition, and promised
him that if he were elected, he would use whatever influence
he obtained politically for the benefit of his friends.

But Cushing's wife died at the time, and he lost his political
ambition; thus Whittier's plan of getting himself elected
did not succeed. Shortly afterwards Cushing did return to
the contest, but he was defeated by the Democratic candidate despite the help Whittier gave him. The deadlock being
broken, Whittier lost his opportunity of running for Congress.

An idealistic spirit now took complete possession of him.
Questioning whether a writer should not devote all his literary
efforts to the cause of humanity, he concluded that poets
should become propagandists in the cause of social justice
and clean politics. In this mood of self-righteousness, he attacked other writers for not serving noble causes. In an unsigned poem 'To a Poetical Trio in the City of Gotham' in
the Haverhill 'Iris' for December, 1832, he urged three poets,
two of whom were William Leggett and William Cullen
Bryant, both of the 'New York Evening Post,' to devote
their pens to the cause of liberty. He told them to follow the
example of contemporary writers in England, like Thomas
Moore, Bulwer, and Campbell, who had turned away from
their old themes to battle for democratic causes. Both
American poets subsequently followed Whittier's advice.

Whittier determined now to do the very thing he was

advising others to do, to serve humanity; he was preparing for a course of action that was to change his entire life. Though he had abandoned poetry and entered politics for selfish reasons, he saw that he could now, divesting himself utterly of any self-seeking motives, use both poetry and politics to further a noble cause — abolition. Rarely had a writer made a greater leap from egoism to idealism. He was like a man who, after hibernating in dark, cavernous depths, suddenly raced up the slopes of a mountain to dwell on its sun-bathed summit.

Possibly he was not conscious that his love catastrophe had prepared him for entering the ranks of the antislavery movement. That a man of Whittier's temperament might have become a reformer without such a motive is not at all unlikely, but his love frustration helped to catapult him into the antislavery movement. Even if he was not aware of the real reasons for his conduct, his course deserves high commendation.

Other external circumstances contributed to Whittier's becoming an abolitionist. Abolition as a propaganda movement for the immediate emancipation of the slaves in America really began with the publication of the 'Liberator' in Boston by Garrison in January, 1831. Garrison, the year after he founded the 'Liberator,' exposed, in his 'Thoughts on African Colonization,' the idiocy and futility of those who advocated colonization, and he showed that they were not interested in liberating the blacks, but only in freeing themselves from the presence of those who had already been emancipated. Garrison asserted that the colonizationists actually retarded the freeing of the slaves.

Whittier, who was at first a colonizationist, had hated slavery before he joined the abolitionists, denouncing it in one of the first editorials he wrote in the 'New England Review.' Contact with Garrison finally sent him into the abolitionist ranks. After he had read Garrison's pamphlet 'Thoughts on African Colonization,' he realized that an intelligent and radical movement to exterminate slavery was necessary.

When Garrison in March, 1833, was preparing for a visit to England to expose the Colonization Society, he asked some woman friends of Whittier in Haverhill to use their efforts to induce him to give up his creations of poetic fancy and his political strife and to throw his support into the abolition cause. Soon he wrote to Whittier himself:

'My brother, there are upwards of two million of our countrymen who are doomed to the most horrible servitude which ever cursed our race and blackened the pages of history. There are one hundred thousand of their offspring kidnapped annually from their birth. The southern portion of our country is going down to destruction, physically and morally, with a swift descent, carrying other portions with her. This, then, is a time for the philanthropist — any friend of his country, to put forth his energies, in order to let the oppressed go free, and sustain the republic. The cause is worthy of Gabriel — yea, the God of hosts places himself at its head. Whittier, enlist! — Your talent, zeal, influences — all are needed.'

A month later Garrison visited Whittier in Haverhill and coaxed him with all the arguments he could muster to become converted to the cause of immediate emancipation. It was an auspicious time. The persecution of Prudence Crandall for founding a school for colored girls in Connecticut was arousing indignation and winning adherents to abolitionism. Whittier cast in his allegiance with the abolitionists, and even arranged for a gathering at the meeting-house, to hear Garrison speak on abolition. He was thoroughly converted, and Garrison departed, leaving behind, a zealous neophyte. Whittier could now speak of himself as he later did of Sumner:

'God said: "Break thou these yokes; undo
    These heavy burdens. I ordain
A work to last thy whole life through,
    A ministry of strife and pain.

'"Forego thy dreams of lettered ease,
Put thou the scholar's promise by,
The rights of man are more than these."
He heard, and answered: "Here am I!"'

Whittier began reading abolition literature. He also read the works of writers who were lovers of liberty. Studying carefully Milton's 'Areopagitica' and other pamphlets, he decided to make the life of Milton a model for his own. Milton had sacrificed a poetic reputation to free the English people from the tyranny of the church, of the press, of the marriage institution, and of the state. He would also abandon his poetical career in the cause of liberty. He read Burke, too, for his sentiments on freedom. He even took up political economy and constitutional law. As the fruit of his studies, he decided to publish a pamphlet against slavery. He knew that the publication of his views would injure his political prospects, but he had no selfish ambitions now; if he was to remain in politics, he would do so from idealistic motives. Whatever political influence he might wield in the future, he would use in the abolition cause. He would begin by trying to convert Caleb Cushing, and, if not successful in that, at least to make him an agent for arousing sympathy for the cause in Congress. He would therefore, continue to support Cushing politically if he showed the least sympathy with the abolitionists. He wrote to him that he would soon send him a pamphlet on slavery, and at the same time he urged him to remain a candidate for Congress.

In June, 1833, Whittier entered the abolition arena by publishing four hundred copies of a pamphlet called 'Justice and Expediency,' for the printing of which he himself paid. Its publication was an heroic act. It sealed his career as a poet, and heralded the most important work of his life.

In writing 'Justice and Expediency' he followed the method of Edmund Burke in his political pamphlets. His study of Burke before writing his book transformed the poet into a controversalist. As a matter of fact, he had been familiar with some of Burke's speeches and writings for a number of years, finding them helpful as models in writing political editorials.

By the publication of the slavery pamphlet Whittier lost many personal and editorial friends. He was soon in a controversy with the Richmond 'Jeffersonian and Times,' and to their charge of fanaticism he penned replies in the 'Essex Gazette.' Garrison reprinted these in the 'Liberator.' Whittier's pamphlet was, meanwhile, reprinted by Arthur Tappan, of New York, as one of the numbers of the first volume of the monthly 'Anti-Slavery Reporter' of New York, and five thousand copies were distributed. It won him friends like Samuel E. Sewall, of Boston, and Nathaniel P. Rogers, of Plymouth, New Hampshire, both abolitionist lawyers.

His chief purpose was to arouse public opinion against slavery, and he made a special plea to women and Quakers. He was not satisfied with the prevailing lukewarm sympathy for the slave. He himself minced no words, as for example: 'The burning, withering concentration of public opinion upon the slave system is alone needed for its total annihilation.' 'The accursed thing is with us, the stone of stumbling and the rock of offense remains. Drag, then, the Achan into light; and let national repentance atone for national sin.'

He was indifferent to the mockery and ostracism that now befell him as an abolitionist. Persecution had been the badge of his tribe; fear of it did not disturb him. He rather felt a welcome relief from the ambition that had been harassing him. He was now spiritually at ease, since remorse for a self-conscious egoism no longer chafed his sensitive spirit.

The change from the career of a poet and editor to that of agitator was so pronounced as to make him wonder whether there had been many literary lives parallel to his own. Though he was no longer eager for a future literary career, the memories of his fame in the past were not unpleasant. During this time he had published several hundred poems in more than a dozen publications — poems that had been widely copied in school readers, anthologies, annuals, almanacs, and newspaper-corners. He was the author of two books of poetry and the editor of two volumes. He had been the subject of many critical eulogies. At the age of twenty-five he had written and published more than had his idol Robert Burns at that age. As a matter of fact at that age when, as he now thought, his own poetical career ended, Burns's had not yet begun; yet he now drowned out the echoes of his own poetic reputation by enlisting as a soldier in the cause of the slave. What a strange prank nature had played upon him by means of one person! Garrison, who had published his first poem in a short-lived village weekly seven years ago had converted him to abolition.

He lost, too, whatever opportunity of political preferment he had, for about this time he had become a candidate for the State Senatorship in Essex County. At the election he was defeated on account of his new course — though by only one vote. Such was the penalty he paid for having become an abolitionist.

In November, Garrison wrote to him that the Boston Young Men's Association wanted to send him as a delegate to the first National Anti-Slavery Convention, to be held in Philadelphia in December. Whittier, in poverty, was fighting the demon of politics, who whispered temptingly into his ear, and he was still in doubt as to his wisdom in the choice of his new career.

'I have as yet done nothing,' he replied. 'I have had no leisure — my time is all occupied with the affairs of my farm; — I must work, or starve, — or do worse, plunge again into the seven times heated furnace of modern politics. I have strong temptations — very strong, to adopt the latter course — but Truth and Conscience and Duty are against it — for so sure as I should enter the lists of political controversy, my lips would be sealed upon the subject, dearest to my heart, the holy cause of Emancipation.' [1]

He finally decided to go to Philadelphia. Here he could be of service in persuading the members of the Society of Friends in Philadelphia to devote themselves to the cause. But he had no funds with which to undertake the journey. Samuel E. Sewall, the Boston lawyer and abolitionist, agreed to defray Whittier's expenses.

With visions of possible tarring and feathering, he made preparations for the journey. As Pennsylvania was a border State, he was apprehensive that Southerners would break up the meeting and inflict personal indignities upon him, which he feared more than physical injuries. He was soon off, with Garrison, his old schoolmaster Joshua Coffin, and others, by stage-coach.

Arriving in Philadelphia, the delegates met with rebuffs when they tried to get some Quakers outside of the abolition ranks to act as chairman. They finally decided to choose one of their own number; they agreed upon Beriah Green, and appointed Whittier and Lewis Tappan secretaries. The meeting was in the Adelphi Building, on Fifth Street, below Walnut, in the shadow of Independence Hall. The convention was made up of more than sixty delegates, most of whom were young; one third of the entire number were Quakers.

Whittier at the convention was thus described by his friend the Rev. J. Miller McKim:

'He wore a dark frock-coat, with standing collar, which, with his thin hair, dark and sometimes flashing eyes, and black whiskers, — not large, but noticeable in those unhirsute days, — gave him, to my then unpractised eye, quite as much of a military as a Quaker aspect. His broad square forehead and well-cut features, aided by his incipient reputation as a poet, made him quite a noticeable feature in the convention.'

In the constitution that they drew up the delegates dis-

---

[1] An unpublished extract from a manuscript letter to Garrison in the Boston Public Library. Pickard published only part of the letter, in Vol. I, pp. 132–133.

avowed acts of violence or attempts to cause insurrections among the slaves. Garrision prepared the platform or declaration of sentiments in the garret of a colored man with whom he boarded. After the usual discussion, the delegates, on the second day, signed the paper, forming thus the American Anti-Slavery Society. They all received copies of it printed on silk. Whittier was proud to be a charter member. He wrote in later years these memorable words: 'I set a higher value on my name as appended to the Anti-Slavery Declaration of 1833 than on the title page of any book.'

The most startling demand in the Declaration was that planters emancipating their slaves should not be compensated. The reasons assigned for this contention were that 'freeing the slave is not depriving them (the holders) of property, but returning it to the rightful owner,' and that 'if compensation is to be given at all, it should be given to the outraged and guiltless slaves, and not to those who have plundered and abused them.'

Having performed the most momentous deed of signing the declaration, Whittier returned to Haverhill in high spirits. Now began his arduous duties and drudgery as an agitator. Shortly afterwards he was appointed an agent for his county, and his duties compelled him to travel in spite of his ill-health. He also became corresponding secretary in the spring for an antislavery society that was organized in Haverhill. He now had to attend conventions and draw up reports. He was not present at the second annual meeting of the New England Anti-Slavery Society which met in Boylston Hall in January, 1834, but he sent a letter — a vigorous, logical plea for immediate emancipation — to the Secretary, Samuel E. Sewall. He attended, however, the important four days convention which met also at Boylston Hall in the latter part of May. Here the abolitionists took up for practical consideration the problems of abolishing slavery in the District of Columbia and the slave traffic between the States. Important leaders in the movement were present — Samuel E. Sewall, David Lee Child, Charles C. Burleigh, Professor Charles Follen, Ellis G. Loring, Amos A. Phelps, and others. Whittier was, with Follen and three others, appointed to a committee to prepare 'An Address to the People of the United States.' The pen of the poet can easily be discerned in this passionate appeal to the American people to exterminate slavery. He was a propagandist now. He sought to convert William Ellery Channing, who had been sympathetic to the cause but had given it no active co-operation. Whittier wrote a letter to him, which apparently swayed him, for not long afterwards the great doctor wrote in behalf of the slaves.

Whittier also used his pen as an antislavery poet, one of his efforts being a long poem on Toussaint L'Ouverture. Another poem of more national appeal was 'To the Memory of Charles B. Storrs,' an elegy on the late President of the Western Reserve College, who had died shortly before the meeting of the Anti-Slavery Convention in Philadelphia, as the result of an indisposition he developed from having delivered a long antislavery address. Whittier's lines, beginning 'Thou hast fallen in thine armor,' sounded through the abolition ranks like the notes of a trumpet. The poem was the earliest of his many elegies on now forgotten abolitionist worthies. It was also the first abolition poem that he contributed to the 'Liberator.'

In 1834 the persecution of the abolitionists, even abetted by the colonizationists, increased. Whittier's pen in behalf of the cause was now more necessary than ever. His poem 'The Hunters of Men,' a mock-rollicking pasquinade directed against the Colonization Society, attracted attention. It is still timely, for it depicts pseudo-philanthropists who are hypocritically more concerned about their own interests than about relief of the oppressed.

Whittier continued to be active with his pen. One of the best of his antislavery poems was suggested by a speech of

Charles Follen, Professor of German at Harvard, who soon lost his position because of his abolition activities. Garrison, who published the poem in the 'Liberator' September 20, 1834, predicted that the blast from Whittier's trumpet of liberty would be heard from Maine to the Rockies. His prophecy proved correct; the poem was quoted and recited throughout the country, some orators making their reputation by declaiming it. The poem, now called 'Expostulation,' is a rhymed editorial, it is true, but it had passionate and commendable indignation. The following stanza was often quoted in antislavery publications:

'What ho! our countrymen in chains!
    The whip on woman's shrinking flesh!
Our soil yet reddening with the stains
    Caught from her scourging, warm and fresh!
What! mothers from their children riven!
    What! God's own image bought and sold!
Americans to market driven,
    And bartered as the brute for gold!'

Whittier was now realizing his early ambition of becoming known as a Howard, a Wilberforce, a Clarkson, rather than as a Byron. With his emergence as an antislavery poet, he was more anxious than ever that his early poems in the files of newspapers and magazines should be forgotten. He wanted to be known only as a propagandist. Furthermore, his religious education had made him avert his eyes from beauty that was not of the soul. His martial instincts impelled him to battle, not to physical battle, but to war for moral justice and social reform. He believed that his antislavery poetry was more important than his poems based on New England legends; in fact, he regretted his past career. When the crying injustice of chattel slavery was abroad, how could he sing love woes? How had he been able to write of love griefs of bewitched ladies and of specter ships, when the cries of mothers separated from husbands and children, sold into slavery, arose about him? Much as he disliked to enter the fray — for he was a sick man, and loved the quiet of his farm and the companionship of his books — he could no longer weave rhymes about sentimental and useless regrets for childhood, when free colored men were being sold at auction in Washington to pay for their jail fees.

Occasionally at this time he did write poems and sketches that did not deal with slavery, but he did this for a livelihood. They appeared chiefly in the 'New England Magazine,' edited by his friend Joseph T. Buckingham.

During this year, 1834, also, he abandoned his allegiance to Henry Clay, whom he had once classed in a poem with Marco Bozzaris, but whom he now regarded as a betrayer of the cause of humanity and as an enemy of freedom.

But Whittier did not — in fact, he never did altogether — abandon his political activities. He now used them in order to further the cause of the abolitionists. He became a candidate for the State legislature, and he supported Cushing, who was again running for Congress, hoping to enlist him for the cause. Cushing nearly lost the votes of the abolitionists, but Whittier came to his rescue. At a meeting of the Essex County Anti-Slavery Society in Danvers in October, 1834, when the delegates decided to write to legislative and congressional candidates for their views on slavery, and to support no one not in favor of abolishing slavery in the District of Columbia, Whittier said that Cushing, in spite of being a colonizationist and opposed to immediate emancipation, would do all in his power to remove slavery from the District of Columbia. He then wrote to Cushing, stating that he had acted without authority in his behalf, but asking him to favor the Society with an explicit answer on his views.[1] This

---

[1] Whittier's letter to Cushing asking him to state his views is dated Nov. 3, 1834, and is in Pickard, pp. 173-174. Cushing's reply, undated, is in Carpenter, pp. 202-204. Carpenter apparently did not know this was the reply, for he merely guesses that this undated letter was 'apparently written in the early part of this period.' Dr. Fuess, thinking that Cushing never replied to Whittier's letter of Nov. 3, 1834, says that Cushing had no intention of becoming Whittier's agent in Congress and saw no reason for gratifying the latter's desires. Apparently Dr. Fuess has not seen the letter in Carpenter. In this undated letter Cushing, fully responsive to Whittier's desires, promised to gratify them.

Cushing did, for he understood very well that Whittier, being the leader of the abolitionists in Essex County, could influence them in voting for him. Since he was running on the National Republican ticket against the Democratic candidate, and since the abolitionists held the balance of power in Essex County, they could help elect him. At Whittier's behest they cast their vote for him and elected him.

Cushing entered the Twenty-Fourth Congress, but did not take his seat till nearly a year later. He then kept his word and presented the petitions of his constituents to Congress for the abolition of slavery in the District of Columbia. Though he himself was not in favor of abolition, he believed in the right of petition. Thus this future Cabinet-member and foreign minister began his political career by the guidance and assistance of Whittier. At the same time Whittier, in spite of his abolition views, was elected to the Massachusetts legislature. His success was proof of the high regard in which the community held him; for an abolitionist running for office in those days was less popular than a Communist today. It was the only time Whittier ever held a political office.

CHAPTER VIII

EMBATTLED FOR FREE SPEECH

WHEN Whittier entered the lower house of the Massachusetts legislature he was not in his element. The farmer-poet who liked nothing better than writing poems about rural life and old legends was neither an orator nor a law-maker; he was peacefully inclined and disliked controversy; yet now he was to help make the laws of his country instead of its songs. His career resembled that of a contemporary German poet, Heine, who also preferred to live a contemplative existence and to weave lyric fancies, but instead was spurring on his nation in behalf of liberty.

As a member of the General Court, Whittier was placed on the Committee on Engrossed Bills. He tried in vain to have capital punishment abolished. He made valuable friendships with men like Robert Rantoul, Jr., and Robert C. Winthrop, both of whom he influenced to some degree to extend their sympathies to the abolition cause.

While attending the session of the legislature he became intimate with George Thompson, the young English orator who had come to this country at Garrison's invitation to plead against slavery. Thompson's presence in America was like a red rag to the American public. Meetings were held in New York, Philadelphia and other cities denouncing him and the abolitionists, and defending the South. The attempt of a foreigner to interfere with our institutions bitterly aroused the ire of the American people. The virulent attacks upon him by the press were directly responsible for the many mobbings to which he was subjected. Whittier, who admired him, not only for his efforts in the cause of the slave, but for his courage in facing mobs, invited him to Haverhill as his guest. Thompson accepted the invitation and came there in August. After staying a few days, he and Whittier went to Plymouth, New Hampshire, to visit Nathaniel P. Rogers and to deliver lectures on abolition. On the way they visited Rogers's brother-in-law, George Kent, at Concord, and arranged for a public meeting on the return trip.

Kent made preparations, and had handbills printed announcing that a meeting would be held at the courthouse, where Thompson and Whittier would answer questions and explain the principles of the abolitionists. The town authorities then took active measures to prevent the announced gathering. The populace became excited and prepared to give the lecturers a reception which they did not anticipate.

After Whittier and Thompson had spent two days with Rogers, they returned to Kent's home in Concord, where at the time a number of women were in session. Whittier soon left the house with some friends to go to the meeting; Thompson was to follow shortly afterwards. On the way Whittier met part of the impatient, howling mob rushing to Kent's house to lay hands on him and Thompson before they could reach the courthouse to speak. They had just attacked a Quaker preacher whom they had mistaken for Whittier. When they now saw Whittier himself, they yelled gleefully. They pelted him with rotten eggs, and shouted as they saw the yellow stains besmirching his black Quaker coat. They hurled stones at him, but these only glanced by him and struck against the fences. Poor Whittier drew his coat over his face and ran on helpless. What a situation for a member of the legislature of a bordering sovereign State to be in!

In an account of his mobbing written shortly afterwards Whittier wrote: 'The good people were lashing each other into a fine frenzy, cursing the Abolitionists as Federalists, etc. The cry was raised "To George Kent's and the wine in his cellar!" [1] Fearing an attack on our friend's house, we

---

[1] From letter dated Boston, Sept. 9, 1835, in *Essex Gazette*. Copied in *Liberator*, October 3, 1835, and from there in Kennedy, II, pp. 93–94.

turned to go back and give warning of the danger. But our friends, the mobites followed us and insisted that I, notwithstanding my Quaker coat, must be the identical incendiary and fanatic, George Thompson. A regular shower of harmless curses followed, and soon after another equally harmless shower of stones, dirt and gravel. These missiles were hurled with some force, and might have done us some injury, had not those who projected them been somewhat overdone by their patriotic exertions in drinking destruction to the Abolitionists.'

Kent's brother rescued Whittier and his companion, taking them into his own house and defying the mob to enter. Being told by a clergyman that the man they had assaulted was not Whittier, they went towards George Kent's house, in search of Thompson. Since he expected that they would be seeking him, he had just escaped accompanied by Kent through a back door. To disperse the mob, a military official was called into requisition. He told them that Thompson was not in the house, that only some ladies were holding a meeting there, and that since they had succeeded in doing what they had intended, preventing the meeting, they might as well disperse. They obeyed him and went away, but they relieved their pent feelings by burning Thompson in effigy.

Whittier, in great anxiety about Thompson, left the house of Kent's brother disguised in the garb of a clergyman and soon found him. They all prudently returned to George Kent's house, for the streets were not safe. The mob, suspecting that Thompson had gone back again, besieged the building. Here they kept up a disturbance till the early hours of the morning, threatening to demolish the structure with the guns and cannon that they had brought with them. In the early morning Whittier and Thompson escaped in a carriage driven by fast horses. After they had passed out of the town limits they stayed at an inn, where they heard themselves discussed and saw handbills about themselves. Whittier, on leaving the inn, told the startled landlord who they were, and they then galloped off in the direction of Haverhill.

Thompson remained here with the poet for a few weeks, winning during his stay the friendly regard of the poet's twenty-year-old sister, Elizabeth.

Several weeks later Whittier was to witness his friend William Lloyd Garrison being carried through the streets of Boston. Whittier had arrived with his sister, he to attend an extra session of the legislature, and she to take part in a meeting of the Female Anti-Slavery Society. Thompson was scheduled to speak, but some 'gentlemen' in Boston circulated handbills offering a reward to anyone who would 'snake' him out and thus help to bring him to the tar-kettle. The mob, unable to find Thompson, broke up the meeting of the Female Anti-Slavery Society, and then laid hold of Garrison. They led him through the streets with a rope around him. Whittier, who was then in the State House, heard the angry shouts of the mob, and became concerned about his sister, who was at the meeting of the Society. He went outdoors, and caught a glimpse of Garrison just as the mayor rescued him and dragged him off to jail. Later he and Samuel J. May visited him in his cell. He was himself warned that the house where he, his sister, and Mr. May were staying might be attacked; nevertheless he remained, and both men kept guard all night.

Though Whittier was now spending his last year on the farm tilling the soil, his pen was not idle. Shortly before he witnessed the mobbing of Garrison, he had written two of his most effective poems — 'Clerical Oppressors,' a violent attack on the clergymen of Charleston, South Carolina, for approving by their presence a proslavery meeting, and the poem called 'Stanzas for the Times,' beginning 'Is this the land our Fathers loved?' He wrote a public letter in reply to Channing, who in his book disapproved of the methods of the abolitionists. Whittier showed that their adopted policy was productive of results and had already disturbed the callous indifference of the community.

He was again in politics, sending Cushing petitions for abolishing slavery in the District of Columbia. 'We shall plague Cushing with it,' he wrote to his friend Thayer about one of the petitions, 'but he had as lief see the old Enemy himself as see it.' He knew that Cushing was not at ease in presenting the unwelcome petitions. He promised him that he would persuade the Massachusetts legislature to support him and to protest against the rejection of the petitions. He continued belaboring Cushing with political advice and soothing him with flattery; he even laid down for his guidance principles of constitutional law, though he was no lawyer and Cushing was one.

Whittier himself was elected for a second term to the legislature, but declined to serve because of ill health; which, however, did not prevent him from pursuing his abolition activities.

About this time President Jackson delivered his famous message denouncing the abolitionists and calling for the passage of laws to restrain their activities. Southern Governors also made insolent demands upon Northern Governors to punish the abolitionists in their States through new legislation. Governor Joseph Ritner of Pennsylvania in a spirited reply refused to heed their intrusive and impudent pretensions. For his noble conduct Whittier made him immortal in a poem. On the other hand Governor Edward Everett called on the Massachusetts legislature to pass penal laws against the abolitionists. Whittier, deeply aroused at this attempt to suppress free speech, wrote a stinging letter for the 'Essex Gazette' addressed to Everett,[1] charging him with trying to do what all the so-called 'patriots' at the time were doing — namely, to stifle any reference to a great wrong. He wrote that he held with Milton that the liberty

[1] Letter to Everett, *Essex Gazette*, Feb. 13, 1836. Copied in *Liberator*, Feb. 20, and from there in part in Kennedy, II, p. 102.

to know, to utter, and to argue freely is above all other liberties, and that he would not consent to 'abstain from discussion,' even though the advice to do so came backed by a cautious intimation of 'prosecution for misdemeanor' or a 'renewal of the old Sedition Laws.'

Fortunately the legislature never passed such a law as Everett recommended.

During the spring of 1836 many of Whittier's writings were on the subject of free press and free speech. For Henry L. Pinckney of South Carolina introduced resolutions in the House against the hearing of the petitions for the abolition of slavery in the District of Columbia, and he was successful in having the resolutions adopted. This was the first of the so-called 'gag' rules which John Quincy Adams, then in Congress, fought.

Whittier, furiously aroused on learning that Pinckney's detestable resolutions were adopted in the House, resented such attacks upon constitutional rights, and wrote his famous lines now called 'A Summons' — one of his most impassioned pleas for liberty. Except in the title, it barely referred to the bill or to the resolutions; its sentiments were such as would be evoked in a lover of liberty by any law that violates the constitutional rights of freedom of speech, press, and opinion, whether economic, political, or religious. Whittier called on the New England people to protest and fight, and not henceforth humbly ask as favors rights that were their own. He pleaded with them to send forth their voice and demand their own ancient freedom, as well as the deliverance of the Negro.

There was also a personal reason for Whittier's pleas for free speech. Dr. Reuben Crandall, a brother of Prudence Crandall, was then being tried in Washington for publishing a seditious libel. His crime consisted in allowing a friend to read and take away the reprint in the 'Anti-Slavery Reporter' of Whittier's pamphlet 'Justice and Expediency.' Whittier, closely following the events of the trial, reflected that while this cultured physician had been languishing for eight months in jail for merely giving away a pamphlet, he, the author of it, was safe at home. Had he been in Washington, he would himself have been tried for sedition. In the bill of indictment some paragraphs, the products of his pen, copied verbatim from the 'Anti-Slavery Reporter,' No. 4, for September, 1833, formed the basis of the charge against Dr. Crandall.

The prosecutor was Francis Scott Key, then District Attorney for the District of Columbia and famous as the author of 'The Star-Spangled Banner.' He was active in the American Colonization Society, but opposed to the 'abominable' publications of the abolitionists. It was even reported that he said he meant to press for a sentence of death if he obtained a conviction. The trial of Dr. Crandall lasted for ten days, and he was finally acquitted. But while in jail he contracted consumption, from which he died two years later. When slavery was abolished, during the Civil War, in the District of Columbia, Whittier in his 'Astræa at the Capitol,' referred to the prison-cell

'Where wasted one in slow decline.
For uttering simple words of mine.'

After Dr. Crandall's acquittal the story of the trial was published in pamphlet form. One of its pages contained the passage from 'Justice and Expediency' for which the doctor was 'charged with Publishing Seditious Libels, By Circulating the Publication of the American Anti-Slavery Society.' Singularly enough a paragraph from this 'seditious' passage anticipated Lincoln's famous speech on 'the house divided against itself.' We thus see that a sentiment the circulation of which at one time put a man on trial for sedition was to send another twenty-five years later to the White House.

About this time occurred two events that affected Whittier's personal life. He became editor of the 'Essex Gazette,' and he gave up the farm at Haverhill. As both his older sister Mary, and his brother Matthew had married, he found that the farm labors were too onerous for him. He, therefore, with his mother, his sister Elizabeth, and his Aunt Mercy, removed to Amesbury, a village a dozen miles away, where they had a more comfortable home.

Shortly before he moved, he took charge on May 7, 1836, of the 'Gazette,' which his brother-in-law, Jacob Caldwell, Mary's husband, now owned. The Whig subscribers were opposed to the poet's becoming editor, not only because he had attacked Governor Everett, but because of his poems on abolition. Whittier nevertheless published in its columns a characteristic editorial on the 'Freedom of the Press.'

'Why are our presses silent?' he asked. 'Their own graves are making. Slavery cannot breathe the atmosphere of Free Discussion. It has sworn upon its own bloody altar to silence the press which utters above a whisper the name of Liberty, excepting always on our Saturnalia of July, when we can speak of any kind of slavery save that of the Negroes of the South, and of any kind of Tyranny save that of slave holding, and of any kind of Liberty save that of the outcast and wretched slave.

'For ourselves, whatever others may do, we go for the full and perfect freedom of the Press as guaranteed by the Constitution of Massachusetts and of the United States. *We shall regard no law which nullifies that guaranty.* We will yield to no laws whatever our freedom of opinion, and constitutional right of expressing that opinion. We are for giving Truth full play. We believe with Milton, in his noble defence of the freedom of the Press.'[1]

Many readers cancelled their subscriptions, though others only protested; Caldwell then sold half his interest to Jeremiah Spofford. The new proprietor forbade Whittier's writing on politics, which was tantamount to telling him that he could no longer continue active on the staff. Though he still published some antislavery poems in the columns of the paper, he resented the check upon his editorial writing

[1] Editorial 'Freedom of the Press,' *Essex Gazette,* June 18, 1836.

and decided voluntarily to give up his position at the end of the year. He was once more on his own resources for a livelihood.

He was now again engaged in drudgery, supervising the publication of reports of antislavery meetings, arranging for lectures to be delivered in and about Haverhill and Amesbury, and writing letters to various officials of the now numerous antislavery societies. In spite of his growing illness, he was always ready to make distant trips in the interest of his cause. Though he did not find traveling very comfortable, he allowed no personal inconvenience to interfere with his idealistic projects.

In January, 1837, he prepared to visit Washington to further the cause of the abolition of slavery in the District of Columbia. Learning on the way that a new 'gag' rule was applied, he ended his journey at Philadelphia. From here he wrote to John Quincy Adams, commending him for his course in bravely presenting the petitions, and promised to get the 'representatives of Massachusetts to enter their solemn and united *protest* against the virtual annihilation of the right of petition involved in the infamous resolution which has passed the House in reference to the petitions and remonstrances of *the people* upon the subject of Slavery.' He boarded with his old friend Thayer, who had moved here. While in the city he became acquainted with Elizabeth Lloyd, who was to figure prominently in his life.

A few months later he wrote an introduction to a collection of letters of John Quincy Adams to his constituents, which originally appeared in the Quincy 'Patriot.' Whittier took charge of the pamphlet because the letters telling of the partiality to slavery in Congress and defending the right to petition were not copied by other newspapers.

While in Philadelphia he entertained hopes of becoming editor of an antislavery publication. In the mean time he went to the antislavery convention at Harrisburg, where he met some of his old friends of three years before. Whittier, though no orator, decided to speak in order to counteract some opposition to a resolution recommending abolitionists not to vote for candidates for Congress in favor of slavery. He began by saying that he did not address them as a political partisan, since as an abolitionist he had abjured all the mere party politics of the day. As all those present were united in the propriety of demanding the abolition of slavery in the District of Columbia, he said that it would be unwise for them to give their votes for a member of Congress who they knew would throw the petitions unread upon the table. If they did so, he went on, they would have no reason to wonder that the Congressman they helped to elect did not make an abolition speech upon the petitions they sent him. As long as they gave their votes in favor of proslavery men at home, he reiterated, so long would the proslavery men vote against the abolitionists in Congress.

While in Harrisburg, Whittier met the Pennsylvania German Governor Ritner, whom he celebrated in a poem for refusing to truckle to the governors of the Southern States.

Whittier soon left Philadelphia, where he could not find the employment he wanted, and returned to Amesbury.

The new President, Martin Van Buren, having taken a decided stand, in his Inaugural Speech against the abolishing of slavery in the District of Columbia, Whittier decided to go to Boston to urge the legislature to pass resolutions in favor of abolition in the District of Columbia. After arriving in Boston, he remained the whole month of March, engaged in sharp and persistent lobbying, though he was so ill that he could not go out in the evenings. The Boston newspapers reprimanded him for his activities, one paper in particular commenting upon his improper and indiscriminate mingling with the members of the House. Nevertheless, owing to the influence he had with old friends, he was successful in his endeavors. As he himself put it, he and his friends caucused in season and out of season, threatened and scolded, pleaded and coaxed, and won the day. He even succeeded, through his friend Robert Rantoul, a Van Buren leader in the House, in having a right-of-jury bill passed for fugitive slaves. He earnestly called on Rantoul to immortalize himself by assisting the abolitionists.

He came back to Amesbury flushed with victory, for he had succeeded in abolitionizing the Massachusetts legislature. He had made Van Buren's own partisans turn against him. Since his efforts in Massachusetts had been successful, he turned eager eyes to Pennsylvania, now the most important State to be won for the cause. There lay the field of battle; there he would eventually go, even if he had to fight the mobs that it was rumored Southerners were trying to stir up, to prevent Pennsylvania from going over to the abolitionists.

The mild poet had in a little over three years become like a horse in battle, delighting in the smell of powder. He no longer tilled the soil. He was frequently at meetings and conventions. Now he was at a meeting of the Essex County Anti-Slavery Society; now at one of the Massachusetts Anti-Slavery Society, and then at that of the American Anti-Slavery Society; — meetings held in different cities. Here he introduced resolutions; he served on committees; he drew up reports. He was even again mobbed at a meeting — that of the Essex County Anti-Slavery Society in Newburyport. Unable to obtain a hall, the abolitionists tried to assemble in a garden, but a crowd beating on tin pans and blowing on fish-horns broke up the gathering.

'As we were being assailed with decayed eggs,' Whittier said, describing the occasion, 'sticks and light missiles, I thought discretion the better part of valor, and hurried away at what my friend N. P. Rogers called "an undignified trot," in company with an aged Orthodox minister, one of the few who had the moral courage to attend an antislavery meeting in those days and who was settled in a neighboring town.'

Whittier developed keen insight into the drift of national

affairs. He showed it when the question of annexing Texas arose. He realized early that the country was hazarding the danger of war with Mexico to increase Southern slave power, and he also foresaw a possible civil war between the North and the South. He wrote to the Secretary of the New Hampshire Anti-Slavery Society: 'For is it not emphatically the question, whether *Slavery* in our land shall be abolished peaceably and happily by the power of moral truth or whether it shall go out like the foul spirit from the demoniac of the parable, rending the union and convulsing the whole land with civil war!' [1]

Convinced that by merely professing antislavery principles, the abolitionists would accomplish little, he urged that they resort to political action. He now differed with Garrison, who was becoming non-resistant in his policy.

In the spring, at the request of Professor Elizur Wright, he came to New York as one of the corresponding secretaries of the American Anti-Slavery Society. His chief companions beside Elizur Wright were Henry B. Stanton and Theodore D. Weld. He shared offices with them and helped edit the 'Emancipator' and the 'Anti-Slavery Reporter.' His new work compelled him to engage in more drudgery, in distributing petitions, in writing appeals and tracts, in getting lecturers, and, incidentally, in helping by the underground railroad to send fugitives off into Canada. He was vitally interested in the Texas question at the time and sent personal appeals to various workers in different parts of the country.

'I send thee a circular from our Anti-Slavery Society, with blank petitions,' he wrote to his friend William J. Allinson. 'They will be circulated over the free states: and it is very desirable that New Jersey should not be neglected. Wilt thou use thy influence and exertions to obtain names in Burlington and vicinity? The Texas question, I am told by John Q. Adams, will in all probability come up at the extra session in the ninth month. Whatever is done must be done quickly,

[1] Letter to John Farmer, dated June 6, 1837, *Liberator*, June 16, 1837.

or Texas, spotted with the plague of slavery, will be fastened upon us. For the testimony of Truth for the cause of freedom and righteousness — let us *act* speedily and efficiently.'[1]

Disliking the dirty city and finding its heat insufferable: he boarded in Brooklyn.[2] Here he met Lucy Hooper, who was to succumb to him, the male coquet.

While in New York, thinking that he ought to embark upon additional missionary work in behalf of abolition, he directed his attention to his former idol Henry Clay. He wrote to him explaining the activities of the abolitionists, which he tried to present in their prope·light. Since Whittier knew that Clay did not approve of slavery, but objected to abolitionism, he endeavored to convince him that no wide abyss yawned between him and the abolitionists. He tried to persuade Clay to use his influence against the annexation of Texas, and to present the petitions of the Friends in opposition to the project. Clay gave him little encouragement, replying that he was opposed to the abolitionists and their methods of immediate emancipation. Moreover, he said that he did not think Texas would come into the Union, but that nevertheless he did not believe in opposing its admission for the sole reason that this would increase the slave power.

Editorial tasks also occupied Whittier that hot summer in New York. He wrote the 'Narrative of James Williams,' based on a tale told him by an escaped slave who professed to be a driver on a cotton plantation in Alabama. The Southern press fell like harpies upon the book, and disproved its veracity. The Society soon withdrew the book from circulation, convinced that Williams had imposed upon them. Whittier also edited with an introduction 'Views of Slavery

[1] Manuscript letter to Allinson, dated New York, June 17, 1837, Cornell University Library.

[2] A manuscript letter to his sister, dated July 4, 1837 (in possession of Harry G. Sperling, of the Kleinberger Galleries, New York), represents Whittier seriously suffering from palpitation and spending his time with Theodore Weld and Charles Follen.

and Emancipation,' by Harriet Martineau, a reprint of the slavery chapters in her book 'Society in America.'

Not long after Whittier arrived in New York, Isaac Knapp, Garrison's publishers, issued in Boston about a score of the poet's antislavery poems, 'Poems Written During the Process of the Abolition Question in the United States between the years 1830 and 1838,' with an unsigned introduction by Garrison. For the first time the public was able to obtain in book form these memorable antislavery poems that were awakening the country. The volume marked a new milestone in the growth of Whittier's reputation; he was to be known for the next quarter of a century as the bard of freedom, the most forceful voice of the antislavery cause. Though the book was not widely reviewed, it made its influence felt.

Whittier soon wrote even greater abolition poems than those in this volume. One of these, 'The Pastoral Letter,' struck, like a bolt of lightning, the General Association of Massachusetts, which had opposed the discussion of slavery, particularly by women. The clergymen had issued a Pastoral Letter directed against the famous Grimké sisters, Sarah and Angelina, who had freed their slaves in South Carolina and come North to lecture on abolition. Though Whittier himself did not believe in introducing the question of women's rights into the abolition movement, he could not sanction the issuing of a ukase that undertook to say who should and who should not enlist in a cause. With ecstatic indignation he penned his poem, publishing it in the 'Liberator' in October, 1837. He was bold and subtle in his attack, for he began by railing against the old Puritans for persecuting witches and Quakers. Then he interrupted himself and declared that he was really aiming his shafts at the clergymen of the present day, for not learning a lesson of tolerance from the errors of their predecessors. The poem is still timely, for it bears on the question whether any body of men has the right to exclude anyone from becoming a mouthpiece for public grievances. It is one of his greatest prophetic utterances.

The year 1837 — the year of the panic — ended with the murder of Reverend Elijah P. Lovejoy, in Alton, Illinois, for persisting in publishing an abolitionist newspaper. Whittier wrote no poem on this supreme tragedy of the abolition movement. With his temperament, he would have had to rage unbecomingly to express his true feelings in verse.

CHAPTER IX

EDITING AN ABOLITION PAPER IN PHILADELPHIA

WHITTIER now accepted a definite offer of a position as editor of a Philadelphia abolition paper. Leaving Amesbury for Philadelphia, he stopped off in New York, where he spent several weeks among his old companions of the Anti-Slavery Society. While here he learned that the colored people of Pennsylvania were being legally disfranchised. He vented his sentiments on this and other topics in the following letter to Francis James, a member of the State Senate, with whom he had previously become acquainted: [1]

NEW YORK 12*th* 2 *mo.* 1838

MY DEAR FRIEND:

... We have been shocked and grieved of Pennsylvania on the subject of Human Rights, especially at the disenfranchisement of the colored people by the miscalled Reform Convention. Are the dark ages returning? Is Pennsylvania about to declare in the ears of the world that she is tired of her early principles — that the maxims of Rush and Franklin are unfit for practise — that after fifty years of trial, of the principles of freedom, convinced of their unsoundness — she had concluded to go back to those of the days of Kingcraft & Absolute Tyranny?

I trust however that you will make one more effort in behalf of Jury Trial for persons claimed as fugitive slaves. Thy own efforts in the Senate have not escaped our notice, — but the Society here should be glad to get an accurate sketch of the debates. We only have a very meagre one. When at Harrisburg last winter, I had the pleasure of an introduction to Senators Darrah and Paul. Please remember

[1] Manuscript letter to Hon. Francis James, sold at Henkle's Auction, Philadelphia, Jan. 19, 1932.

me to them. I know and love the men who in a body like that of the Pennsylvania Legislature dare to stand up the devoted advocates of unpopular truths.

Things cannot always be thus in Pennsylvania. The adamant of party will crumble before the power of truth; and a day of tremendous reaction will atone for the present disgraceful progress towards despotism. The overthrow of the V. Buren party alone, will not do much for you. The state must be *abolitionized* before it will go back to the old & pure principle of '76.

I have been spending some weeks in this city, & of course, do not know, all that is doing in my own state of Massachusetts but Stanton & Birney are at Boston addressing committees of the Legislature. They have a special committee on Slavery in the District of Columbia & another on Texas.

Truly thy friend
JNO. G. WHITTIER

HON. F. JAMES.

In March he arrived in Philadelphia to assume the editorship of Benjamin Lundy's weekly paper, 'The National Enquirer.' The Pennsylvania Anti-Slavery Society had bought it and changed its name to the 'Pennsylvania Freeman.' Joseph Healy was its financial agent. Whittier's name as editor appeared in the issue of March 15. The next issue contained one of his most famous abolition poems 'The Farewell of a Virginia Slave Mother.' More aggressive than Lundy's 'Enquirer,' and containing more original contributions, the 'Freeman' now challenged comparison with the 'Liberator' itself. It gave reports of speeches, and printed articles by leading antislavery writers. The correspondence column, with letters always addressed to 'Friend Whittier,' established a personal relation between the editor and his readers. Whittier, however, would never allow himself to be swerved by subscribers who wanted the paper to take up other causes, no matter how much he was in sympathy with these. The paper was the typical partisan sheet. Whittier often quoted the Southern papers, repelling their pro-slavery arguments with remorseless logic and blazing indignation. Though he handled the bondman's cause 'not with gauged and softened tone,' he announced his opposition to all forms of violence. Not being a revolutionist, he merely sought to awaken moral indignation at a great wrong, and to accomplish his ends by political action.

In an editorial called 'The True Character of Slavery'[1] he replied to those who held that there was a moral excuse for slavery in the mutual beneficial effects upon master and slave resulting from their relationship. In answer to the theologians, he maintained that slavery was against the order of God. He wrote in conclusion: 'IT IS NO EVIL TO BE MITIGATED, BUT A CRIME TO BE ABOLISHED. No modification of it can make it right, which does not amount to a formal and virtual abolition of it.'

In May he made a brief visit to New York to attend the annual meeting of the American Anti-Slavery Society. Here he presented a resolution to harmonize the growing discordant elements in the organization, but he was unsuccessful in carrying it through. Disappointed, he came back to Philadelphia, to face the most startling event in his antislavery career.

The office of the 'Freeman' had been transferred to a beautiful new building, Pennsylvania Hall, just erected on the southwest corner of Sixth and Haines Streets, below Race Street. Since abolitionists and other reformers had often found difficulty in obtaining halls for the purpose of free discussion, they constructed this magnificent edifice — a temple of liberty. The dedication ceremonies lasted several days, on one of which Charles G. Burleigh read Whittier's poem 'Pennsylvania Hall,' specially written for the occasion. The abolitionists held their meeting on the third day, Wednesday, May 16. Antislavery men,

[1] 'The True Character of Slavery,' *The Pennsylvania Freeman*, April 12, 1838.

PENNSYLVANIA HALL, PHILADELPHIA

including Garrison, had come from different States to attend the celebration. Whittier during the afternoon session offered a resolution against voting for candidates to political office who opposed the abolition of slavery in Congressional territory. He also attended the evening session and listened to many famous women speakers, among them Maria W. Chapman, Lucretia Mott, and Angelina E. Grimké, the South Carolinian who had recently married Whittier's friend Theodore Weld. On this occasion a mob of fifteen hundred people gathered outside and attacked the building, breaking some windows; but the chairman merely ordered the blinds drawn. Whittier went to press, indignant at the mob outrage that had been perpetrated, little suspecting the calamity that was to follow. In his editorial he comforted himself with the thought that mobs had never put down abolition societies, and prophesied that abolition would eventually triumph over lynch law in Philadelphia.

The next day witnessed a most disgraceful scene. Since a crowd had been gathering all day, Daniel Neall, the president of the managers of the Hall, fearing some impending disaster, called on Mayor Swift for protection. The Mayor suggested that the abolitionists hold no meeting that night, but turn over the keys of the building to him. This was done. At night he confronted the mob and assured them that no meeting would take place. He asked the people to be his policemen, saying, 'We never call out the military here.' As soon as he had departed, the mob, encouraged by the last remark, spurred on by Southern medical students, and angered by rumors of the hobnobbing of colored and white people of both sexes, crashed in the doors of the building. They pillaged what they thought of value, and then set the building on fire with kindled abolition books and copies of the 'Freeman.' Whittier, seeing his newspapers and manuscripts being consumed, decided to save what he could. Disguising himself in a wig and white overcoat, and pretending to be one of the mob, he rescued some of his precious manuscripts. Meanwhile the fire spread, the flames leaped higher, and soon the building was a roaring furnace. The mob would not even allow the firemen to extinguish the flames.

In the next issue of his paper, Whittier wrote an account of the catastrophe, laying particular emphasis upon the plundering:

'Then came the plunder of the book depository and the scattering of its contents among the crowds, the flash of the lighted torch along the deserted aisles — the heaping of light combustibles on the speaker's forum, and firing the pile — the wrenching of the gas pipes from their places, and adding their quickly kindled current to the rising flames — the shout which greeted the outbursting conflagration, as it rolled along the walls, and roared and crackled in the fresh night breeze, while the motto of the beautiful Hall, "Virtue, Liberty and Independence" shone clearly for a moment in the dazzling light, and was then effaced forever — the foul-like cry which went upward as the roof fell in, a blazing ruin; and smouldering and blackening walls alone remained, in place of the costly and splendid edifice.'

This act of vandalism was never effaced from his memory. He always treasured a large engraving of the burning hall. His poem 'The Relic' was inspired by the presentation to him of a cane made from woodwork spared by the fire.

Shortly after the fire, he was again in New York, William H. Burleigh, the antislavery poet, brother of Charles C. Burleigh, conducting the paper in his absence at the new office on Ninth Street below Arch. After a short stay in New York, Whittier went to Boston to attend the meeting of the New England Convention, where his friends Garrison, Henry B. Stanton, and Nathaniel P. Rogers were to be the leading speakers. Debates about the right of women to vote and take active part at abolition meetings disturbed the convention. Though he was opposed to the introduction of this irrelevant subject, in his letters to the 'Freeman' he assured the enemies of abolition that such inevitable dissensions among the antislavery men would never hurt the cause. He also vehemently denounced the clergy, for their lukewarm attitude on the abolition question. He did not agree with his friend the Reverend John Pierpont, the anti-slavery poet, who thought that the clergy merely needed to be enlightened; he believed that they ought to be castigated. No little courage was necessary to send in signed letters containing attacks upon the church.

He returned to Philadelphia at the end of June, and resumed control of the 'Freeman.' He now directed his attention to the colonizationists, referring to them as 'the Sanballats and Tobiahs of Colonization around us, summoning against us the Ammonites and Ashdodites of the mob.' He had good cause for this, as they were suspected of exciting mobs against the abolitionists.

He would sometimes pass by the ruins of the Pennsylvania Hall, and gaze sadly and wistfully at the blackened ruins. He could not understand why anyone should burn a building which some idealists wanted to use as a forum for open discussion. In such a mood he one day caught a glimpse in a hotel window, of an advertising sheet adorned with a picture of the burning of Pennsylvania Hall accompanied by the words 'Destroyed by the People on the night of May 17.' Rushing to the office in hot haste, he penned an editorial 'Base and Contemptible Servility,' [1] in which the burden of his message was that slavery was an economic, and not a moral, issue. Speaking of the Northern foes of abolition, he said, with justice and persuasiveness:

'Their love of the Union should be interpreted, love for their pockets. Their horror of amalgamation, dread of losing the custom of Southern amalgamators. Their jealousy for the honor of the city, a concern for their Southern trade. Their pious fear of "dividing the church" anxiety to divide with Southern slave-holders the gains of oppression. The hypocrisy is manifest, the secret is out. The Pennsylvania

---

[1] 'Base and Contemptible Servility,' *op. cit., Freeman*, Aug. 2, 1838.

Hall was destroyed for the benefit of the Southern trade — a "business transaction" — a commercial speculation, — the result of mercantile forecast and prudent calculation of profit. *SHAME*, SHAME upon this vile bartering of humanity for gold! This sacrifice of principle to the sordid and base spirit of gain.'

During the summer, Philadelphia clergymen harangued against the abolitionists, the politicians abused them in the newspapers, boys hawked daily through the streets penny sheets with caricatures of Garrison and the abolitionists. Whittier came to the defense of his friend from the attack of the 'Saturday Courier.' The editor had charged Garrison with being animated by hopes of either notoriety or pecuniary reward, but not by interest in the slave. Whittier, knowing how little regard Garrison had for money, told how he had suffered for his ideals by imprisonment in Baltimore. The poet gave personal testimony of the inward impulse that alone moved his agitator friend to do away with the oppression. He also added a few words showing in what respect Garrison's theories were weak:

'Had he [the hostile editor] accused him [Garrison] of excess of zeal — of unnecessary harshness of language — of a want of cold, calculating prudence, — and of an austere and stern intolerance towards the oppressor and his apologists, there would have been some plausibility in the charge. But to accuse him of acting from an overweening love of fame and notoriety, is wrong and unjust. We know him thoroughly. He was one of our earliest and most intimate friends.'

Though Whittier was editor of the 'Freeman' for two years, he was not actually in the city for more than twelve months. He participated very little in social life, and mingled still less with the literary circles.

He did not seek entrance into literary circles; he did not contribute to 'Godey's Lady's Book,' which was edited by his old friend Sarah J. Hale from Boston, nor did he try to be admitted to the famous parties at Dr. Wistar's house on

Fourth and Locust. He thought most of the literary men of the city unfaithful to their trust, and they despised him as an abolitionist.

He associated chiefly with the abolitionists here and those from the surrounding counties — Chester, Bucks, Delaware, and Lancaster. His intimate circle of friends consisted of William J. Allinson, of Burlington, New Jersey; his old editor Abijah W. Thayer; clergymen like Joseph Parrish and J. Miller McKim; the two brothers William and Charles C. Burleigh; Daniel Neall, and Joseph Healy. He saw young girls, especially his cousins Ann E. and Margaret Wendell and Elizabeth Lloyd.

Soon his health broke down, and it became imperative for him to seek rest. He returned in October to Amesbury for the necessary recuperation, leaving the paper in charge of Charles C. Burleigh.

When he reached home, instead of taking his ease, he plunged into the whirl of local politics; but circumstances beyond his control had forced him to do so. It was the time of the Congressional election in Essex County, when Cushing, candidate for election a third time, was losing the confidence of the antislavery men, then in convention at Salem. Whittier went to Salem and found that the delegates wanted Cushing to state his views on slavery more definitely than he had done in a recent letter, in which he had said that he stood by his record. Since his evasions did not meet with their approval, they resolved not to support him. Cushing complained to Whittier about the decision of the delegates.

Whittier at heart was in accord with the delegates, but, not wishing to wound Cushing's feelings, he appealed to his practical sense. Cushing agreed to sign a letter that Whittier wrote. It was found satisfactory, and Cushing was elected for the third time by Whittier's help.

While Whittier was absent, Joseph Healy, with whom Whittier boarded at 72 North Seventh Street above Arch, issued a volume of fifty of his poems. About half of them were antislavery poems, most of them having appeared in the earlier volume. It had a large proportion of weak religious poems and sterile compositions in which the author paraphrased texts in the Bible. One of the best of them, 'Christ in the Tempest,' had been the first poem of his to appear in a school reader, being selected by B. D. Emerson for his 'First Class Reader.'

Bryant in his first anthology, 'Selections from American Poets,' published in Harper's 'Family Library' in 1839, selected three poems from Whittier's volume — 'The Female Martyr,' 'The Worship of Nature,' and 'Pentucket.' Griswold, a few years afterwards, in 'Poets and Poetry of America,' added 'The Frost Spirit' and 'Palestine' to the poems Bryant chose. It will be noticed that neither Bryant nor Griswold included any of the abolition poetry. Apparently Whittier was satisfied with these selections, for he retained them in his collected poems.

Still physically indisposed, and indifferent to the fame which the new volume brought him, he continued sending signed letters to the 'Freeman.' Unable to attend the meeting of the Pennsylvania Anti-Slavery Society in Coatesville, to which he had been elected delegate, he sent a letter to Burleigh, who published it because it was 'full of the vital energy and glow of thought and feeling which are wont to warm almost into breathing life the page over which his pen glides.' That Burleigh had cause for his enthusiasm is apparent by the following passage: [1]

'You will assemble at a time of trial and difficulty, with all the baser elements of the community moved and excited against the unpopular truths which you are called upon to assert. Around you, on every side, gathers and blackens the frown of a corrupt and wicked public sentiment. Interested and mercenary merchants, — selfish and heartless politicians, — time-serving priests and their deluded followers, — hypocrites in Church and State, — bloated aristocrats and

[1] Whittier's letter dated Amesbury, Oct. 26, 1838, *Freeman*, Nov. 15, 1838.

counterfeit democrats, — all are combined against you. The whole atmosphere of that beautiful country which stretches from the Delaware to the Mountains, is corrupted by the proximity of slavery. Every breeze that blows over you from Maryland and Virginia comes loaded with the moral pestilence. Along your valleys and beneath the shadow of your forests, the fugitive from the Southern prison-house, steals onward towards the grateful boon of a homeless and penny-less freedom in the wilds of Canada; while the echoes of your free hills ring with the shouts of the pursuing man-hunters, BLOOD HOUNDS, too often of Pennsylvania growth, who howl for hire in the tracks of oppressed human-ity. This is not all. The rights of the colored citizens of Pennsylvania have been immolated on the Altar of Southern Slavery, — the elective franchise which they have peacefully exercised for nearly half a century, has been wrested from them — a trial by jury has been denied to men upon the question of their liberty or slavery in the courts of Pennsyl-vania.'

It will be observed that Whittier had not been able, in spite of his activities, to realize the hopes that he had ex-pressed to Senator James before coming to Philadelphia; the elective franchise were wrested from the colored people, and a jury trial was not granted to fugitive slaves.

About this time began the controversy between Whittier and his old friend Garrison, who was frowning upon Whit-tier's political activities and his refusal to agitate for women's rights. Garrison, now classing Whittier with Clay as a re-conciliationist, said that the poet might eventually truckle to the slave States. No statement could wound Whittier more deeply. He wrote to Garrison, asking if it was not hazardous on his part to experiment upon his complacency while suffer-ing from protracted indisposition — or, in less rhetorical language, to attack him when he was ill. He went on: 'No visions of future treachery haunt and disturb me in my com-munion with my anti-slavery brethren; no shadows and omens of thick-coming disasters throng before me; no ghosts of treason, wearing the similitude of loved and familiar friends, scowl on me from the shadow World of the Future. My sphere of vision is mainly limited to the Actual and the Present.' He trusted that he would not evince any faltering when real difficulties came. Garrison printed his letter in the 'Liberator,' [1] but tactlessly widened the breach between them by adding that Whittier was for obtaining peace at the expense of consistency, if not of principle.

This thrust from the leader of the cause in which he fought did not abate the violence of Whittier's charge upon the common enemy. Atherton, of New Hampshire, who was responsible for a 'gag' rule received a merciless lashing from Whittier in the poem 'The New Year.' [2] Another foe arose in the person of the newly elected governor of Pennsylvania, David Rittenhouse Porter. Though Porter defeated Ritner for re-election, Whittier had been hopeful that the new governor would take up the same position on the slavery question as his predecessor had done. He had reasons for his hopes, because Porter, when in the Legislature, had voted to instruct the Congressional delegates from Pennsylvania to use their influence to abolish slavery in the District of Columbia. But Whittier was disillusioned, for the new governor in his inaugural message decried agitation on the slavery question, on the ground that it had been settled by our Constitution, and said definitely that the efforts of the antislavery men would meet with no encouragement at his hands.

Whittier, as he read the message while sick at home, was chagrined at the *volte-face* of the new governor. He wrote a poem against him for the 'Freeman.' [3]

[1] Whittier's letter to Garrison, dated Amesbury, Feb. 24, 1839, *Liberator*, March 8, 1839. In Kennedy II, pp. 148–150.

[2] *Freeman*, January 10, 1839. I have found an unknown broadside of the poem in the Pennsylvania Historical Society.

[4] The poem on Porter, 'Stanzas for the Times,' *Freeman*, Feb. 28, 1838, was reprinted in the 1849 edition under the title 'Response' and then dropped. It may be found in Kennedy II, pp. 125–126.

Possibly the prose editorial against Porter in the same paper was written by

In his letters to the 'Freeman' Whittier continued to discuss topics of interest to abolitionists. In one letter he pleaded for reconciliation and compromise in the ranks, insisting that sectarian differences need not prevent the members from working for the common cause. Why, then, should other differences disturb their allegiance to the cause? he asked. 'Of what consequence is it that Garrison is a "Perfectionist," and Phelps an "Orthodox Minister," that the editor of *The Freeman* is a "Quaker" and the editor of the *Emancipator* a "Presbyterian"? Are we not all brethren — abolitionists all — with our hearts yearning for the consummation of one glorious object?' In another letter he directed his attacks against the Northern proslavery apologists. He assailed the politicians who held that abolition was not a political matter because they did not want it to interfere with vote-getting; and he attacked the theologians who said abolition was not a religious matter because they did not want it to interfere with church support from the slaveholder. Whittier said, properly, that the slavery question was a matter related to both religion and politics, for it concerned human justice. The fact that a slaveholder could plate sin with gold was no reason for taking the question out of the pale of the law or of the church. In still another letter he wrote an attack upon his old idol Clay, who had made a speech in the Senate from which some of the Whigs concluded that he believed in the right of the abolitionists to present petitions. Whittier, perceiving the weakness of

Whittier. It is immaterial who wrote it; what is worthy of mention is that the writer made a satirical suggestion to the governor that he might as well drag up the 'old sedition law' from its grave of infamy for resuscitation by the Democracy of Pennsylvania. Of course, no one ever dreamed that a sedition law *would* be passed in Pennsylvania eighty years later, long after slavery was abolished, and immediately after a world war — a law which among other things provides that a judge shall have the power to send to jail for twenty years and impose an enormous fine upon anyone who publishes anything that brings the national or State government into hatred or contempt, or who even injures the State property of a public official. This law has been found constitutional by a higher court, and there have been convictions under it — in the State founded by William Penn, one of the greatest modern apostles of tolerance.

Clay's argument, was annoyed by the maudlin pathos, the overstrained affectation of patriotism, and the shallow sophistries with which it abounded. He even resented Clay's compliment to the Quakers upon their love of peace, for he saw in it a scheme to get votes from both Southerners and Quakers. Whittier did not believe that the Friends wanted peace based on compromise with the sin of slavery.

In April, 1839, Whittier was well enough to return to Philadelphia. In an article entitled 'The Editor at His Post' he maintained that the abolitionists should present a united front to the enemy. As he observed the dissensions in New England, he became convinced more than ever that he ought to oppose the introduction of any extraneous issue into the abolition platform.

In the summer he wrote a magnificent editorial on the subject of mobs — an editorial he was competent to write by reason of his own experiences. He made an interesting distinction between the mobs in European cities, who were ready to give their lives to make the principle of liberty triumph, and those in America, who were anxious to give the principle its death-blow. The editorial was sanely reasoned, and characterized by a subdued tone of indignation. He chides rather than rants; he speaks like a journalist, like a statesman, like a philanthropist, and like a poet — all in one. He concludes however like a prophet, warning the North that if it countenances mobs it plays into the hands of revolutionists.

'The spirits of mobocracy may yet tear in pieces the magicians who have raised them. The inventor of the brazen bull perished in his own instruments of torture; Haman mounted the gallows which he had set up for his neighbor; the hounds of Acteon devoured their own master. Let the instigators of mobs beware. What if it should be ascertained that it is as easy to destroy a bank as a Hall of Free Discussion! that deeds of warranty and mortgage are as combustible as anti-slavery papers: that the hoarded heaps of the capitalist are

as accessible as the "incendiary documents" of the Abolitionist.' [1]

Though Whittier denounced mobs for violating the law,
he himself refused obedience to it when it was in conflict
with the dictates of his conscience. Since Pennsylvania
denied fugitive slaves a right of trial by jury, he refused to
be instrumental in sending back to slavery a man who possibly might be a free citizen. He would not kidnap men,
though the law called on him to do so.

Towards the end of June, 1839, Whittier again announced
to his readers that the indisposition from which he had been
suffering for some time compelled him to resign in part the
charge of the 'Freeman' to his friend and cousin Moses
A. Cartland. He decided to take a trip in parts of central
Pennsylvania for his recuperation. He could at the same time
engage in propaganda and induce Pennsylvania-German
orators to address the people in their own language on the
subject of abolition. He went with Henry B. Stanton, stopping off at various places — at Harrisburg and Carlisle,
where he visited his friend J. Miller McKim and the retired
Governor Ritner. 'We have been recommended to some
half-dozen Schloshenburgers and Quackenbosches and Kaker-
spergers and Slambangers with unpronounceable Dutch
names enough to crash the jaws of any Anglo-Saxons, whom
we hope to interest in our cause,' he wrote to Elizabeth
J. Neall, daughter of Daniel Neall, in Philadelphia. He then
spent some time in Gettysburg, lost in revery at the sight of
the beautiful hills, never dreaming what blood would be shed
there in a slavery struggle between the North and the South.
He returned to Philadelphia and wrote an excellent editorial,
'The Cause,' [2] dealing with the prospects of the abolition
movement in central Pennsylvania.

I cite the following passage, the sentiments of which were
undoubtedly suggested by personal experience:

'It is comparatively a small thing to suffer for a good cause,

[1] 'Mobs,' *Freeman*, June 20.   [2] *Freeman*, July 25, 1839.

in the midst of sympathizing friends, and in common with a multitude of our fellow-laborers. Heart gathers from heart a strength for endurance even unto death. But the man who, alone and without sympathy, stands firmly up against popular prejudice, — with no voice of encouragement in his ear, — no kindly glance of approval resting upon him — but meeting, wheresoever he turns, an eye of hatred or contempt, the finger of his neighbors pointing after him in scorn — the drunken howling mob in his track, or breaking the miserable repose of his afflicted family, — and who knows that for all this endurance he can acquire no earthly praise — that his thousand sacrifices and trials will find no record among his fellow-men — that, if he perishes in the struggle with his enemies, the verdict of his contemporaries will be, like that pronounced over the grave of the Israelitish warrior, "*Died Abner as the fool dieth,*" — such a man, opposing his single breast to the beating storm of universal censure — in opposition to the passions, the interests, the prejudices all around him — moving onward in his path of duty — uncheered even by any decided fruits of his exertions, and hearing on all sides, —

<blockquote>
'the world's dread laugh,
Which scarce the firm philosopher can scorn'
</blockquote>

is the true martyr of our cause, and, even, while living the crown is resting on his brow.'

He next attended the convention at Albany to give his aid in smoothing over factional differences. He and Garrison were chosen members of the business committee, but Garrison refused to serve, because he would not countenance any political endeavors whatever to extirpate slavery. The convention committed itself to action by the use of the ballot-box, but not by means of a separate party. Many abolitionists, however, wanted a distinct antislavery party, though Whittier at this stage was not ready to join them. His main views on the wisdom of political action, nevertheless, underwent no change. In a letter to the Secretary of the Philadelphia Anti-Slavery Society, he advised the organization to continue presenting petitions for the abolishment of slavery in the District of Columbia. He reiterated his belief that antislavery protests would prove meaningless and harmless unless translated into political action; the reformer must press on and fight with the ballot, he said.

After a month's rest in Amesbury he returned to the arena in Philadelphia, at the new office of the 'Freeman,' No. 31 (old number) North Fifth Street, above Arch Street.[1] About this time he noticed that a young writer who had arrived here late in the preceding summer was attracting attention in literary circles. His name was Edgar Allan Poe, and he had just become editor of Burton's 'Gentleman's Magazine.' We have no record that Whittier and Poe ever met, but it would be very singular if they did not at least see each other on a number of occasions, for the business section of the city covered less than a square mile.

Not very long after Whittier had left Philadelphia, Poe recorded his opinion of Whittier:

'Mr. Whittier is a fine versifier,' he wrote, 'so far as strength is regarded independently of modulation. His subjects, too, are usually chosen with the view of affording scope to a certain *vivida vis* of expression which seems to be his forte; but in taste, and especially in *imagination*, which Coleridge has justly styled the *soul* of all poetry, he is ever remarkably deficient. His *themes* are never to our liking.'

In an editorial that Whittier wrote with messianic zeal, 'The Cause of Emancipation,'[2] he virtually identified himself and his coworkers with the early martyrs in the cause of Christianity. In eloquent words he showed that one of the humanitarian acts of the early Christians was bringing liberty to the slaves.

'Were our anti-slavery *organizations* to cease tomorrow,'

[1] The office of the *Freeman* was at 29 North Ninth Street (old number, below Arch) from June 14, 1838 to January 3, 1839, and at 72 North Seventh Street (old number, above arch) till October 10, 1839.

[2] *Freeman*, Jan. 9, 1840.

he assured his readers, 'the anti-slavery FEELING would still live on and gather strength. It bears about with it the indestructible vitality of Truth. It appeals with certainty of success to the best emotions and sympathies of our nature. To arrest its progress there must be a change effected in the very elements of the human mind. All that discovers and vindicates the relationship of man to his Creator must be annihilated. Every ennobling trait, every generous impulse — the kindlier nature of brute instinct itself — must give place to the utter depravity of the fallen Angel, before the anti-slavery excitement can be arrested.'

Though his health was getting worse, he thought it expedient to go to Washington to protest against the 'gag' rule. Here he called with some friends upon John Quincy Adams, who recorded in his diary a brief account of their visit and conversation in the following words:

'Whittier said he thought this last outrage upon the right of petitions, the establishment of a rule refusing to receive or entertain any abolition petition, might perhaps be the best thing that could have been done to promote the cause of abolition. It was, at least, casting off all disguise.'

Adams was not an abolitionist, though he was in sympathy with the movement and had visited Lundy.

'I had much conversation with these men,' he wrote, 'upon the discussion among the anti-slavery men and abolitionists and concerning the late Benjamin Lundy.'

Whittier soon returned to Philadelphia, in worse health than ever. He remained with his paper as long as he could, but on the 20th of February he published a farewell editorial entitled 'To Our Readers.' He explained to his friends that he had tried to carry out his editorial policy of concentrating all his efforts on the antislavery cause. He then delivered a sermon, in which the fiery agitator was merged in the benevolent preacher.

CHAPTER X

LUCY HOOPER

WHITTIER'S work as abolition poet and editor did not occupy all his energies, either in New York or in Philadelphia. He liked and sought the society of women. While boarding in Brooklyn he met a young poet, Lucy Hooper, who had come six years previously from Essex County, from the vicinity of Whittier's own home. He found much in common with her since she was an abolitionist, and he encouraged her poetic work.

She succumbed to his blandishments. Yet he did not wish to appear fulsome: 'No, I do not wish to flatter thee'; he wrote to her, 'first, because I should despise myself for the meanness of the attempt, and second, because I know that by so doing I should deservedly forfeit thy esteem. But in perfect sincerity allow me to say that I believe thee able to produce within six months of this time a poem which would be received with general commendation on both sides of the Atlantic.'

He tried to persuade her to write a long poem, expressing the opinion that length would add an attribute to her poetry that would be conducive to its survival, and he flattered her by telling her that she was greater than some of the leading poets of the day. He predicted a great future for her, and offered to get her a publisher. What more was necessary to turn the head of a girl of twenty-one? Even had he not been a tall, slender, handsome man, with markedly brilliant dark eyes and curly black hair, he would have impressed her by his poetic reputation and his abolitionist career.

When, in the following spring, he became editor of the 'Freeman,' he generously offered her the use of its columns as a medium for the publication of her work. He published

her poem 'The Lock of Hair,' commenting upon it that
'there were touches of exquisite beauty and tenderness in it
true to the holiest affection of our nature.' [1] Several months
later he published a poem by her celebrating the emancipation of slavery in the West Indies, again adding eulogistic
comment.[2]

'The following,' he wrote, 'is one of the most beautiful of
the many poetical effusions which the late glorious change in
the West Indies Island has elicited. We need not say to its
author that her writings will always find a ready welcome to
our column, especially when, as in the present instance, they
are consecrated to the cause of Religion and Humanity, —
and to their intrinsic beauty is added the holier aim of
Philanthropy.'

During the spring of the next year reports circulated that
Whittier and Lucy Hooper were engaged. The friendship
of the two poets with similar literary tastes made such
rumors seem plausible. The young man of thirty-two and
the girl of twenty-two were of marriageable age; they were
both poets, deeply religious and fanatically abolitionist.
But there were obstacles to Whittier's becoming engaged to
her. Lucy was not of the Society of Friends, but an Episcopalian; unfortunately, she was also consumptive. Whittier
was too poor to marry, for he had a mother and sister to
support, and, besides, he was not really in love with her.
When he saw that she was infatuated with him, he suffered
from twinges of conscience. The entire episode was, alas!
a repetition of the Evelina Bray affair. He was to take a last
walk with her and hint that both his poverty and Quaker
faith made marriage to her impossible, and he was even to
write a poem commemorating the final meeting and farewell.

In August, 1839, he and Lucy happened to be in Essex
County on visits. He had recently left Albany, where he

[1] 'The Lock of Hair' and comment on Lucy Hooper in issue of the *Freeman*, April
19, 1838.

[2] Lucy Hooper's West Indies Emancipation poem and Whittier's comment,
Freeman, Aug. 16, 1838.

attended the convention. What induced Lucy to make
a trip to Essex County at the same time we do not know.
Whittier, however, was no longer deeply interested in Lucy,
for he had other woman friends — among them Harriet
Minot, of Haverhill, who had been concerned about his
rumored engagement; Ann E. Wendell, whom he had just
encountered again at a meeting in Newport; and Elizabeth
Lloyd, of Philadelphia. Nevertheless, he met Lucy and took
a stroll with her on the banks of the Merrimac River. He
celebrated this walk in the elegy he wrote in 1841 when Lucy
Hooper died from tuberculosis. In the poem he recalled
the summer two years before, when he heard her soft voice
mid the lapping of water; he declared that the memory of her
loveliness would smile around his weary pathway; he stated
that Nature would have a tender meaning for him, because
he had studied Lucy's noble ideals in her verse.

He ruined his poem with theology, mentioning even that
he did not approve of the religious rites with which she was
buried, and that he did not acknowledge her creed, though
he was willing to concede her sincerity. His religion was
absorbing him more than ever, as is apparent in the recently
written 'Memories,' in which also he dwelt on the religious
differences that lay as a barrier between him and his old love,
Mary. From the importance he assigned to religion in these
two poems, it is evident that he had determined never again
to think of marrying 'out of meeting.'

At the time Lucy died Whittier paid a tribute to her in
the 'Anti-Slavery Reporter.' He called her 'a pure-spirited
and noble woman, who had the firmness to defend and
advocate the cause of emancipation — to throw her literary
reputation on the altar of reform — and to consecrate youth,
beauty, genius, to the vindication of unpopular truth.' [1]

We have not direct and indisputable evidence of Lucy's
feelings towards Whittier, because Whittier destroyed the
letters she sent him. In her poems she makes no mention of

[1] *American and Foreign Anti-Slavery Reporter*, Sept. 1, 1841.

his name, but she refers in several of them to an unnamed famous person whom she loves; she complains that her reputation does not bring her the happiness that love would have brought. In one of her poems, 'Last Hours of a Young Poetess,' she alludes to an 'absent idol,' who is unquestionably Whittier:

> 'Again it comes
> That half reproachful voice that she hath spent
> Her life at Passion's shrine, and patient there
> Hath sacrificed, and offered incense to
> An absent idol — that she might not see
> Even in death — and then again the strength
> Of a high soul sustains her, and she joys,
> Yes, triumphs in her fame, that *he* may hear
> Her name with honor, when the dark shades fall
> Around her, and she sleeps in still repose.'

One wonders what the poet thought as he glanced through the posthumous volume of her 'Poetical Remains' and read this passage. Did he blame himself for having allowed her to pine in silence for him during the four years of their friendship? Did he feel remorse for having increased her sufferings? Did he justify himself for not having proposed to her? He must have felt that he had again been the male coquet. He must have realized that he had again trifled with human affections, that he had this time hurt a noble, talented invalid, bruised a sensitive soul. He noted poems in the volume that were apparently mild rebukes to him. When she sang of a lover poet so absorbed in his dreams of fame as to allow his sweetheart to pine away, she must have meant him. Did she have him in mind in the poem where she makes a girl waiting in vain for her dallying lover cry out in despair:

> 'Is there no brow so high that falsehood's traces
> May not rest upon its glorious surfaces?'

Whittier, who had never suspected that she loved him so deeply, lived over her sufferings by recalling the agonies he went through in his love for Mary.

Seven years later, when a new edition of Lucy Hooper's poems appeared, he reviewed it in the 'National Era,' but he said nothing about the personal poems in the volume. Instead, he selected for quotation and praise the poem that Lucy had written in the late thirties celebrating the emancipation of the slaves by the British in the West Indies. He now made the suggestion that Lucy's beauty of character may have induced the public and the critics to place an exaggerated value upon her poetry. But he did not contradict the rumors that associated her with 'Memories,' for he was proud of his friendship with her. He caused her pain but he immortalized her in verse. Her own poems are forgotten, but she will always be remembered, because of Whittier's poem.

CHAPTER XI

A MODERN TYRTÆUS

AFTER Whittier left Philadelphia and returned to Amesbury in March, 1840, he was not only ill in body, but disheartened and disillusioned. He was on the verge of a mental crisis similar to the one he had undergone eight years previously, and he was also suffering from a physical ailment which affected his heart. He was still in almost hopeless poverty, for he now had no means of support. At the same time he lost by death several intimate friends — among them Professor Charles Follen, who was burned to death on a steamer. He was also alienated from Garrison, who now publicly criticized him. The bosom friend who had discovered him as a poet and had been instrumental in converting him to the anti-slavery cause now expressed a sense of relief that Whittier was no longer editor of the 'Freeman.'

'J. G. Whittier has retired from the editorial chair of the "Freeman"!' wrote Garrison in the "Liberator." "The time has been when we should have deeply regretted to make this announcement; but, in his present state of mind, as it respects political action and "new organization," and in view of the course he has thought proper to pursue in regard to the state of things in his native commonwealth, we are reconciled to his withdrawal.'

There was a slap in the face! That was his reward for the sacrifices he had made. The hopeless state of his mind is apparent from the following letter to his friend the Rev. Samuel J. May:[1]

AMESBURY 27*th* 3 *Mo.* 1840

MY DEAR BRO. MAY:

This will be handed thee by *Rev. Mr. Smith* of this place — a true hearted friend of the Slave. I have been now at home

[1] Manuscript letter to Samuel J. May in the Morgan Library.

some three weeks — and the absence of excitement has contributed to render my state of health more comfortable — but I fear not permanently better.

I read thy line with great pleasure — and should have answered it had I not been in that situation in which even the grasshopper is a burthen.   My strong faith in my early fellow-laborers remains — I cannot (for the Lord's sake & the slaves sake I dare not) seek occasion against any one who feels an interest in the cause of the slave. 'Judge not that ye be not judged,' has to me an awful meaning. But I cannot see eye to eye with Garrison & Mrs. Chapman. They do injustice, as I think, to those who dissent from them. There is a dictatorial censorious intolerant spirit about them which I cannot fellowship. I loathe this whole quarrel — it is not *Christian* and, the less I see of the papers containing it, the more peace of mind, and true regard for the great interests of humanity, I feel. Is there to be no end of it?

Most gladly would I accept thy invitation to visit Scituate were I in a condition to do so. It is very uncertain about my going to England. It might be of more injury than good to my health.

My mother, sister & Aunt desire to be affectionately remembered to thee. Give my kindest regards to Mrs. May & believe me ever &

truly thy friend,

John G. Whittier

I have just heard of the death of the venerable & beloved Dr. Parish of Philada one of the earliest friends of the Slave. What a loss we have met with in Dr. Follen — and in Benj. Lundy.

> 'Like clouds that rake the mountain summit
> Like waves that know no guiding hand
> How swift has brother followed brother
> From sunshine to the sunless land.'

Yet a little time & we shall follow them. May the mercy

of our Heavenly Father & of His dear Son be with us! I feel that I at least need it.

Brother Smith will take a letter for me. He is a fine spirited man — and yr difference in religious opinions need not prevent your being good friends.

He was interested in the Liberty Party Convention, which met in Albany to discuss for the first time the advisability of putting forth candidates for President and Vice-President. Though the convention was composed of representatives from six States, five sixths of the entire number of delegates were from New York. The reason for this disproportion was that the New York State Anti-Slavery Society, which was in favor of political action, called the meeting; the Massachusetts Abolition Society and two other New England societies denounced the proposed meeting with bitter invective. Whittier, always eager for reconciliation in the abolitionist ranks, but unable to attend the meeting, sent a letter to a friend in which he suggested that the political abolitionists make no nomination and forego their vote at the national election. He thought they would make their political aims more effective by passive action, by supporting neither the Democratic President Van Buren, who was a candidate for re-election, nor General William H. Harrison, the Whig candidate, and by putting forth no independent candidate themselves. But the abolitionists, not heeding his advice, nominated James G. Birney for President and Thomas Earle for Vice-President. Though Whittier declined to have his name on the electoral ticket, he gave these men his support.

Another matter that excited his interest keenly at the time was his prospect of going to London to the World Anti-Slavery Convention, which he was anxious to attend. He was at first cheered by a letter from his friend Rev. J. Miller McKim, of Philadelphia, informing him that the executive committee had chosen him as a delegate. But he saw two obstacles to the journey facing him: one, insufficiency of funds, and the other, objection by his physician. As Dr. Bowditch finally advised him not to make the voyage, predicting that if he did the excitement of the convention might be of serious consequence to him, Whittier reluctantly abandoned his plan of going abroad. It was a great disappointment, but he resigned himself to his fate. 'It sometimes seems strange that I cannot do as others around me,' he wrote bitterly to his sister, 'but I try to suppress any feeling of repining or murmuring.'

At this time the Pennsylvania Anti-Slavery Society held a meeting in Philadelphia. In spite of his poor health he took the long journey and attended it, staying with his cousins the Wendells. He found it bracing to see his old friends, especially Elizabeth Lloyd. Having caught a bad cold, with much pain in his head and chest, he became dispirited. On his recovery he and his cousin Joseph Cartland rode up to Joseph Healy's farm in Bucks County, overlooking the Delaware River and about half a mile northwest of the Cuttalossa Creek.

While here the most important event in the history of the abolition movement took place in New York City, the disruption of the American Anti-Slavery Society and formation of a new organization in favor of political action — the American and Foreign Anti-Slavery Society. Though Whittier was heart and soul with the new organization, he had not gone to the convention, because he knew that he would find it painful to witness the strife. He came from Philadelphia to New York after the secession had taken place. Although he had been elected to the Executive Committee, he was compelled to decline serving on it because of his ill health. At the same time, he wrote a letter to the 'Emancipator,' reiterating his dissent from the non-resistant policy of the old organization.

The rumor spread that he was no longer in sympathy with abolition. He was, on the contrary, more interested than ever, but he merely shook himself free of all trammels. He returned home from New York harassed and bewildered, so distracted, in fact, that he thought of taking a trip to Halifax, but he was too ill to do so. His bitterness was increased by attacks upon him by friends who remained with the old organization. Even the women, Lydia M. Child and Maria Weston Chapman, denounced him. The latter was reported to have said that she wondered whether Whittier was a fool or a knave. He nevertheless began again writing for the cause.[1]

Unwisely and gratuitously he plunged into a double controversy with Garrison and Nathaniel P. Rogers, who also remained with the old organization.[2] Though the controversy broke out after they had both returned from the London Convention, it had had its inception before the convention began. Garrison had sneered at Whittier's poem written for the occasion, but the poet bided his time to reply. He soon found the opportunity to strike at Garrison by aiming at Rogers. When the British delegates had refused to admit women to the convention, Garrison did not take his seat. Rogers had also been incensed at the conduct of the British abolitionists; after returning to America he attacked them. Whittier, in a letter to his old paper the 'Freeman,' now edited by Charles C. Burleigh, said Rogers's attack was too bitter and unjust, and he criticized him for being a dreamer and seeking to make the whole world free from all oppression. Burleigh replied to Whittier in the 'Freeman,' and Garrison, also coming to Rogers's defense, called Whit-

---

[1] There are two letters of Whittier in the *Freeman* for Oct. 22, 1840, and Oct. 29, 1840, in the former of which, 'The Cause,' he advocates open refusal to obey the Fugitive Slave Law, and in the latter of which he delivers a eulogy on Thomas Earle, candidate for Vice-President on the Liberty Party ticket.

[2] The controversy with Rogers, here bibliographically indexed for the first time, is covered in very long letters as follows:

Freeman, Nov. 20, 1840, Whittier's first letter dated Sept. 24, 1840.

Op. cit., Dec. 3, an anonymous reply by the editor, Charles C. Burleigh.

National Anti-Slavery Standard, Dec. 10 and Dec. 17, 'John G. Whittier' — reply by Rogers.

Op. cit., Dec. 24, Whittier's rejoinder.

Op. cit., Jan. 4, 1841, 'John G. Whittier,' Rogers's final reply.

tier's letter 'very reprehensible' and 'somewhat contemptu-
ous.' Rogers himself answered Whittier in the 'National
Anti-Slavery Standard,' which he then edited. He also
practically read the poet out of the abolitionist movement.

Whittier, writing to Rogers directly, replied in part as
follows:

'If brother Rogers should so far shut up the bowels of his
compassion as to quote my own poetry against me, and as in
the case of poor Cinna, the poet in Shakespeare's "Julius
Cæsar" condemn me for my bad verses, however I might
writhe under the infliction, I don't know as I could complain.

'But if Nathaniel P. Rogers means (what his language
somewhat strongly implies) to impeach my character as an
honest man — to assail my moral integrity — to brand me
with the foul suspicion of treachery and hypocrisy; as one
fully recreant to the cause of emancipation — I have only
to say that his recent voyage "in search of a World's Convention" has wrought in his head a "sea change" which would
have astonished the tenants of Prospero's Island, transform-
ing the generous and high-minded Christian gentleman into
a false "accuser of his brethren" — a Titus Oates swearing
away more than the life of his friend.'

Rogers answered again, and the matter there ended.

It was a year of agony for him, and he sometimes wondered
if he had not taken a mistaken course in joining the anti-
slavery ranks and abandoning the muse. Such thoughts
were, however, only momentary. In a self-revealing poem,
'Looking Backward,'[1] which he contributed at the time to
a scrapbook of his early poems owned by Elizabeth Nicholson, of Philadelphia, he showed that he did not allow the
bitterness of controversy to affect the general satisfaction he
felt in his abolitionist career:

'Oh for the power to dedicate anew
Heart, soul and spirit to the right and true —

---

[1] First published by Pickard in *The Independent*, June 7, 1906.

> To offer up on Duty's holy shrine
> The morning incense of a heart like mine!
> But vain the wish! Let the time past suffice
> For idle thoughts and worse than vanities.
> Thy will, oh Father! hath it not been shown?
> Thy gentle teachings have they not been known?
> Have I not heard amid life's stormy din
> The voice of bland entreaty entering in
> When midst my selfish aims of power and fame,
> The mournful sighing of the captive came.'

Entering upon a religious crisis, he paid more attention to theological questions than previously. He was going through a harrowing ordeal, and well-meaning friends were trying to make him look for solace more than ever in religion. He found consolation in corresponding with his cousin Ann E. Wendell, of Philadelphia, to whom he confided his growing religious struggles. The correspondence barely transcended Platonic friendship. The death in New York, at the time, of the eminent foreign Quaker Friend and Missionary Daniel Wheeler, moved him deeply, and at Ann Wendell's suggestion he wrote an elegy upon him for the Philadelphia Quaker paper, the 'Friend.' [1] He gave an account of the missionary's work, but in it he showed that he did not think all was right in the world. He simply became resigned:

> 'His will be done,
> Who seeth not as man, whose way
> Is not as ours.'

He found consolation in the journal of John Woolman, in which he saw 'beauty such as Goethe pictured, such as Shelley dreamed of.'

As his illness continued he turned for consolation to his muse and temporarily stopped writing abolition literature. He gained entrance into the 'Knickerbocker Magazine,' to which he contributed some able poems in his old vein. But he felt inert and apathetic; he could take no interest in life,

---

[1] *Friend*, Aug. 1, 1840. By a curious error the poem is assigned in the list of Whittier's writings in the Cambridge edition to the year 1847. I have also discovered a broadside of the poem in the library of Yale College.

and he wandered back in memory to his childhood days. He suffered grievously, but tried to resign himself to God's will. He developed a view he often later entertained — a sick man's philosophy — that illness fans the half-extinguished conscience into life. However, things could not continue in this manner. He decided to go to New York or Philadelphia to escape the cold; he thought again of undertaking editorial work, or plunging into politics. He did take a hand in Cushing's re-election to Congress, but he did not have to wage a strenuous battle for him this time.

After the new year, 1841, began, he determined to shake off his despondency. He would continue to write with the same moral earnestness as before; he could not lie down and sleep when duty was calling him. In an unpublished poem that he contributed during this time to an album, he dwelt with emphasis upon the value of an unselfish life: [1]

TO ANN REBECCA

As, in the garland rich and rare
The girl weaves around her hair;
'Midst rose and pink and violet
　　The darker laurel leaf is set,
So, in this tasteful wreath of thine
Where only *flowers of Thought* may shine
"Still with the gladsome and the gay
Be mixed the moralizing lay."
　　And nought be left upon its page
　　To shame the eye of after age.

Yet a few years — and thou wilt look
　　With other eyes on this fair Book, —
A saddened and a serious gaze
　　Upon this lay of girlhood's days:
　　For many a name, now kindly penn'd
By relative, or school-day friend,
Will waken thoughts but of the dead,
Cold, sleeping, in their narrow bed, —

[1] Manuscript poem 'To Ann Rebecca,' dated Jan. 28, 1841, in Morgan Library,

Gone, from the blessed light of Day,
And sound of living voice, away!
Oh! — then, if memory calls to mind
No selfish act — or word unkind
Towards those who never more can know
A sense of human joy or woe —
    Who in the dwelling of the dead
    Heed not the tears above them shed, —
This record of their names will be
    A Blessing and a Joy to thee!

Fortunately an event happened that saved him. Joseph Sturge, the English philanthropist, prior to his visit to America to study the slavery question, wrote to Whittier asking him to accompany him on his travels and offering to defray all expenses. Whittier took advantage of the offer. He met Sturge in New York in April, and they were soon off together touring the East. Though Whittier's illness often interrupted their travels, they visited many of the large cities. In Washington they met Clay, who, though he treated the poet as a deserter from his own banner, discussed abolition with him and the attitude of the Friends towards it. They talked to John Quincy Adams, who welcomed them, and they called on President John Tyler, who treated them coldly. They saw the prison in which Dr. Reuben Crandall had been confined for sedition, because he lent Whittier's slave pamphlet to a friend. They travelled to Philadelphia, to New York, and to Boston, where they visited Channing and Garrison. Whittier also entertained Sturge as a guest at his home in Amesbury. Sturge's visit aroused attention, and a letter, addressed to Whittier and published in a newspaper, giving a vivid account of the horrors of slave establishments, was widely discussed. Before Sturge returned to England he left a thousand dollars with Lewis Tappan for the use of Whittier in his illness; but it seems that Whittier never availed himself of this fund. Sturge published a book, 'A Visit to the United States in 1841,' for which Whittier wrote the preface.

Whittier's association with the Quaker English philanthropist was bracing; it cleared his brain and purged his soul.

Whittier was also cheered by a visit from Stanton and his
celebrated wife, Mrs. Elizabeth Cady Stanton, who, on
returning from England after nearly a year's stay, found the
poet somewhat recovered in health and an entertaining host.
Mrs. Elizabeth Cady Stanton in her account of the visit in
her autobiography has given us the best picture we have of
the poet's home life at this time:

'I enjoyed, too, the morning and evening service, when our
host's revered mother read the Scriptures, and we all bowed
our heads in silent worship. There was at times, however,
an atmosphere of solemnity that was oppressive. There was
a shade of sadness in even the smile of the mother and sister,
and a rigid plainness in the house and its surroundings,
a depressed look in Whittier himself that the songs of the
birds, the sunshine, and the bracing New England air seemed
powerless to chase away, caused, as I afterwards heard, by
pecuniary embarrassment, and fears in regard to the delicate
health of the sister.... Whittier's love and reverence for his
mother and sister, so marked in every word and look, were
charming features of his home life.'

It was at this time that Whittier spoke to Mrs. Stanton of
the love of his youth to which I have previously referred.

He now returned to public life. He tried to help an old
friend, Samuel E. Sewall, by asking Cushing to sponsor his
appointment as a Federal Judge, but Peleg Sprague had
a prior claim on the office. Having by this time become
a party man, he wrote the Liberty Party Petition calling for
a general convention of voting abolitionists in Massachusetts
to which prospective converts to political abolitionism were
invited. He also took up editorial work again. In September
and October he edited two issues of the 'American and Foreign Anti-Slavery Reporter,' the not very successful periodical of the new organization. In an editorial, 'Slavery
in the District of Columbia,' he wrote one of his first attacks

upon Daniel Webster for becoming a renegade. Webster was then Secretary of State, having remained in the Cabinet of John Tyler when the rest of the members resigned. Whittier now charged him with accommodating his principles to his position, and deplored that the man who three years previously in a debate with Calhoun had declared himself in favor of abolition now joined hands with a proslavery President for the sake of a Cabinet position. He showed that the people who countenance abuses in their own day are loudest in condemning similar abuses of a past age. He wrote another editorial praising Joseph Sturge. In the next issue he had another vigorously condemning Edward Everett. Everett, who had once urged the Massachusetts Legislature to pass penal laws against the abolitionists, now professed to be converted to their views, because he wanted the support of the Massachusetts abolitionists for his appointment as Minister to England. Whittier, not believing in his sincerity, charged him, after the confirmation of his appointment by the Senate, with having obtained the abolition votes of Massachusetts under false pretenses.

In another editorial, 'Our Political Responsibility,' Whittier, placing great faith in securing victory for the cause of abolition by means of the ballot-box exclusively, now advised the voters to abandon party allegiance. He was neither a believer in non-resistance nor a revolutionist, but sought to achieve his ends by the ballot through a new party. His work on the 'Reporter,' however, could not save the paper, and he transferred his activities to the 'Emancipator,' which had been moved to Boston. Being now a Liberty Party man, he concentrated upon political action.

During this time his poetic pen was idle. Rogers took him to task for this neglect, attributing it to his too great preoccupation with political abolitionism. Calling on him for more poetry, he wrote in the Concord (N.H.) 'Herald of Freedom,' which he now edited:

'Where is Whittier now, that we no more see his verses

starting up like a "meteor to the troubled air"? What has palsied his muse? Why does he no longer furnish the anti-slavery cause the poetry for her movement? New organization has touched his genius with her torporific wand and it soars not above the dunghill of Third Party.'

Whittier was too busy with politics to write. He now showed more skillfully than before his master hand in the game, for he had to meet a situation fraught with peril to the cause. Caleb Cushing was showing himself refractory on the slavery question. Whittier was taken off his guard, for he had tried in the spring of 1841 to have him appointed to succeed Webster as Senator, when Webster resigned to become Secretary of State in Harrison's administration. When President Harrison died, Tyler, who succeeded him, promised Cushing a position in the Cabinet. Cushing found it expedient to break with the abolitionists to ingratiate himself with the new proslavery President. It was at this time that Whittier, not knowing of Tyler's promise to Cushing, tried to convert him altogether to the cause.

Cushing had also broken with the Whigs and knew that they would not nominate him to Congress. He wanted the nomination, though he knew he would not be elected. In order not to suffer the disgrace of a defeat he obtained the nomination but had someone decline it in his behalf; he was now able to say that he had been nominated but had refused to run. Even John Quincy Adams tried to persuade him to go over to the abolitionists, but in vain. After Cushing's term in Congress expired, Tyler nominated him for the office of Secretary of the Treasury. Whittier was furious. 'We shall see,' he said, 'whether Cushing will eat back this explanation for the sake of being premier or anything else under John Tyler of Virginia.' He then published the letter with the abolition sentiments that he himself had dictated in 1838, and which Cushing had signed to insure his re-election. The Senate rejected the nomination three times successively.

Meanwhile the nominees for Congress who were put forward by the Whigs and Democrats were men of whom Whittier did not approve. At this stage, to prevent a pro-slavery man from being elected, he himself entered the campaign as a candidate on the Liberty Party ticket. He caused a deadlock for a year, remaining a candidate out of 'cussedness,' for he did not expect nor want to be elected. He polled many votes, and finally Webster told the Whigs that they might as well elect Whittier. A Boston newspaper, however, said that the Whigs could never come to Whittier's support till they lost all regard for principle and self-respect! But soon the Whigs were ready to support him, and when he saw that he might be elected, he withdrew, after having caused a deadlock for a year. He was too ill to be active in Congress. He thus deliberately cast aside a great political opportunity.

Whittier's re-entry into active politics in the summer of 1842 gave Garrison an opportunity of mockingly chiding him:

'Where is John G. Whittier?' he asked. 'At home, we believe, but incapable of doing anything important for the cause, except to write political, electioneering addresses for the "Liberty Party." New organization has affected his spirit to a withering extent, and politics will complete the ruin, if he "tarry in all the plain."

When Whittier became himself a candidate for Congress, Garrison, who was for disunion, again attacked him, for supporting a 'bloody instrument' like the slavery-supporting constitution.

Whittier was now hardened, for he had become a thorough politician. 'I am not much affected by the whirl of politics,' he wrote to Ann E. Wendell in the summer of 1842. 'I act because I believe it to be my duty, decidedly and vigorously, but my inward self is calm. The ambitions and selfish hopes of other years do not disturb me. Why it is so, I know not, but I can mingle in the exciting scenes of an election without feeling the excitement to any extent. My enthusiasm has been tamed by that hard and cross-grained mistress Experience.'

In the fall of 1842, when he was campaigning for the Liberty Party and also trying to put his friend Samuel E. Sewall in the Governor's chair, an event of great importance to the abolitionists occurred. An escaped Virginia slave, George Latimer, was captured by the Boston authorities and claimed by his Virginia master. Sympathizers with Latimer made an attempt to secure for him the right of trial by jury under the Massachusetts Law of 1836. The Chief Justice, however, following a decision of the United States Supreme Court that held that such a State law was unconstitutional, refused Latimer a trial. Public indignation meetings were held, the most important one being that at Faneuil Hall, where Sewall, of counsel for Latimer, presided. Here Edmund Quincy made a reputation for himself by an address, and Wendell Phillips, when interrupted by a mob, pronounced his famous curse on the Constitution.

Latimer's freedom was purchased, but the matter of the attempted return of a person into slavery without a jury trial became one of national significance. Massachusetts finally sent to Congress a petition under the charge of John Quincy Adams signed with sixty-five thousand names praying that the Constitution be amended, so as to free Northern States from the obligation to return fugitive slaves. Bitter fighting occurred and acrimonious words were exchanged between Northern and Southern Congressmen. Of course, Congress passed no such amendment, and the Southern members only heaped indignities upon the State of Massachusetts. Her citizens responded by holding conventions simultaneously in the various counties on January 2, 1843. At the Essex County Convention in Ipswich, a poem, 'Massachusetts to Virginia,' written for the occasion by Whittier, electrified the audience. It was the first important antislavery poem he had written in several years, but in it he made up by fervor and genius for his long silence. Garrison, in spite of his attacks upon Whittier, published it in the 'Liberator.' Members of both the old and the new organizations admired it. A young writer named Thomas Wentworth Higginson idolatrously asked Whittier for permission to shake the hand that wrote the poem.

Whittier contrasted very effectively in his poem the Northern and Southern attitudes on slavery. Massachusetts would not interfere with the institution in the Southern States, but she would have no slavery in her domain. The South could handle the problem in her own borders as she wished, but she would have to make peace with her own conscience. He took the position that there was a higher law than the Constitution, and that such a law never sanctioned the return of a runaway slave.

Like Tyrtæus,[1] the poet who twenty-six centuries before by his song and his valor had led the Spartans in the second Messenian War, Whittier by word and deed arrayed the abolition forces against the common enemy.

[1] *The Emancipator* for June 19, 1838, had an anonymous poem, 'Ode for the First of August to John Greenleaf Whittier, the Tyrtæus of Our Holy Warfare.'

CHAPTER XII

HIS FIRST MASTERPIECE: 'LAYS OF MY HOME'

In 1843 Whittier, relaxing his antislavery labors, turned his thoughts again towards his literary career. He had been recently attracting attention by his contributions to the 'Democratic Review' and the 'Knickerbocker Magazine' on themes from New England legends, by poems on reform and by personal lyrics. Griswold included in his 'Poets and Poetry of America' two poems of this period, 'The Funeral Tree of the Sokokis' and 'St. John.' Lowell succeeded in obtaining from him for his magazine the 'Pioneer' one of the best poems he ever wrote, 'Lines Written in the Book of a Friend' (now called 'Ego'). Whittier, who had issued nothing in book form since the 1838 edition of his poems, except a revised edition of 'Moll Pitcher' and 'The Minstrel Girl,' thought it time that he publish a new collection. As an abolitionist he was unwelcome in publication circles, but fortunately he knew James T. Fields, who had made a connection with the firm of William D. Ticknor, of Boston. He suggested that Fields publish a volume to be called 'Legends of the Merrimac.' He had written to him as early as January 24, 1842, with singular modesty: 'I am wholly unacquainted with booksellers, and have never published anything of consequence.'[1]

In the spring of the next year Whittier gave Fields a list of the poems he wanted included in the volume, most of them being new. The book, with the title changed to 'Lays of My Home,' was issued in May, only a month after he concluded negotiations with Fields about the publication.

The volume took the public by surprise, for it had begun

[1] Manuscript letter to Fields, dated Jan. 2, 1842, in possession of Carroll A. Wilson, Esq., of New York.

to think of Whittier as an unpolished rhymester of the caliber
of Ebenezer Elliott, a propagandist without art, an agitator
with no sense of beauty. When it found in the new volume
tender poems like the elegy on Lucy Hooper, and the beautiful sentimental reverie on his lost love, 'Memories,' it bowed
in submission to his claims upon it as poet and artist. It saw
that in this so-called abolitionist fanatic a gentle heart
throbbed beneath the agitator's cloak. It realized that he
loved beauty and quiet, that he was equally at home in
painting a landscape or in detailing the conflicts of his own
soul. In short, it saw in the volume American poetry of a
high order, making a bid for literary immortality. Whittier
now took his place alongside of Longfellow, who had recently won popular esteem and critical eulogy.

In 'Cassandra Southwick,' the best ballad in the book,
the rhythm was perfect. The measure — iambic hexameter
and heptameter with rhymes in couplets — gave the poem a
swinging and ringing effect. The tale was historical, dealing
with Puritan intolerance and Quaker humility in Colonial
times. In the form of a monologue the heroine, Cassandra,
related the account of her life in prison and of her temptations to abandon her ideals in order to be let out of jail. She
enumerated the pleasures of youth that she had foregone, to
spend her life in a cold prison-cell. Whittier made her the
symbol of his own inner trials, for he too had shut himself
out of the light of this glorious world. He too had made
sacrifices — his literary and political career; he too had let
love and wealth pass him by; truly, he was also in prison.

Whittier by this poem disproved the charges of the critics
who said that by turning trumpeter in the cause of abolition
he had desecrated his gifts and buried his genius. He showed
that, on the contrary, as a result of his practice in writing
abolition poetry, he voiced his poetic utterances more ecstati-
cally and prophetically than ever.

The volume contained not only one of the best ballads he
ever wrote, but some of his greatest poems, 'Memories,'

'Massachusetts to Virginia,' and the not so well-known autobiographical poem 'Lines Written in the Book of a Friend,' now called 'Ego,' to all of which I have referred. Recounting in the last poem the story of his spiritual evolution and change from the career of a poet of romance to that of an abolitionist, he gloried in his self-sacrifice and dwelt on the consolations he found. The poem — his 'Apologia Pro Vita Sua' — is one of the very best of his subjective poems; in fact, one of the great poems in American literature. The following lines teem with rich idealism:

> Deep as I felt, and stern and strong,
> In words which Prudence smothered long,
> My soul spoke out against the wrong;
>
> Not mine alone the task to speak
> Of comfort to the poor and weak,
> And dry the tear on Sorrow's cheek;
>
> But, mingled in the conflict warm,
> To pour the fiery breath of storm
> Through the harsh trumpet of Reform;
>
> To brave Opinion's settled frown,
> From ermined robe and saintly gown,
> While wrestling reverenced Error down.

The book also contained some of his ablest poems of reform, among which were his declamations against capital punishment, 'The Gallows' and 'The Human Sacrifice,' both giving vigorous expression to the growing sentiment against the death penalty. They were indirectly a reply to Wordsworth's sonnets in favor of capital punishment, but chiefly a counterblast to some clergymen who had published pamphlets defending the gallows. In these poems Whittier, always aroused to a frenzy when the so-called men of God defended cruelty and vengeance, gave them a scorching castigation for their views. The poems should be read today by the members of the legislature of every State in the Union.

Besides these poems, the book had such a masterpiece as

'To —— with a Copy of John Woolman's Journal' and such favorites of anthologists as 'Raphael' and 'Democracy.' He included only two or three abolition poems, and two of earlier vintage — 'The Demon of Study' and the selection from 'Moll Pitcher' which he called 'Extract from "A New England Legend."' There was as usual in his books a sprinkling of religious poetry, such as 'Follen,' an argument for immortality of the soul.

He knew that he had produced a volume of poetic merit, and he preserved every one of these poems in the final collected edition of his works. Yet, in spite of the obvious merits of the book, the 'North American Review' was critical and patronizing in its notice of it.

Shortly afterwards, Edwin P. Whipple, in an article on Griswold's anthology, took issue with the reviewer by extolling Whittier in the very periodical where he had been recently criticized.[1] To this notice Whittier used to attribute his acceptance as a poet by the literary world.

[1] Whipple's notice on American poets appeared in the *North American Review*, January, 1844. Reprinted in *Essays and Reviews*.

CHAPTER XIII

IN MILTON'S FOOTSTEPS

DURING the year 1843 Whittier was taking a breathing-spell from his arduous abolition labors and diverting himself by studies in the superstitions of New England. Yet he found time to address a letter, 'What is Slavery,' in which he incorporated many passages from an old editorial in the 'Freeman,' to the Liberty Party Convention at New Bedford. This was one of the conventions that endorsed Birney, who had, at Buffalo in August, again been nominated for President.

Whittier wanted to go to the antislavery convention in Philadelphia at the end of the year, but he was too poor. In a letter to the Rev. J. Miller McKim he wrote about his poverty as follows: [1]

'I hear you are to have a great meeting in Philadelphia on the 10th January of the Am. A. S. Soc. I should rejoice to be with you; but see no possibility of it. I cannot travel in the cold season without suffering severely & besides, I may as well confess that, the *expense* is with me no trifling matter. In my state of health I can do but little in the money-making line — & I am therefore under the necessity of *calculating* with all the proverbial minuteness of a true Yankee. It is a pitiful business, sadly belittling a man — but what help for it? I for one know of no way of realizing of Brownson's theory of the "Supremacy of man over his accidents."

'Talk as you will of the mind; higher element of intellectual banquets &c — the bread & cheese — the pork & greens are also essential. Heaven help us! What a combination of angel aspirations, animal appetites, is this marvel & mystery we call man!'

[1] From manuscript letter to McKim, dated Haverhill, Oct. 12, 1843, in Library of Cornell University.

The next year he was again in the arena, and was writing political editorials for the Essex 'Transcript,' an Amesbury paper. As he wrote to Lowell, he had the principal charge of the weekly paper, and the trouble and responsibility of an active politician of the Liberty stamp working steadfastly to roll up votes for Birney. At Stanton's request he drafted the resolution of the State Convention and gave it publicity in the 'Transcript.'

Meanwhile the old organization was going rampant and calling for a dissolution of the Union. 'No union with slave-holders' had become their cry — a sentiment with which men like Phillips and Quincy and Charles C. Burleigh were in sympathy. But some of the members of the old organization — Richard Hildreth, the historian, Ellis Gray Loring, David Lee Child, and George Bradburn — were opposed to such a policy. Of course the political abolitionists were incensed at this stand. Whittier, though not a disunionist, for a while preferred disunion to the annexation of Texas. Gerrit Smith addressed a public letter to him in which he showed that the Constitution was an antislavery document.

In the latter part of July, 1844, Whittier became editor of the antislavery weekly paper the 'Middlesex Standard,' of Lowell, Massachusetts. He moved into the town and prepared himself for the arduous and exacting work before him of working for the Liberty Party, in behalf of Birney for President. In the very first issue of the 'Standard' under his editorship, July 25, 1844, he plunged into the fray with a long article entitled 'Who is Birney?' on the front page of his four-page paper. And the next week there was an editorial called 'The Hour and the Man,' telling more about Birney. From this time on till election day, the young editor hammered away at his readers on the merits of his candidate, and on the virtues of the principles of the Liberty Party. He pleaded with voters not to be misled by the professions of both other parties that were inconsistent with their practice, not to be seduced from their steadfastness by the 'sounding brass of Whiggism' on one hand or the 'tinkling cymbals' of Democracy on the other.

But his interest in Birney did not make him forget his hostility to the churches that supported slavery. In the second issue of the paper appeared 'Slavery and the Church,' one of his most devastating articles on the clergy.

'Men who maintain the doctrine that slaveholding is a divine institution, and consistent with the holy attributes of Deity,' he wrote, 'have no more claim to the character of Christian than the worshippers of the Scandinavian Odin, or the devotees of Brahma and Vishnu. The Deity which they profess to worship, and on whose altars, reared with the unpaid toil and cemented with the blood of human victims, they offer the fruits of robbery and tithe the gains of oppression, is not the God of the Bible. A monster not outwardly fashioned of wood and stone, but a moral abomination, originating in the mind of a slave-holding priesthood, has been set up on the high places and under every green tree of the South, and even at the North is too frequently found like one of those idol gods described by Milton,

> ... 'who dared abide
> Jehovah thundering out of Zion, throned
> Between the cherubims — yea, often placed
> Within the sanctuary itself their shrines.
> Abominations! and with cursed things
> His solemn feasts and holy rite profaned.'

'Who has not shuddered at reading the disclosures of the existence of a religious sect in India, called Thugs, who worshipped the being in Hindoo mythology represented as the God of Murder, and who actually lived by the robbery and murder of travellers making a religious rite of their horrible vocation? Yet, in what essential particular does their case differ from that of slaveholders, who, to give sanctity to a crime of which Nature and Revelation testify their abhorrence, discard the God of Mercy, and Love, and Justice, and fashion in their own imaginations a Being who can look down approvingly upon American Slavery, the pollutions of which reek up to Heaven, the blood of whose innocent victims the earth cannot cover, and which includes in itself all the crimes forbidden by that Voice which spoke amidst the thunders of Sinai? And yet these men are received among us as Christian brethren. The Priesthood of the god of Slavery stand up in Northern pulpits, and lift in mockery of prayer to the Father of Mercies hands red and reeking with the blood of human sacrifices offered to their own horrible idol.'

He was now anxious to persuade the leading American writers either to write in behalf of abolition or to engage in active propaganda. James Russell Lowell had already joined the abolitionists, chiefly because of his admiration for Whittier, though his wife also influenced him. Whittier was now cheered by the prospect of a greater proselyte — Ralph Waldo Emerson, who, though he had at one time been hostile to the abolitionists, was gradually growing more friendly to them. On August 1st Emerson was scheduled to deliver an address on the celebration of West India Emancipation at the Concord courthouse. Whittier was very curious to know what Emerson would have to say. He had heard him speak before and had read his writings, but regretted that the notable thinker and lecturer had held aloof from the abolitionist cause. That Emerson should pay no heed to the rising sentiment on the subject was a great discredit to him, in Whittier's opinion. Men like Garrison, Channing, John Pierpont and John Quincy Adams engaged in different degrees in heroic service for the cause, but Emerson had remained silent while men were being murdered and imprisoned for speaking and writing against slavery. On a drizzling rainy day Whittier journeyed to Concord with other passengers in a closed carriage, and reached the courthouse where the famous transcendentalist was to speak. It was a great occasion. Thoreau rang the bell to summon the audience, and Hawthorne's wife spread the 'collation' tables for the feast. Whittier listened enraptured, and although he missed the rhetorical beauty which had impressed him in a previous lecture, he was pleased because he found that Emerson properly suited his delivery to the worthy occasion by entering into a simple narrative of the story of the emancipation and by making just reflections upon it.

During the next week, Whittier wrote of Emerson in his editorial, 'The First of August at Concord — A Day's Excursion':

'With quiet sarcasm he alluded to our pleasant obliging representatives in Congress, who so amiably deferred to the wishes of their Southern friends, and queried whether it might not be well to send thither some a little less obliging and amiable.'

In spite of the rain, he had spent a delightful day at Concord; he had seen and heard a most important convert.

He returned to the subject a month later when he read the address published in pamphlet form. He admitted that he had at one time felt half indignant that a man like Emerson had not supported the abolitionists in their struggles against the popular current. He had contemplated with pity the spectacle of Emerson 'brooding over his pleasant philosophies, writing his quaint and beautiful essays, in his retirement on the banks of the Concord, unconcerned and "calm as a summer morning."' Now he read the address with a glow of the heart, with silently invoked blessings. Emerson, greatly pleased with Whittier's tribute, sent him a copy of the second series of his 'Essays.'

Whittier sought to enlist in the cause another writer, Longfellow, whom he tried to persuade to run for Congress on the Liberty Party Ticket, and who he believed might be elected on account of his popularity. Longfellow was in sympathy with the abolition cause and had in fact published a pamphlet called 'Poems on Slavery' — an act that required courage in those days. Whittier now wrote inviting him to join the ranks of the abolitionists in behalf of liberty and run for Congress. Imagine Longfellow's surprise when one day he received the following letter: [1]

LOWELL 9th 9 mo. 1844

DEAR FRIEND:

I do not know as thy views on the question of anti-slavery entirely coincide with mine but I do know that thy little collection of poems on Slavery have been a great and important service to the Liberty movement. From my heart I thank thee for them.

I write now to inquire of thee whether thou art with us in the great question of Liberty which is about [to] be decided at the ballot box, and if so, whether we may not present thy name as the Liberty candidate of the 4th Congressional District, at our Convention at Acton on the 16th. Our friends in the 4th say they could throw for thee 1000 more votes than for any other man. The cause is taking a deep hold on the best hearts and minds among us. A line from thee at thy earliest convenience would be acceptable. With high respect & esteem,

J. G. WHITTIER

Since Whittier himself, in spite of his love of poetry, scholarship, and retirement, was engaging in active service in the cause of the oppressed, he cannot be blamed for his mistaken zeal. He did not realize that a man of Longfellow's temperament could not run for Congress! He must have been chagrined when he received the following reply:

'It is impossible for me to accept the Congressional nomination you propose, because I do not feel myself qualified for the duties of such an office, and because I do not belong to the Liberty Party. Though a stray antislavery man, I am not a member of any society and fight under no single banner.

'I am gratified that the Poems on Slavery should have

[1] Manuscript letter to Longfellow, in Longfellow House, Cambridge.

exercised some salutary influence & thank you for your good opinion of them. At all times I shall rejoice in the progress of true liberty; and in freedom from slavery of all kinds; but I cannot for a moment think of entering the political arena. Partisan warfare being too violent, too vindictive for my taste & I should be found but a meek and unworthy champion in public debate.'

Whittier was of a different stamp, for he was running for the State Legislature — to which he was not elected.

Of the violent abuse that the Whigs, upon losing the election, heaped upon the Liberty Party, Whittier received his share. In defending himself for his hostility to Clay, their candidate, he wrote emphatically that no lover of liberty could support the 'champion of the vilest oppression on which the sun looks.'

The chief criticism that may be directed against Whittier during his residence in Lowell is for his lukewarm attitude towards those members of the laboring class, the girls in the mills. It is true that he did not approve of their long fourteen-hours work day. But, as he said, he was unable to see how a 'ten-hour' system could be realized; he believed that both the working-girls and the stockholders would object to it, the former on account of a loss of wages and the latter because of a decrease in profits. Had he and others been just as hopeless of the success of the abolition cause, he would never have witnessed its triumph. He never imagined that an eight-hour day would actually become established. Again, he knew that the girls after paying their board averaged in wages two dollars a week, and that they lived several in a room in the boarding-houses. Yet he wrote that the work of the women was 'adequately rewarded,' and he complimented the employers on having removed the social disabilities of women by not discriminating against them. In short, the employers were doing the women a favor by giving them work!

Whittier swallowed whole the propaganda spread at the

time by the employers to show that in Lowell the working-
girls were benevolently treated by the corporations. Were
they not allowed to have a magazine of their own, 'Lowell's
Offering'? Did not the Merrimac Manufacturing Company
take care of their morals and interest itself in their religion
and education? Whittier did not realize that though the
employers may have been men of good character, they were
profiting by the faults of the economic system. He was too
naïve to notice that the stockholders increased their wealth
because they exploited the girls with the sanction of the law.

Probably it is unjust to Whittier to say that he was altogether uninterested in the cause of labor, for he did write
two or three sympathetic editorials on the subject, but his
position was at best Laodicean. He gave no support to the
various associations in Boston and Lowell who were agitating
for shorter hours and were trying to gain ground lost by the
failure of recent strikes. He did bestir himself to write two
editorials one day, 'The Curse on Land and Labor' and
'Labor,' but they were of no service to the labor cause. They
appeared in the issue of October 31st when the election
campaign was practically over, when Whittier, merely
curious whether Polk or Clay won, was resting from his
labors. Yet what did Whittier urge in these editorials? In
the first one he answered those who complain that God had
cursed the earth with labor, by saying that man has cursed
himself more by changing the fruit of his labor into poison
when converting cane-sugar-juice into rum! In short Whittier made the sufferings of the workers a text for a temperance sermon. He did better, however, in the other editorial,
though he had an axe to grind there also, namely, to induce
the workingman to vote for the Liberty Party. He began
nobly:

'It is a truth too obvious for argument, that labor the
world over, is not looked upon as it should be. Wherever
oppression is practised — it is the laborer who is oppressed.
Wherever any class of men are degraded and crushed — it

is the laborer who suffers. Wherever the rights and privileges of any men are taken away or curtailed — it will be found to be the laborer who is injured. Such being the universal experience of the world, it certainly becomes workingmen — to be careful to whom they delegate power.'

He went on to tell the laborers to vote for men who would take care of their interests, and then, blaming the Southern slaveholder for the oppression of the Northern laborers by the Northern employer, he sought to persuade them to vote for the Liberty Party. While he was right in urging laborers to vote for a party that was against oppression, he was dragging a red herring across their path. He knew that no immediate results in alleviating the conditions of labor could be attained by the Liberty Party, which was primarily interested in the slave and which was sure of defeat. He said nothing about labor unions or strikes by which the working-men were beginning to seek remedies for their grievances.

But let us not think that Whittier was not interested in any other cause of liberty than that centering around the slave. While after the defeat of Birney he fought most vigorously against the annexation of Texas, he did not hesitate to plunge into other battles for freedom. He defended the rights of the foreign born in America and those of the Irish across the water. At this time the nativists in America were forming leagues to render it difficult for a foreigner to become naturalized. Hostility especially to the Catholics was increasing and soon led to the forming of the American, or Know Nothing, Party. In a noble editorial, 'The Naturalization Law,' copied, as were some other editorials, from the 'Essex Transcript,' to which Whittier had continued to contribute, he pleaded in behalf of the immigrants.

A far bolder editorial appeared in the issue of February 27, 1845, headed 'Ireland — The Pope vs. O'Connell and Repeal.' It is particularly noteworthy because Whittier in later life proved recreant to the cause of Irish freedom. He was interested in his early years in the career of the Irish orator Daniel O'Connell, about whom he had written an article in the 'Pennsylvania Freeman.' News had reached America of a singular effort to thwart the cause of Irish liberty through the Pope. 'For the sake of plundered and outraged humanity,' Whittier wrote, 'and for the sake of the cause of civil and religious liberty throughout the world, we fervently trust that when thus called upon to decide between liberty for Ireland or blind subjection to Papal authority, every Irishman will stand by his Father Land.'

Whittier only occasionally commented upon European affairs. He was more interested in fighting the proposed annexation of Texas. This possibility stirred him to write more poems and editorials than any other current event. He feared a double calamity by the entrance of Texas into our Union — a victory for the cause of slavery and a war with Mexico. He brought into service various resources besides writing — lobbying and circulating petitions to prevent annexation. Even before he joined the 'Standard,' the reverberations of his poem 'Texas' were heard throughout the country.

In the fall Mr. C. L. Knapp joined him in his editorial labors on the 'Standard.' Now that the election was over, they both turned their attention to the Texas question. Whittier wrote editorial after editorial, though he saw the battle was lost. From the end of October till March, when Texas was finally annexed, he conducted an indignant and smashing campaign, calling on the people to protest vigorously in conventions. The editorials appeared under various titles — 'Texas and Democracy,' 'Petition against Texas and Eternal Slavery,' 'Texas — The Crisis,' 'The Deed Done! — The First Vote on the Texas Question,' 'Annexation by Joint Resolution,' 'Great Anti-Annexation Meeting at Faneuil Hall,' 'The Anti-Texas Convention,' etc. He anticipated great results from a meeting of protest to be held in Faneuil Hall and he tried with his poem 'To Faneuil Hall' to make the gathering as large and vociferous as possible. He published the poem in the 'Standard,' and Garrison, in spite of his differences with the poet, copied it. It was one of Whittier's clearest clarion calls.

When his hopes were not realized, he still did not relax his efforts to make the annexation useless to the slave power. Striving to prevent Texas from becoming slave territory, he sent an article he wrote with directions to Alden Morse, of Essex County, to circulate it with a petition for signatures against the admission of Texas as a slave State. In the midst of these activities the 'Standard' was consolidated with another paper.

He now contributed editorials more frequently to the 'Essex Transcript.' [1] In one of these, 'No Union with Slaveholders,' he attacked Garrison for seeking to dissolve the Union. Whittier preferred to have Texas come in as a slave State, rather than to have the Union broken. In the fall he was again busy traveling and electioneering — actually making speeches. In December he was in Washington with Henry Wilson, as representative of the Liberty Party to present to Congress the petition signed by sixty thousand voters against the admission of Texas as a slave State. While there he wrote the poem 'At Washington,' in which he contrasted the splendor and fashion of Washington society with the miseries of the slave-market.

His chief work now was writing editorials for the 'Essex Transcript.' He would stroll daily down to the office, greet the compositor, and read over the newspapers. When he became affected by some act of injustice, he would nervously write his editorial in a paroxysm of rage. He was furious at

---

[1] There is no file in existence of the *Essex Transcript*. I found a few stray issues in the American Antiquarian Society in Worcester. Miss Annie C. Pettengill, of Amesbury, daughter of the proprietor, has sent me two issues dated January 27, and February 3, 1843, both of which contain eulogistic references to Whittier, who was then a candidate for Congress. The only articles by Whittier from the *Essex Transcript* accessible besides those I mention are the few where he quoted from himself in the *Standard*, and one he wrote on Torrey, which he reprinted.

The editorial 'No Union with Slaveholders' is unsigned and is in the issue of the *Essex Transcript*, Aug. 22, 1845.

the time because of the imprisonment of his friend the Rev. Charles F. Torrey in Baltimore for assisting some slaves to escape. He regretted that he had not been able to help him in any way, for he had promised to do so, and had written to him to 'keep up a good heart and hold out firmly.' [1]

He had taken up the cudgels in behalf of Torrey since his arrest. The first issue of the 'Standard' under Whittier's direction contained news about Torrey. Then it had letters from Torrey himself, sent from jail, accounts of various efforts in his behalf — even in Scotland, where the case attracted attention, copies of editorials from other papers about him, and finally reports of the trial and the sentence. In all there were more than a dozen articles by or about Torrey within five months.

After leaving the 'Standard,' Whittier was much concerned about the illness which Torrey developed in jail. He wrote to Gerrit Smith that when he thought of Torrey wearing out his life in the slaveholder's dungeon, he was almost ready to call for fire from heaven.

Torrey died of his sufferings in jail during the spring of 1846. Whittier, after attending the special funeral held in Boston, described his feelings in his account of it in the 'Essex Transcript.' 'We longed to see the wicked apologists of slavery — the blasphemous defenders of it in Church and State — led up to the coffin of our murdered brother, and there made to feel that their hands had aided in riveting the chain upon those still limbs, and in shutting out from those cold lips the free breath of heaven.'

During the summer, in a signed editorial in the 'Transcript,' 'Questions For The Clergy of the U.S.,' [2] he returned to his old task of baiting the ministers and propounded to them several questions: Was the Gospel of Jesus designed to improve man? Was slavery consistent with it? Should not the clergy rebuke slavery? Should not the churches be free

---

[1] Line from manuscript letter to Torrey, dated Lowell, Oct. 14, 1844, in Congregational Library, Boston.   [2] June 25, 1846.

from slavery? Did the Bible sanction slavery? If it did, was
it the will of God? and Wherein was Christianity better than
Paganism? He then gave his own answers:

'If slavery is practical Christianity, say so, and let the
Northern churches continue to hug to their bosoms those who
come among them foul and reeking with its abominations.
But if it is anti-Christian, anti-Scriptural, if God and humanity cry out against it, let the truth be told, let Christianity
be vindicated and its purity be preserved by an entire separa-
tion from the cursed thing.'

In the fall his career nearly came to an end. While he was
gathering grapes in the arbor in the garden, two boys were
firing at a mark, and one of them, not seeing him because of
a high fence, shot him in the cheek; the bullet just missed
entering his brain. Probably the neuralgia from which he
suffered the rest of his life was partly caused by this accident.

During the year 1846 there appeared another collection of
his poems, 'Voices of Freedom,' containing most of the anti-
slavery poems from his last three volumes and those he had
written since, as well as poems that have no bearing on human
freedom.

Whittier, not yet forty years old, was now recognized
as the greatest bard of Freedom in America.[1] He increased
his reputation with 'The Pine Tree Shilling,' a poem inspired
by Charles Sumner's speech at a Whig convention denouncing the delegates who had rejected an antislavery resolution.
He also wrote 'The Reformer,' the poem by which he at one
time wanted to be most remembered, as embodying his sentiments. Here he disclosed that his sympathies were with
those who tear down old institutions. He symbolically presents a strong man, deaf to all pleas, striking down shrines
sacred to the church, to art, to custom, and romance, and

---

[1] 'His anti-slavery songs,' said Dr. William F. Channing, a son of William Ellery
Channing, 'were stronger than the laws, and moulded the future more than anything
else in contemporaneous literature, within my knowledge, either in this country or
Europe.' From an unused manuscript written for Pickard and now in the possession
of Dr. Thomas Ollive Mabbott.

declares that only by the destruction of the old can such reforms as universal peace, the extirpation of slavery, repeal of capital punishment, and abolition of imprisonment eventually triumph. Apparently the so-called waster, Whittier points out, is really a builder, for the new structure springs from the ruins of the old. The true reformer must not be hindered from rooting out wrong and evil. Whittier draws a lesson from the Hindu doctrine that nature is revivified by destruction, and he finds only good emerging from the ruins made by the reformer.

Whittier saw that the war against Mexico which broke out in 1846 was one of unjust conquest — merely a step to increase Southern slave power. President Polk had begun the war by ordering General Taylor to the Rio Grande, who won his first victories in the spring, before war was declared. Whittier, who sympathized with the enemy, attacked the government's policy by a subterfuge, writing a battle hymn for the Mexicans under the pseudonym of José de Saltillo of Vera Cruz. Garrison was probably aware of the true authorship for he published it in the 'Liberator' in the summer of 1846. Whittier never collected the poem, but acknowledged it as his forty years later.

He was somewhat compensated for the disappointment of finding the country in a war for slavery, by the first significant political victory for the antislavery cause. In the fall of 1846, John P. Hale, of New Hampshire, an antislavery man, though not an abolitionist, after a memorable fight, won a seat in the United States Senate. Whittier had been in correspondence with him for a year, having himself begun it by writing to him in praise of his speech against the annexation of Texas. During the campaign on an Independent Democrat platform Hale followed Whittier's advice in various matters, thus obtaining the Liberty Party votes that elected him. Whittier was instrumental in making Hale Senator, just as he had been in helping send Cushing to Congress.

'He has succeeded,' he wrote of Hale to a friend in New Hampshire, 'and his success has broken the spell which has hitherto held reluctant Democracy in the embraces of slavery. The tide of anti-slavery feeling, long held back by the dams and dykes of party, has at last broken over all barriers, and is washing down from your northern mountains upon the slave-cursed south, as if Niagara stretched its foam and thunder along the whole length of Mason and Dixon's line. Let the first wave of that northern flood in its dashes against the walls of the capitol, bear thither for the first time an anti-slavery senator.' [1]

At last Whittier was avenged for the indignities he had suffered from the Concord mob. In a spirit of mockery and hilarity, he sent to a Boston newspaper an anonymous poem, 'A Letter,' in which he twitted and taunted the defeated pro-slavery voters about their mobbing him and Thompson ten years before.

It was during these years that the spirit of Milton rested upon him more than ever. In 1845 in 'The Training' he said that Milton influenced him more even than some of his Quaker idols:

'Blind Milton approaches nearly to my conception of a true hero. What a picture we have of the sublime old man, as sick, poor, blind, and abandoned of friends, he still held fast his heroic integrity, rebuking with his unbending republicanism the treachery, cowardice, and servility of his old associates! He had outlived the hopes and beatific visions of his youth; he had seen the loud-mouthed advocates of liberty throwing down a nation's freedom at the feet of the shameless, debauched and perjured Charles II, crouching to the harlot-thronged court of the tyrant, and forswearing at once their religion and their republicanism.'

Whittier considered Milton's prose works the greatest productions of his genius. Much as he appreciated 'Paradise

[1] Extract from Whittier's letter about Hale in the article on Hale in *Appleton's Cyclopædia of American Biography*.

Lost' he reverenced most the author of 'Areopagitica' and the pamphlets on religious and civil liberty. He admired Milton the republican, who advocated a free Commonwealth without a king or lords; he stood in divine awe before the aged poet who held fast to his views even when his neck was in danger. He told Mrs. Fields that his whole life felt the impress of Milton's writing. Mrs. Woodman, his cousin, in her excellent account of Whittier dwells on Milton's influence upon him. Whittier himself has said that he loved Milton's controversial works 'for their stern dignity and terrible invective, the bitter scorn, the annihilating retort, the solemn eloquence and devout appeals.' Nothing illustrates better how steeped he was in the spirit of Milton's radicalism than his numerous references to him. It is for this reason a mistake to couple Whittier's name chiefly with Burns, for Milton is the spirit more akin to his.

In later years Archdeacon Farrar of England wrote to Whittier, when asking him to contribute some lines on the great poet for George W. Child's memorial window, 'I think if Milton had now been living, you are the poet whom he would have chosen to speak of him, as being the poet with whose whole tone of mind he would have been most in sympathy.'

CHAPTER XIV

THE RADICAL

In the beginning of 1847 Whittier became contributing editor of the 'National Era,' a weekly paper started in Washington by the American and Foreign Anti-Slavery Society. Its editor was Dr. Gamaliel Bailey, who had edited Birney's 'Philanthropist' in Cincinnati, and had seen three printing-presses of that paper thrown by a mob into the Ohio River. He edited the new paper till his death in 1859. Whittier remained contributing editor till 1860, when the paper expired. He sent to it most of the poems, literary essays, and political articles he wrote during those years.

Whittier at this time became more radical than ever in his antislavery views. He would not compromise like Webster and Everett with the slaveholders, though he did not hesitate to engage in political maneuvers to win over voters to the cause of abolition, for he hoped for final victory through the ballot. Whittier himself best stated his radical stand on the occasion of Edward Everett's death shortly before the end of the Civil War.

'My pronounced radicalism on the great question which has divided popular feeling rendered our political paths widely divergent. Both of us early saw the danger which threatened the country. In the language of the prophet, we "saw the sword coming upon the land," but while he believed in the possibility of averting it by concession and compromise, I, on the contrary, as firmly believed that such a course could only strengthen and confirm what I regarded as a gigantic conspiracy against the rights and liberties, the union and life, of the nations.'

Though he took an uncompromising attitude towards slavery, he resorted to measures of expediency for the purpose of increasing the political power of the antislavery party. He now discreetly urged that some man with abolition tendencies who was outside of the Liberty Party should be nominated for President. He believed that such a course would induce many Whigs and Democrats not in sympathy with the pro-slavery sentiment of their parties to break party lines and support such a candidate. In short, Whittier sought to build up a larger antislavery party through concessions, by enlisting sympathizers from all parties. Deciding that John P. Hale was the best choice for the Presidency, he prepared the way for him by eulogies in the columns of the 'National Era.'

In the summer he began plying Hale with sagacious counsel as to how to placate the Liberty Party men. He advised him to disconnect himself from the two old parties but still to avow his Democratic faith in the doctrine of Jefferson, and to adopt stricter antislavery principles. In an editorial in the 'National Era,' 'The President — the Man for the Hour,' September 2, 1847, Whittier definitely advocated Hale's nomination. He now asked Hale to write a letter with antislavery sentiments, shrewdly saying at the same time: 'I trust thee will not permit thyself to be troubled with "constitutional" difficulties. The Constitution has been a mere ruse of war in the hands of Slavery for half a century. It has been made to say and be just what the South wished. We must take it out of the custody of slavery and construe it in the light of Liberty — "as we understand it." We must bring it out of the land of bondage, just as David did the ark from the Philistines to Obed Edom. At all events, with the Constitution or without the Constitution, *Slavery must die.*'

In the October convention of the Liberty Party at Buffalo, Hale was nominated after much opposition. In the next year the Whigs nominated General Taylor, and the Democrats Lewis Cass — both proslavery men. Dissension arose in all three parties. The members of the Democratic and the

Whig parties who were opposed to slavery seceded and joined
with the Liberty Party men in forming a new party called
the Free Soil Party. Thus the abolition ranks were aug-
mented by the so-called 'Conscience Whigs' and the Democratic 'Barnburners' and replenished with leaders who were
among the ablest men in the country. The delegates met at
Buffalo in August, 1848, to agree upon a candidate. They
decided to accept Martin Van Buren, who had been put forth
as a candidate by the Democratic 'Barnburners,' for he had
become sympathetic to the abolition cause, and had even
opposed the annexation of Texas. Whittier was too ill himself to attend the Free Soil Convention and do what he could
to promote the earlier nomination of Hale, whose rejection
and humiliation by the convention he deplored. He was
opposed to Van Buren's nomination, for he doubted his
sincerity, though he eventually decided to support him. He
wrote an editorial in the 'National Era' (September 7, 1848),
'Bygones,' in which, after referring to Van Buren's former
proslavery attitude, he called on all in favor of abolition to
support him since he had allied himself with their cause.
Whittier himself was an elector from his district on the
ballot of the Free Soil Party, which polled nearly three
hundred thousand votes and sent William H. Seward of New
York and Salmon P. Chase of Ohio to the Senate.

About the time Whittier launched the movement to
nominate Hale for President — in September, 1847 — the
Mexican War was virtually ended by General Scott's capture of Mexico. Whittier expressed his disapproval of the
war, not only in the poem previously mentioned, signed with
a pseudonym, but in his editorials. He began by attacking
Cushing who had joined the army as a General. The spectacle of a man who had received support from the abolitionists
now fighting a war which was waged to increase slavery, a
war which the Southern slaveholders had brought about, exasperated, yet amused Whittier.

'It is a poor compliment,' he wrote, 'to civilization, religion and humanity of our age and country, that a man like Caleb Cushing, with a mind highly gifted by nature, enriched by varied learning, and capable, if rightly directed, of exerting a healthful influence upon his countrymen and the world, is able to find no better employment than that of leading off a company of deluded unfortunates thousands of miles to shoot men, with whom *they* at least have no quarrel, or be shot by them; and this too, without the plea that the welfare of the country requires it or its true honor demands it.'[1]

In another article he charged the government with being guilty, in prosecuting the war, of a greater crime than Danton's instigating the September massacres during the French Revolution. After the treaty with Mexico was signed, Whittier, while reviewing the second volume of Lamartine's 'History of the Girondins' (February 17, 1848), wrote these burning words:

'There is a Satanic sublimity in this sacrifice — this laying of conscience, self-respect, and honorable fame on the altar of the public weal. Here was a man [Danton] willing to make himself infamous — to burden his soul with crime — to stamp murder on the forehead of his memory for all time — in obedience to what he regarded as the dictate of patriotism. We can scarcely see how those who adopt the atrocious maxim "Our country right or wrong" can censure him. Is there anything more dreadful, after all, in the massacre of venerable priests, high-born nobles, and beautiful women, in the prisons of Paris, than in the slaughter of women and children in the bombardment of Vera Cruz? Does not every poor soldier who bleeds away his life suffer as much as did the Bishops and Princes who fell under the daggers of the Parisian mob?... It may well be doubted whether the "glorious victories" for which Thanksgiving and praise are offered in our Christian temples are not as hateful as the massacre of September, over which the world has shuddered for half a century.'

[1] *National Era*, Jan. 27, 1847.

As Whittier was in Washington at the time his editorial appeared, he apparently was defying the authorities to arrest him for sedition, but they did not do so. While there he called on the eighty-year-old veteran John Quincy Adams and heard him talk more vehemently against slavery than ever. A few days later he was shocked to learn that Adams had been stricken with apoplexy at his post of duty in the House of Representatives and had died. Whittier wrote to his friend Sumner about the dramatic end of Adams's glorious career, and later published in the 'Era' a brief account of his interview with Adams.

Whittier hoped that Adams's son Charles Francis Adams, who was even more devoted to the antislavery cause than his father, would be chosen as his successor. However, another able man, the great educator Horace Mann, was elected by the 'Conscience' Whigs instead. Shortly afterwards Charles Francis Adams received the nomination for Vice-President on the Free Soil Ticket.

It was about this time that Whittier entered into the service of the labor cause. He was deeply interested in the revolution then going on in France and in the fight for liberty throughout Europe. Being a Quaker, he naturally was always opposed to violence, entertaining no belief in revolutionary methods, but relying only upon the use of the ballot. Yet he was a radical, and in an editorial on the revolution in France — one of the boldest and most courageous he ever wrote — he even attacked representative government.

'The world has been cheated long enough,' he wrote, 'with the idea that Governments are instituted chiefly as police regulations to keep the people as they are, the feet of one class on the neck of another.... Under our present system, the protection of property, and not of man, is still the great object of Government.... When the rights and immunities of Property are the special object of Government protection to the neglect of the rights of men, it matters very little to the millions, whether they are ruled by Senate or Kaiser, Constitutional

King or Provisional Committee.... Not the least of shams is the notion that a nominally republican form of government necessarily secures the freedom and happiness of People who live under it.... These inequalities... these monstrous contrasts, which shock and pain us wherever we look — are none the less evil, in themselves considered. It is nevertheless our duty to labor, as a way may be opened, for their removal. We would advocate no violent measures, no injustice to any class; no unsettling of rightful tenures of property, no compulsory distribution.'[1]

Other reformers, however, feeling that he did not go far enough, believed that his religious orthodoxy prevented him from being more sweeping and drastic. The 'Harbinger,' the old Brook Farm paper to which he himself had contributed, disapproved of an editorial he wrote about Robert Owen, and it charged him with clinging to the 'tattered remnants of a strong and rigid old fanaticism.' To this criticism he replied as follows:

'I have never joined in the popular clamor against those who are so unfortunate as to doubt or disbelieve the divine origin of the Gospel; I have on all occasions, and at some cost, vindicated their rights of speech, and fair hearing; and have, at the risk of misapprehension and obloquy, rebuked the intolerance of and bitter spirit of some of their assailants, who had undertaken to be God's avengers in the matter. Fully sympathizing with the free and hopeful spirit of the age, a humble and toiling member of that party of Reform and Progress, which is the future of the great Free Party of the Future, I cannot, even for courtesy's sake, admit the correctness of the charge preferred against me, of clinging to the "tattered remmants of a strong and rigid old fanaticism." I reverence whatever is good and true and heroic in the past, not because it is old, but because it brings with it the freshness and newness of an immortal life, and it is not merely a part of the past, but of the present future also.'[2]

[1] From article 'Labor — The French Revolution,' *National Era*, April 27, 1848.
[2] *National Era*, March 11, 1847.

By his own words 'unfortunate as to doubt the divine origin of the Gospel' he gave Unitarians greater offence. The free-thinkers were only amused at his rejection of reforms merely because these were not in accordance with the doctrine of Christianity.

Whittier was, nevertheless, attracted to all characters who, like Ibsen's Dr. Stockman, suffered persecution for espousing unpopular doctrines. He was always ready to recount tales of men who boldly defied prevailing public opinion to follow their inner light. In his well-known ballad of 'Barclay of Ury,' contributed to the 'National Era,' he depicted such a person. Whittier admired, not the soldier Barclay, who fought under Gustavus Adolphus in Germany, but the converted Quaker Barclay, who now bore meekly the taunts and mockery of the crowd. Whittier knew from his own experience what Barclay's sufferings were.

In poems like this he indirectly defended himself for having deserted the muses, for no longer sporting 'with Nærilla in the shade.' He sought to justify his own course in now living for others instead of for himself and in casting aside the rewards he could have had.

In spite of his geniality in private life, he was personal and abusive in his attacks upon those who were hostile to his cause; in fact, he made himself amenable to the libel laws on more than one occasion. But though he stormed against those who incurred his wrath, he was thinking rather of the pernicious views and cruel practices for which they were sponsors. He never hated the slaveholder; he was merely opposed to the holding of slaves.

Like the contemporary editors, he indulged in virulent abuse, blasting especially statesmen and clergymen with his wrath. His attacks upon the latter are singular, coming as they did from one who was pious and believed in the Bible, from one who wrote tributes to many noble clergymen, from one who composed many fervent hymns himself. But he became exasperated when he saw the clergy lending their sanction to policies not in accord with the ideals of the religion they professed. He was especially incensed at the attempt to find support for slavery by appeals to the Bible. Many of his tirades are just as timely today as when delivered; for it was not a particular clergyman whom he assailed for quoting the Bible to defend slavery; he denounced the paid hireling of vested interests; he was righteously indignant that a body of men who should have been supporters of liberty were its enemies.

In a poem published in the 'National Era,' 'The Curse of the Charter-Breakers,' he praised an old custom of the Catholic clergy of England in invoking a curse upon those who infringed that foundation of liberty, Magna Charta. He regretted that the priests today were not as bold as those ancient ones.

He was an enemy of creeds only when they interfered with liberty of speech, press, or conscience.

In a letter in later years he wrote to a Catholic admirer who complained of some of his strictures upon the church:[1]

'As to what I have said of the Catholics, it has no theological animus. I only hate bigotry, intolerance and persecution, and the sin against the Holy Ghost in opposing every movement of the age for freedom and humanity. It is thy church as a vast political power that I dislike. During our long struggles for Emancipation here, the Catholics almost without exception took the side of Slavery.'

[1] Manuscript letter, dated Amesbury, Oct. 24, 1877, in Library of Yale College.

CHAPTER XV

SELECTING CHARLES SUMNER FOR SENATOR

In THE early part of 1850 Henry Clay introduced a new Fugitive Slave Bill in Congress to give the South a more stringent law than that then in force. Webster, coming to Clay's support, made his famous Seventh of March speech, defending the bill. He asserted its constitutionality and demanded its passage for the purpose of conciliating the South and preserving the Union, and at the same time he made an onslaught upon the abolitionists. They now fell upon him tooth and nail and charged him with angling for Southern votes to obtain the Presidential nomination. Not only Garrison and Phillips, but authors like Lowell and Emerson, exhausted their vituperative vocabulary in berating him. Whittier assailed him in the poem 'Ichabod,' but, by making no allusion to him by name, or to the law for which he stood sponsor, inflicted wounds as though with the barb of a spear; for he made his thrusts at Webster by innuendo, in fact put forth repeated pleas to remember his past services, and not to abuse him, thus rendering the taunt cumulatively catastrophic. The merits of the poem do not depend upon the question whether Webster or Whittier was in the right.[1] Its sentiments are applicable to any person who has proved recreant to the ideals of liberty and has compromised with the oppressor. Whittier wrote it, not in a partisan spirit, nor with personal enmity to Webster; he was prompted only by fear that the whole country would become a hunting-ground for slaves. The poem is a lament for one who had deserted a noble cause, rather than a personal lampoon on Webster; it belongs to the same class as do Shelley's poem 'To Wordsworth' and Browning's 'The Lost Leader.' Though Whittier

[1] I myself emphatically dissent from some recent historians who have rushed to the defense of Webster.

never retracted his judgment on Webster for his support of the Fugitive Slave Bill, he later made amends for his attack by writing another poem about Webster, 'The Lost Occasion.'

While the bill was pending, Whittier tried to create hostile sentiment against it and prevent it from becoming a law, by writing 'A Sabbath Scene,' one of his most powerful and seditious poems, in which he showed the cruelty caused by a clergyman's compliance with the old law. As the parson goes up to his pulpit, a fugitive slave girl, pursued by her master, runs into church seeking refuge. The minister calls on the deacon to trip her with the heavy Polyglot Bible, and when she stumbles, and falls, he himself ties the knots to bind her. He then defends his course with Biblical texts, but he does not drown out the cries of the girl, as they rend the air when her master leads her away.

Whittier could have become State senator at this time, for the Democrats wanted to nominate him on the eventually victorious coalition ticket then being formed between them and the Free Soilers against the Whigs. He refused to run for any office, on the ground that as a public official he would have to support the new obnoxious law. In declining the nomination, he wrote: [1]

'Since the passage of the *Fugitive Slave Law* by Congress, I find myself in a position, with respect to it, which, I fear, my fellow citizens generally are not prepared to justify.

'So far as that law is concerned, I *am a Nullifier*. By no act or countenance or consent, of mine, shall that law be enforced in Massachusetts. My door is still open to the oppressed whether fleeing from *Austria* or *South Carolina*.'

A year later in his poem 'Kossuth' he rode full tilt against Webster a second time. This assault arose out of the belief that Webster would officially welcome Kossuth, who had just come to America. Webster's services in rescuing Kos-

[1] Whittier's letter declining the nomination, dated Oct. 4, 1850, was published in the newspaper *The Bay State*, Lynn, Mass. Reprinted by Albree, pp. 113-114.

suth in Turkey from the efforts of the Austrian government
to apprehend him in violation of international law made him
the logical person to offer him the hospitality of the country.
But Webster, realizing that as a public official he could not
properly extend a special welcome to a political refugee, decided to remain at his post in Washington. Whittier, an admirer of Kossuth, meanwhile had penned a poem of greeting
to him, expressing the hope that no renegade to the cause of
freedom would welcome an apostle of liberty, and regretting that John Quincy Adams was not alive to act as host.
In this poem, as in 'Ichabod,' he does not mention Webster
by name.

> 'Who shall be Freedom's mouthpiece? Who shall give
>   Her welcoming cheer to the great fugitive?
> Not he who, all her sacred trusts betraying,
>   Is scourging back to slavery's hell of pain
>   The swarthy Kossuths of our land again!
> Not he whose utterance now from lips designed
>   The bugle-march of Liberty to wind,
> And call her hosts beneath the breaking light,
> The keen reveille of her morn of fight,
>   Is but the hoarse note of the bloodhound's baying,
> The wolf's long howl behind the bondman's flight!'

This sally kindled the indignation of Webster's admirers,
who now thought it time to call the poet to account. They
were bolstered up by the hope that they could convict him of
treason for this poem, and were further encouraged to believe
that they would succeed in doing so because he had recently
reprinted his old seditious diatribe against Governor Porter
of Pennsylvania. Webster himself undoubtedly had nothing
to do with their proposal. However, someone anonymously
issued a four-page leaflet headed 'Abolition Treason,'[1] in
which the Kossuth poem and the old poem against Governor
Porter were reprinted as proofs of the poet's amenability to

[1] This leaflet is mentioned in *American Book Prices Current*, 1931, as sold Dec.
2, 3, 1930, by the American Art Association, Anderson Galleries, from the Library
of the Honorable Frederick W. Lehman.

arrest for treason. The text of the leaflet began as follows:
'Abolition Treason is no new thing. It was even set in
rhyme as long ago as 1838, by the Quaker poet, Whittier, as
the following will show.' The poem against Porter under the
title 'The Response' followed. The text then continued:
'The traitor still alive. Here is another production fresh
from the pen of the same treasonable rhymester. Where is
the Attorney General?' Then came a reprint of the Kossuth
poem.

This document shows that there were quite a number of
men who regarded our reputed inane, harmless poet as too
vituperative and dangerous to be at large.

Some of Whittier's most denunciatory writing is in the several poems that grew out of public attempts to defy the enforcement of the Fugitive Slave Law and rescue its victims.
In his 'Moloch in State Street,' written on the rendition of
Thomas Sims, the escaped slave, he impugned the motives
of the merchants who, out of greed and fear of loss of the
Southern trade, aided in returning the Negro.

When in 1854, Massachusetts was again disgraced by the
return of the slave Anthony Burns, Whittier wrote in 'The
Rendition' that he no longer felt love of home, or pride of
birthplace, as he saw Liberty marching 'handcuffed down the
sworded' street. Walt Whitman also wrote a poem on the
occasion, 'Boston Ballad.' When some citizens determined
to rescue Burns by force, however, Whittier deplored the attempt, as the following letter to Samuel E. Sewall, counsel
for Burns, shows:[1]

AMESBURY *29th 5 mo.* 1854

My dear Friend:
I do earnestly hope and pray that no violence or brute
force may be resorted to by the friends of freedom. I would
die rather than aid in that wicked law; but I deplore all for-
cible resistance to it. I know the case is an aggravated one,
but in the end forbearance will be best for all parties. I feel

[1] Letter to Sewall, in *Samuel E. Sewall*, by Nina Moore Tiffany, p. 79, 1898.

sure that thy influence will be on the side of peace; and I beg thee *to take especial pains with our colored friends to keep them from resort to force.* May God in his mercy keep us from evil, in opposing evil.

Thine ever,
JOHN G. WHITTIER

Nevertheless, when Wendell Phillips, Theodore Parker, Thomas Wentworth Higginson, and others were arrested for treason, for their interference in behalf of Burns, Whittier secretly rejoiced that they acted in accordance with the dictates of their consciences. In a poem 'To Friends under Arrest,' which he later entitled 'For Righteousness' Sake,' he maintained that no common wrong provoked their zeal, but said that he would not repeat their 'hot words,' since his own lips were 'trained to caution.' The bills of indictment against the men were afterwards quashed.

When Massachusetts passed a personal-liberty bill in an attempt to free her citizens from carrying out the provisions of the Fugitive Slave Law, Whittier took heart and celebrated the event in a poem whose title, 'On the Passage of the Fugitive Slave Bill,' he later changed to 'Arisen at Last.'

> 'Southward the baffled robber's track
> Henceforth runs only; hereaway,
> The fell lycanthrope finds no prey.'

Though Whittier was not able to prevent Congress from passing the Fugitive Slave Law, he was forging a bolt that was to pierce the armor of slavery. He was putting forth Charles Sumner as the candidate for the United States Senate under the coalition entered into between the Democrats and Free Soilers against the Whigs.

Whittier, originally attracted to Sumner by his famous oration against war, had become friendly with him in the last five years, and had successfully urged him on to secede from the Whig Party. He admired Sumner's integrity and scholar-

ship and, above all, his unselfish devotion to the cause. In
the coalition taking place at the time, the Democrats agreed
to appoint a Free Soil Senator, if the Free-Soilers would help
them elect George S. Boutwell, their candidate for Governor.
It was Whittier's belief that Sumner's reputation made him
the most available person for the Senatorship, then held by
Winthrop.

He called on Sumner at Phillips Beach, Swampscott, and
revealed to him his plan of having him chosen as Senator in
the coalition. Sumner had never held political office — except that of Federal Court Reporter — and really did not wish
to become a Senator, preferring the life of a student of law and
literature. Whittier had to resort to many persuasive arguments to induce him to consent to the use of his name. They
contended and argued — the young scholar and the poet —
on the subject of Whittier's plan. That summer day the
poet shaped 'a large future' for the scholar, as he later wrote
in his poem on Sumner. Here was the shy Quaker poet, un-
educated, a power in politics, handing an office, as it were, on
a plate to a young lawyer and scholar, who had already refused to accept the Whig nomination for Congress, and who
had run for Congress on the Free Soil ticket only because he
knew he could not be elected. Here was an unselfish and shy
bard offering to put in Webster's seat a scholar-politician
who did not want the honor. After much debating, Sumner
finally promised to take the office if the State legislature
elected him.

Though the coalition seemed an unholy alliance to many
abolitionists, and horrified the young Henry Adams, son of
Charles Francis Adams, the results of the election were gratifying to the Free-Soilers. By their vote they not only elected
George S. Boutwell Governor, but they sent Robert S. Rantoul, Jr., to Congress and re-elected Henry Wilson State
Senator. Whittier was especially pleased by the success of
the latter two, both personal friends of his. He now looked
to Wilson to use his efforts to induce the Democrats in the

legislature to perform their part of their agreement, and send Sumner to the Senate. He wrote Wilson the following letter:[1]

AMESBURY, 18*th* 11*mo*. 1850

MY DEAR FRIEND:

Thy notification of the meeting of the State Free Soil Com. & other friends at the Adams House tomorrow morning, has just reached me, & I should be glad if I could answer it in person. But as I cannot well be with you, I can do no less than offer my congratulations upon the measure of success which has attended the 'Union ticket', — a ticket to which I reluctantly assented at the outset, but which has succeeded thus far beyond the anticipation of the most sanguine in its behalf.

I had, I confess, but a single object in voting it, the election of a Free Soil U. S. Senator. Give me this, and I am willing that Hunkerdom shall have all our State offices. I fear, however, that we are by no means sure of this object. You have some twenty or thirty Hunker Democrats headed by Caleb Cushing directly in the way. In our town the Dem. candidate for her representation openly declared that he preferred a Webster Whig to a Free Soil Democrat.

If I were in the Legislature I would demand first of all a pledge signed by the Democratic members that they would vote for the Free Soil Senatorial candidate. Without some *positive* assurance of the kind, I for one wd. never vote for Geo. S. Boutwell. I would break off the 'union' at once & stick to our own noble & true Phillips.

But Boutwell's inaugural address disturbed the Free-Soilers, who now feared that the Democrats would not carry out their part of the agreement to choose a Free Soil Senator. In the following spring Whittier watched with anxiety the sharp contest going on in the legislature for the senatorship. Believing now that he had made a mistake in helping elect

[1] Manuscript letter to Wilson, then editor of the *Republican*, in the Ford Collection of the New York Public Library, presented by John P. Morgan.

Boutwell Governor, he advised Sumner to abandon the contest. Sumner decided to follow his advice, but the Free-Soilers urged him to continue the fight. Sumner, distracted, begged Whittier to come to Boston and give him the benefit of his counsel. But Whittier was sick at the time, and in fact was so nonplussed that he did not himself know what to suggest. It was hazardous to withdraw and rely on the next legislature, since then the Whigs might be in the majority and elect one of their own party; yet it seemed hopeless, if not fatal, to continue the contest. He asked Sumner to call on him at Amesbury, which he did; they again discussed the situation, and Whittier finally advised him to remain a candidate. Sumner heeded him — very fortunately, for he was chosen Senator, by one vote on the twenty-sixth ballot. Whittier, though at this time so ill that he did not expect to recover, was exultant.

'Sick abed,' he wrote to Sumner, 'I heard the guns — Quaker as I am — with real satisfaction.'

Thus the plan that the poet had worked out the summer before at Phillips Beach came to fruition. Though Wilson as President of the State Senate led the fight which placed Sumner in the United States Senate, Whittier originated the plan, advised Sumner during the fight, and spurred Wilson on to the battle.

For himself he sought from Sumner no rewards and no office, though his own finances were at a low ebb, as he had a meager income. He had put up Sumner for the office to serve the cause; that was all he wanted him to do. As he himself said in an autobiographic sketch published in later years, 'While feeling, and willing to bear all the responsibilities of citizenship, and deeply interested in questions which concern the welfare and honor of the country, I have, as a rule, declined overtures for acceptance of public stations. I have always taken an active part in election, but have not been willing to add my own example to the greed of office.'

A few years later, Whittier undertook to help politically

Robert C. Winthrop, Jr., the Whig candidate whom Sumner defeated for the Senate. But Winthrop would not join the Free-Soilers, or the new Republican party soon to be formed. When, in 1854, the Kansas-Nebraska Bill, which was to repeal the Missouri Compromise, came before Congress, Whittier was one of those who saw the need of a new party. He tried to arouse Winthrop's interest in it, and to make him its leader. He wrote to him as follows:

AMESBURY 4th 2nd Mo. 1854

DEAR FRIEND:

I cannot doubt that the threatened and too probable repeal of the Miss. Compromise by the Bill now before the Senate, backed by the whole power of the Executive, is as repugnant to thy feeling & convictions as to my own. Permit me to inquire if something cannot be done to avert this great and terrible evil — a broad, generous Northern movement, not confined to the various grounds of party. I know of no one so well able as thyself to take the first step in this movement — none whose antecedents are so likely to secure a candid hearing from the whole country. The honored name of Winthrop has ever been dear & sacred to the decendants of the Pilgrims, & I mean no empty compliment in saying that it has lost nothing in thy possession.

At this crisis I cannot feel or speak as a party man. Would to God that all our old dissensions could be buried & forgotten & that all who love freedom & the good old ways of the fathers could unite for their preservation. I know that I am not alone in looking to thee at this time. Providence has placed thee in a position to speak & act with effect; & surely the power to do so on thy part involves a duty.

Pardon this abrupt appeal & believe me with great respect & esteem thy friend,

JOHN G. WHITTIER

Two months later Whittier again wrote to him:[1]

AMESBURY 10th 6th Mo. 1854

MY DEAR FRIEND

I have just been reading over for the second time thy admirable sketch of Algernon Sydney, the just & generous sentiments of which confirm my long-cherished belief that thou canst do more than any other Northern man, at this time, to organize the people of the free States irrespective of party, in opposition to the encroachments of Slavery, & in so doing save our beloved country from utter disgrace & degradation or the horrors of bloody revolution. I fully believe that the people of New England — the vast majority — are ready to unite in a movement having for its object the restriction of Slavery to the States where it now abides, the repeal of the Fugitive Slave Law, & the Nebraska perfidy.

I enclose a little article of mine published a day or two ago in the Commonwealth; and my object in now writing is to ascertain thy views of this proposition. That the Free Soil party are ready in good faith to abandon their organization & support Whigs or Democrats who will go for the measure above indicated, I am quite sure. Doubtless we may have erred in many of our movements — much has been said & written which I regret, — but the great body of the antislavery party have been honest & true men. Let all that is calculated to irritate & divide the Northern sentiment be forgotten & forgiven; and let the strong & wise men of all parties take counsel together to avert the common danger. The crisis is upon us; we cannot avert it if we would. It must be met, either with the wild violence of excitement; or the calm & deliberate wisdom of law-abiding but liberty-loving men.

With sentiments of real respect & esteem

Thy fr.
JOHN G. WHITTIER

HON. R. C. WINTHROP

[1] Manuscript of both letters to Winthrop in the Massachusetts Historical Society.

Nothing but the assurance from myself & other friends of peace that a Great Northern movement was on foot prevented a fearful outbreak in your city in the case of Burns. If this hope fails — if such men as thy self do not come forward & lead the popular feeling in the safe channel of legal & constitutional action, the next attempt to execute the F. S. Law in N. England will be resisted to the death — armed, organized revolution. I am using no idle words. I beseech thee to seriously consider this matter in the light of personal duty & in view of the responsibility which attaches to one in thy position.

He wrote to Emerson, who was also interested in the new party, that he believed that Robert C. Winthrop held in his hands the destiny of the North and that 'by throwing himself on the side of this movement he could carry with him the Whig strength of the north.'

But Emerson had proved himself a better judge of Winthrop than Whittier did; he had estimated him at his true worth in a lecture on the Fugitive Slave Law, calling him an enemy of liberty, though not mentioning him by name. Referring to an address delivered by Winthrop, Emerson said that the speaker 'professed his adoration for liberty in the time of his grandfathers,' yet 'proceeded with his work of denouncing freedom and freemen in the present day; much in the tone and spirit in which Lord Bacon prosecuted his benefactor Essex.' [1]

Whittier was not successful in winning Winthrop over to the cause. Winthrop did not join the newly formed Republican Party — one of his reasons being that he did not approve of its leaders — and by his refusal sealed his political career; he allied himself with the Know-Nothing, or American, party.

[1] Emerson alludes to Winthrop, though not by name, in his lecture delivered in New York, March 7, 1854, published in *Miscellanies*, pp. 242–243.   In his *Journals*, Vol. VIII, pp. 307–310, under date of July 8, 1852, Emerson mentioned Winthrop by name and wrote the words against him that he afterwards used in the lecture. This was despite the fact that Winthrop had voted against the Fugitive Slave Law.

Whittier, after having succeeded in helping to form the Republican Party, terminated his career as an active politician. For he was a sick man; he had done his greatest work, and he left younger men to take up the burden. He was proud of his accomplishment and scented victory in spite of discouraging signs. He wrote to Mrs. Lydia M. Child:[1]

'Just think of Massachusetts as she was in the fall of '35 and of what she is now in '56. The seed then sown in weakness, is springing up in power. My chief regret, personally, is that I cannot do much for the good cause. The state of my health is such that sometimes for many [days] together I cannot write a word without great suffering.'

He continued writing antislavery poems till the end of the Civil War, but he did not excel his earlier abolition poems. He wrote poems about the difficulties in Kansas and campaign songs in behalf of Frémont's election. Though one or two of the Kansas poems, like 'Burial of Barber,' became popular, his Kansas poems did not seethe with such indignation as did those of the undeservedly forgotten Richard Realf, who, having moved to Kansas, nobly sang about the scenes in which he took an active part.

One of Whittier's last and most fiery abolition poems was 'On a Prayer-Book,' suggested by seeing a prayer-book that contained a frontispiece of Ary Scheffer's 'Christus Consolator' Americanized by the omission of the black man. He wrote he would never kneel before such a praying-book, reminding us of Wordsworth when he said that he would rather be a Pagan than a Christian who could not appreciate nature. Whittier burst forth:[2]

'I, for one,
Would sooner bow, a Parsee, to the sun,
Or tend a prayer-wheel in Thibetan brooks,
Or beat a drum on Yedo's temple-floor.
No falser idol man has bowed before,

---

[1] Manuscript letter to Mrs. Child in Pennsylvania Historical Society.
[2] 'On a Prayer-Book,' *The Independent*, Sept. 15, 1859. *Poems.*

In Indian groves or islands of the sea,
 Than that which through the quaint-carved Gothic door
Looks forth, — a Church without humanity!...
Better the simple Lama scattering wide,
 Where sweeps the storm of Alechan's steppes along,
His paper horses for the lost to ride,
And wearying Buddha with his prayers to make
The figures living for the traveller's sake,
Than he who hopes with cheap praise to beguile
The ear of God, dishonoring man the while.'

Yet the old hatred for abolitionists has extended down to our own day; popular Northern American historians belabor them with abuse and compare them to fanatical prohibitionists or contemporary quacks. It seems strange that a body of noble men who displayed such unselfish devotion should still be misunderstood. They were reformers who had absolutely nothing to gain for themselves by their zealous efforts. Their activities were like rays of light in the dark places of our history, at a time when political corruption was at its height, when Northern statesmen betrayed their constituents to the South and when the clergy with few exceptions justified slavery.

Many people who still think Garrison was an incendiary hold that Whittier was a harmless poet. As a matter of fact his poems of freedom are too dangerous to be introduced into the schools. They still breathe that 'blasphemy' and 'sedition' of which vested interests are in mortal fear. Their author accuses the clergy of using religion as a cloak for crime, theft, injustice, and exploitation; he attacks the state for its servility and unwarranted vindictiveness; he calls upon the public to agitate against encroachments upon its liberties. These poems, therefore, belong to radical and revolutionary literature; they take their place with some of Milton's sonnets and Shelley's lyrics.

CHAPTER XVI

DEVOTION TO THE MUSES

IN SPITE of Whittier's antislavery work he never forgot that he was primarily a poet. At times, with a feeling akin to that of dereliction of duty, he did compose verses that had no bearing on the antislavery cause at all. He was not altogether unconcerned about his poetic reputation, even though he did little to advance it. By his 'Lays of My Home' he had shown the public that he was also an æsthetic poet, who could write on other themes as well as on the abolition of slavery. He even became interested in spreading his purely poetic reputation in England. When his friend Elizur Wright went abroad in 1844, Whittier asked him to supervise a volume of his poems there, and sent him a selection from the poems of the Philadelphia 1838 volume and the 'Lays of My Home,' together with some poems that he had recently published. The book duly appeared with an introduction by Wright; thus an American antislavery poet was introduced into England by an antislavery worker.

Whittier knew that his poems were defective artistically and psychologically, but he was cognizant of their true value in furthering the cause of liberty and justice. Towards the end of 1847, when he was forty years old, he penned his famous 'Proem,' which hereafter he always placed as the introductory poem to every edition of his collected poetical works. He gave us in the poem a good criticism of his faults, dwelling on his jarring words, his deficiencies as a finished artist, his failings as a nature poet and as a psychologist.

An album poem of the period, December, 1847, written for Mary Bagley, sister of Anna, of Amesbury, also shows how much the subject of liberty occupied him then:

TO MARY [1]

As one who to the wave-washed sand
 His name and record gives;
Or, on the casement's frosted pane
 A frail memorial leaves,
My lines upon thy page I trace;
My name within thy book I place.
Yet, ere the wave sweeps o'er the sand,
 Or melts that frosted line,
 Some eyes before the record there
 With deeper joy may shine;
And the frail characters impart
A gladness to some human heart.

I leave my name upon thy page —
 In trust that it will be
 Link'd, if but humbly, with the cause
 Of truth and Liberty;
And, not unworthy, hence to share
A place within thy album fair.'

Whittier's reputation as an antislavery poet reached its height when he published the beautiful Boston edition of his poems in 1849. At the head of the book was the long, weak Indian poem *The Bridal of Pennacook*, which had appeared a few years previously in the 'Democratic Review,' and 'Mogg Megone.' The Pennacook poem could, like 'Mogg Megone,' without any loss to Whittier's reputation, have been relegated to the appendix of the later collected edition. It has no significance in his career as a poet, except to show that, in the midst of his antislavery poetry, he retained his interest in Indian legends. The volume contained old poems, most of those in the 'Voices of Freedom,' and some that he had recently written for the 'National Era' and other publications. There were ballads like 'The Exiles,' 'The New Wife and the Old,' 'Barclay of Ury,' and 'The Angels of Buena Vista,' favorite poems which helped to wean the public away from the view that Whittier was only an abolition poet.

[1] Manuscript 'To Mary,' dated Dec. 10, 1847, in Morgan Library.

The best notice of the volume was by James Russell Lowell, who recognized in Whittier a prophet and a bard of liberty.

'If we should attempt to depict the peculiar characteristic of Whittier,' he said, 'we should say that of all poets he the most truly deserved the name orator.... He is the Quaker Peter Hermit and crusade preaching is his natural vocation. ... His oratory is that of a prophet, rebuking, denouncing, forewarning, seeing the evil day afar off. If ever a man deserved the title of poet (maker), John Greenleaf Whittier does.' [1]

The year after the appearance of the collected poems, Fields published Whittier's 'Songs of Labor and other Poems.' Popular as these once were and still are, they are of importance chiefly in an historical sense, representing the first attempt to celebrate the workingman in our literature and to bring home to him the poetry and dignity of physical toil. The charge may be brought against Whittier that he sought to narcotize the laborers in their slavish condition, and to prevent them from advancing themselves materially; that he put a weapon in the hands of employers by which to hold laborers to their menial task, and that he has proved an ally to exploiters in withholding ample payment for labor. Whittier, in his 'Dedication,' said that he wanted to make the toiler gain 'a manlier spirit of content.' But did he forget that he wrote in the essay 'The Factory Girls' [2] in his book 'The Stranger in Lowell': 'There have been a good many foolish essays written upon the beauty and dignity of labor'?

He did not write the poems for thinking men, he said in later life. He painted homely and yet enchanting pictures of laborers at the various occupations of fisherman and lumberman, of drover and shipbuilder. The only two forms of labor with which he had personal familiarity were shoemaking and

[1] The uncollected Lowell review was in the *National Anti-Slavery Standard* for Dec. 21, 1848.

[2] He did not preserve this essay in his collected works.

farming. The husking poem, with its corn song, is the best of the group; its picture of country life has fascinated the American people. Whittier was a forerunner of Whitman in making humble occupations the theme of song.

Whittier's attitude towards the labor question was undoubtedly naïve. He sought merely by appealing to the generosity of the employers to obtain a few more crumbs for the laborer; he never tried to solve the economic question in a more scientific way. He outlined his position in a letter in which he hoped to refute the Alabama Senator Jeremiah Clemens's charge that the New-Englanders treated their factory workers worse than the Southern planters did their slaves. Harriet Farley, who had worked in a Lowell mill, and was editing the famous magazine 'Lowell's Offering,' asked Whittier to write to her about the conditions of the factory workers at Amesbury; and in a pamphlet in reply to the Alabama Senator she published the poet's reply. In it Whittier spoke of the 'paternal care' extended to the 'help' by one of the employers. He also stated that the owners employed no one under fourteen years of age, and that they closed their mills at night. As a matter of fact, the girls worked in summer fourteen hours a day, from sunrise to sunset, and at the end of the week like the factory girls of Lowell had two dollars wages clear after the cost of board and lodging was deducted. Whittier did not comment on this and apparently saw nothing wrong in the treatment of the operatives. The workers were, however, not satisfied, for not very long afterwards they went on a strike, because an agent named Derby had refused them the long-exercised prerogative of leaving their work for a few minutes in the morning to get luncheon. The operatives lost the strike, and foreigners replaced them. It is said, however, that Whittier was in sympathy with the strikers; that he had even used the local paper, 'The Villager,' in behalf of a ten-hour bill — a bill which did not become a law till many years later.

Critics, like Parrington, while admitting that Whittier anticipated Whitman in singing about labor, have frowned upon his half-hearted attitude on the wrongs of the working-man.

In his 'Songs of Labor' Whittier developed the tendency that became almost an obsession, of bringing in the Lord's name, no matter how irrelevant to theology the topic under consideration might be. If we did not know the poet was sincere, we might charge him with cant. He spoiled his poems, as St. Augustine did his autobiography, by the continual addresses to God. He ruined a beautiful nature poem, 'The Lakeside,' by introducing doctrinal discourses, after putting his reader under a spell by a beautiful description of the mountains. He preached to him, on a text derived from the translation of the Indian name of the lake — Winnipiseogee ('Smile of the Great Spirit') — and, using a false and ludicrous analogy, showed him that this name was proof of the tender love of God, and of His benevolent and merciful will. The poet became lost in the Quaker exhorter; the optimistic believer kept peeping out from beneath the broad-brim. Whittier never learned that a poet limits his universality by charging his blunderbuss with doctrinal bullets.

'The Chapel of the Hermits,' the poet's next collection of poems, published three years later, made up mainly of poems originally contributed to the 'National Era,' was, as a whole, superior to the preceding volume. The opening poem, from the title of which the volume derived its name, is a long sermon in the form of a narrative, based on an account by Bernardin de Saint-Pierre of a visit to the Chapel of the Hermits in company with Jean Jacques Rousseau. Whittier gives us two excellent portraits of these writers. The volume was miscellaneous in character; it had a tender poem inspired by an old sweetheart, 'Benedicite,' an historical poem on the capture of Derne by General Eaton in the Tripoli War, a poem to his old schoolmaster Joshua Coffin, and another to Wordsworth. It also included one of his most intellectual poetic compositions, 'Questions of Life,' in which he showed the conflict in his mind as he unfolded various theories on the nature of life. Anticipating the theory of evolution, as Whitman did about the same time, he wondered if man were not part of the same scheme as the animal kingdom, and whether he was really not related to it. He finally turns back to the witness of God in his own heart, but he does not succeed in allaying the doubts he raises in the reader's mind on religious dogma.

'The Panorama and Other Poems,' his next book of poetry, was perhaps the most significant volume he had published thus far, for it contained the popular pieces 'The Barefoot Boy' and 'Maud Muller,' both of which had had prior publication.[1] These poems had been copied far and wide and had immediately 'caught on.' The former, by its sentimental ecstatic reveries on the rural scenes of childhood, and the latter, by the universal sentiments born out of retrospective glances to fruitless love affairs, stirred all classes anew. Many who disapproved of him as an abolitionist were ready to forgive him. The scholarly and pedantic Professor of Greek at Harvard, Charles C. Felton, who signed a letter approving Webster's Seventh of March speech, wrote to Whittier that the poem on the barefoot boy made him forget his Greek and vividly recall his boyhood days.

The poems in the book — most of which had been published in the 'National Era' — showed all his strength and weaknesses. In it were mingled poems vastly different in treatment and theme — ballads, lyrics, sermons, satires, elegies, religious tracts, nature poems, and personal revelations. He spoiled good ballads by astoundingly commonplace moralizing, and he wove the texture of dull stories out of the woof and warp of theology. Giving expression freely to his religious yearnings, he more chivalrously than ever rushed to the defense of the Lord, to show that He was always good and just. Lacking the courage of a Tennyson

[1] 'Maud Muller' appeared in the *National Era*, Dec., 1854. 'The Barefoot Boy' was in the *Little Pilgrim*, Jan., 1858, edited in Philadelphia by Grace Greenwood.

who admitted that life preyed on life, he vehemently insisted upon proving God's goodness by absurd illustrations, as in the ballad 'The Ranger.' Because the girl in that poem saw the realization of her never-failing hope in the return of her absent lover, long given up as dead, Whittier established it as a universal law that hope and prayer are always efficacious; and he offered the barren comfort that life is sweeter and love is dearer for trial and delay. He continued his moral axe-grinding when he told us of the doubting preacher 'Tauler,' whose life was changed by a stranger's assurance that men are in God's hands and that they cannot lose His presence. He converted a beautiful poem like 'Summer by the Lake-side' with its fine touches of nature, into an obtrusive sermon by informing us that God wills no evil to his creatures and that sooner or later He makes recompense to all. The popularity of poems like these made the more intellectual critics distrust the public judgment about Whittier. One must surrender the heritages of one's intellect to yield to the seductiveness of literature of this kind.

Fortunately some poems in the volume were beautiful in their simplicity, and others had a universal yet rational appeal. There is the Burns poem, with its picture of the effect of the Scotch bard upon Whittier's boyhood dreams; there is the touching elegy on that noble politician Robert Rantoul, Jr., who had recently died while serving in Congress; and there are the tributes to Samuel G. Howe and Charles Sumner. There is 'Mary Garvin,' the ballad of a Quaker girl who, after being kidnapped by the Indians, married a Catholic, and who on returning to her Quaker home taught her grandparents a lesson of tolerance — 'Creed and rite perchance may differ, yet our faith and hope be one.' One of the best poems in the book, not so well known, is 'The Voices,' wherein Whittier recorded his struggle with the tempter, who urged him to give up his ideals.

The most popular piece in the volume, 'Maud Muller,' a poem that has been parodied more than any other poem in

American literature with the possible exception of 'The Raven,' deserves separate consideration. The public did not know its significance in the poet's life, since he concealed the true story of his rejection by Mary Emerson Smith on account of his poverty. In the poem he not only voiced a universal regret for the barrenness of the past, but he declaimed against those who set wealth and social position above love. In the misfortune of Maud Muller whom the judge refused to marry because she was a poor farm girl, he symbolized his own tragedy. Mary Emerson Smith had rejected him because of his poverty and social inferiority, and had married a judge. Whittier looked back regretfully with the feeling that he might have been happier in life had Mary, unspoiled by notions of wealth and position, married him, hence he bewailed the foibles of society in worshipping wealth and position.

The close of the year brought its cares — illness of his mother and poverty so extreme that he accepted money from his old friend Joseph Sturge in order not to be compelled to mortgage his home. At this time Whittier had no source of livelihood except his meager book royalties and his small salary as contributing editor of the 'National Era.' As the year closed, his mother died, the shock leaving him stunned. 'The world looks far less than it did when she was with us. Half the motive force of life is lost,' he wrote.

In 1857 he published a collected edition of his poems in two volumes. It is chiefly the heroic Whittier, now forgotten, who speaks to us in this edition of his poems. Had he died at the time it appeared, he would have stood as high as ever as an heroic character and poet. It is on the basis of this 1857 collection that his reputation will most likely endure — though it does not contain 'Snow-Bound,' or 'Barbara Frietchie,' or 'In School Days,' or 'The Eternal Goodness,' or others of his later well-known and artistic poems. I do not mean to imply that these later poems are not often better, and at times of more universal interest, than those he

published before his fiftieth year; I simply mean to say that
the work of Whittier as the poet of freedom and the singer
of the oppressed really ended with his fiftieth year.

His life now underwent a change, for he turned more and
more to literature. At a dinner given by the publisher of the
new magazine, the 'Atlantic Monthly,' he again met purely
literary men like Longfellow, Lowell, Holmes, and Emerson,
instead of out-and-out abolitionists. He had avoided the
company of littérateurs since the old days in Hartford and
Boston, when he mingled in literary circles gathered around
Mrs. Sigourney and Mrs. Hale. We have seen that after he
had entered upon his career as an abolitionist, he associated
exclusively with orators, politicians, propagandists, editors,
philanthropists, reformers, and even cranks, for he was
absorbed in the same topics that occupied them. Though
some of the abolitionists, such as John Pierpont, William
Burleigh, Maria Chapman, and Garrison himself, wrote
poetry, Whittier was drawn to them by devotion to a common cause. He now again became interested in the writers
of the day who were pursuing literary careers divested from
propagandic purposes.

The 'Atlantic Monthly' and the 'Independent' became
the chief vehicles for his poetry. The poems he now contributed to these periodicals made his fame undergo one of
the strangest metamorphoses in the history of poetic reputations. His renown as an antislavery poet began gradually to decline, to yield to that of balladist and singer of
the legends of Colonial days, and of portrayer of rural life.
He became the mouthpiece of the common people, giving
them the sentiment they sought and preaching the moral
in which they delighted. He acted in the double rôle of
a singer of hymns to console the aged, and a composer of
songs to please the children. He voiced also the ideals of the
middle class, and he was no longer in the vanguard of the
stalwart radical minority.

We must reassign to Whittier a just and proper place in

American literature. He is held in popular esteem more for his later innocuous and even puerile work than for the poems that represent him at his best — the bold, courageous, independent, and fiery prophecies of his middle life. If the English public had completely overlooked Wordsworth's 'Lyrical Ballads' and Swinburne's 'Songs Before Sunrise' and had attached more significance to their less vital and less revolutionary work of later years, it would have treated their reputations as unjustly as we treat Whittier's. Our usual consideration of Whittier as the poet of 'In School Days' and 'The Barefoot Boy' makes us forget he was the perpetrator of laudably 'seditious' and delightfully 'blasphemous' poetry. To quote the words of his biographer F. H. Underwood, 'The poetry of the anti-slavery movement in the United States exceeds in bulk, as it does in inspiration power and beauty, all the poems written on subjects of great national importance in the latter centuries.' [1] And of this abolition poetry Whittier's was the best and has alone survived.

[1] The quotation is from Underwood, pp. 204–205. A whole page and a half embodying this quotation is lifted, with one or two minor changes, without quotation marks, in W. J. Linton's *Whittier*, 1893, pp. 123–124. Linton was then past eighty years of age. The entire passage sounds very much as if Whittier had written it himself and given it to Underwood.

CHAPTER XVII

THE NEGLECTED PROSE WORKS

WHITTIER penned most of his prose works with the purpose of furthering the cause of freedom. If he wrote critical essays about literary men, his prime object was not to appraise their æsthetic gifts or to expatiate on their style; he sought texts from which to preach against oppression.

Having been an editor and editorial contributor for many years, he wrote more prose than poetry during the course of his life. He once said that his collected prose would occupy at least twelve octavo volumes. He assembled more articles from the 'National Era' than from any other periodical for which he wrote. He included sketches here and there from the 'New England Magazine,' the 'Pennsylvania Freeman,' the 'Middlesex Standard,' the 'Democratic Review,' and some other periodicals. He reprinted practically none of his prose writings in the early newspapers with which he was connected.

Whittier published his first book, 'The Stranger in Lowell,' which had appeared serially in the 'Middlesex Standard,' anonymously in 1845.[1] He never reissued the work as a whole, but he retained most of the essays in his collected prose works. It is unfortunate that he destroyed the identity of this unique and charming volume, for it contained some of his most beautiful prose and embodied his most courageous sentiments. In these sketches, composed as a diversion from editorial writing, he displayed much variety, combining the whimsicality of Charles Lamb and the force of Burke, two of his favorite writers. The intricate personality

---

[1] *The Stranger in Lowell* had eighteen essays, four of which Whittier never reprinted. In one of these latter he showed a sympathetic attitude towards mesmerism.

of the quiet home-loving Quaker and militant reformer is always present, enlivening the pellucid and unaffected style.

In his sketch 'Yankee Gypsies' he dwells with loving care upon the foibles of vagabond fakirs and peddlers. He evokes all the vagabond types he encountered in his boyhood days. The tone of the essay is distinctly autobiographical.

Among the masterpieces in the volume were 'The Training' and 'The Scottish Reformers,' containing his tributes to Milton and to radicals, respectively. These essays are good examples of his tendency to introduce irrelevant discourses on liberty into books where logically they are anachronisms.

Whittier's second book in prose, 'Supernaturalism in New England,' published in 1847, was a reprint chiefly from the 'Democratic Review.' In it he betrayed his old interest in the New England superstitions — an interest he could not suppress in spite of his antislavery activities. He never reprinted this brochure, although he preserved some of its essays in his collected prose works. It contained a verse dedication to his sister, in which, fearing criticism from his fellow-workers for these trifling scholarly studies in times of great stress, he apologized — poor conscientious soul — for seeking recreation from his labors in the cause. He knew, he said, that she would overlook his lapse from duty because she was aware how his life had been

> 'A weary work of tongue or pen,
> A long, harsh strife with strong-willed men.'

One of the chief external interests attached to this book is an uncollected review of it in the 'Literary World,' by Nathaniel Hawthorne, an authority on the subject of the volume. No one was more competent to pass judgment on this aspect of Whittier's work than he, though he did not sympathize with him in his main work as an abolitionist. 'Mr. Whittier's name,' he wrote, 'has been little other than an accident of exertions directed to practical and unselfish purposes, — a wayside flower, which he has hardly spared the time to gather.... We doubt not he will return to the battle of his life with so much the more vigor, for this brief relaxation.'[1]

Hawthorne did not agree with Whittier that there really was a supernaturalism in New England. He also thought that her superstitions had a more sordid, grimy, and material aspect than they bore in the mother country from which they were transplanted. He ventured to add that Whittier made his style sparkle too much, that he talked too learnedly and quoted too frequently.

'We conclude with the frank admission,' he said, 'that we like the book, and look upon it as no unworthy contribution from a poet to that species of literature which only a poet should meddle with. We hope to see more of him, in this, or some other congenial sphere. There are many legends still to be gathered, especially along the seaboard of New England, — and those, too, we think, original and more susceptible of poetic illustration, than these rural superstitions.'

Shortly afterward Whittier was able to requite the novelist by getting one of his tales published in the 'National Era.'

Whittier had a very high estimate of Hawthorne's New England tales as we know from a letter to their common publisher a dozen years later. 'The weird and subtle beauty of his legendary tales,' he wrote, 'early awakened my admiration, and rebuked and shamed my own poor efforts in a similar direction. We all know how the promise of that authorship has since blossomed and borne marvellous fruit — how he has peopled for us the realms of fancy — with what life he has clothed the grim skeleton of old Puritanism — with what richness of coloring he has painted for us the immortal frescoes of his story of Rome and Italy!'[2]

Whittier published his most ambitious book in prose, a

[1] Hawthorne's review of *Supernaturalism in New England* appeared in the *Literary World*, April 17, 1847, Vol. I, p. 247.

[2] Manuscript letter of Whittier dated 9th 7th mo., 1860, in possession of Carroll A. Wilson, Esq., of New York.

work of fiction, 'Margaret Smith's Journal,' in 1849.[1] Except for 'Uncle Tom's Cabin' it was the most important book that appeared serially in the 'National Era.' At the time he was working on it, he was engaged in political editorial-writing in behalf of the Free Soil Party. In this book he displayed unusual powers of concentration on an historical theme, and facility in making a fictitious narrative appear authentic. Based on contemporary documents and bristling with names of real people and events, it purports to be the diary of an English girl visiting New England in 1678 and 1679. The book, not inferior in its beauty and simplicity of style or in interest to some of Hawthorne's stories, is one of the best accounts of Colonial life, and captures the spirit of the times with amazing fidelity. Whittier also speaks constantly through Margaret herself, and draws his own portrait, finding in her, though she was no Quaker, a kindred spirit who radiated tolerance and human sympathy. He even went out of his way to take a fling at an old Puritan clergyman for owning a slave — to such an extent did he imbue the work with his own personality.

It is difficult to determine which features of this book to praise most. We are carried away by beautiful pictures of New England scenery and farm lands, as well as by the tale of Goody Morse, the witch about whom Whittier had written in his youth. We meet the old characters throbbing with life; we see Endicott again fretting and we hear Eliot haranguing on his missionary ambitions among the Indians. We recognize in the vivid pictures of liberal and narrow clergymen forerunners of antislavery and proslavery ministers of Whittier's own day. We note the contrasted types, the broad-minded Mr. Richardson and the bigoted Mr. Norton, as we hear arguments against, and in behalf of, persecution, from their own mouths. We obtain an insight into the minds of the men who were in favor of punishing witches and Quakers.

[1] 'Margaret Smith's Journal' appeared in the *National Era* from June 1, 1848, to Nov. 9, 1848.

Whittier insinuates that the arguments used in favor of persecution in those days were akin to those used in suppressing freedom of expression in his own time. The journal is really a disguised tract on tolerance, and yet it never bores us with didactic discourses. Since the author carefully eradicated traces of original sources, he presents scenes in so startling a manner as to make us think he was an eye-witness. The character-portrayals are particularly excellent, as, for example, that of Margaret's brother, who unable to tolerate the narrowness and prejudices of the clergy rallies to the support of Peggy Brewster, the persecuted Quaker maiden, and who finally, foregoing his own clerical ambitions, braves popular opinion by marrying her.

Robert Pike, however, wins our hearts — Robert Pike, the noble youth who was jilted by his cousin Rebecca Rawson in favor of a wealthy baronet. Whittier understood Pike's feelings only too well, for had he also not been rejected by Mary Emerson Smith for a wealthier suitor? Whittier was attracted to the famous Puritan love-story about Rebecca Rawson because in some phases it resembled his own love tragedy. Robert Pike, a prototype of the poet, had loved his cousin since childhood, and studied and toiled to make himself acceptable to her as a husband. Rebecca hesitated between him and the new candidate for her affections, Sir Thomas Hale, who boasted that he was a nephew of the great Sir Matthew Hale. When Robert asked Rebecca's father for her hand, he replied that he preferred for her an alliance with a gentleman of estate. Rebecca, influenced by parental prompting, decided, though not without doubts and superstitious fears, to accept Sir Thomas. Robert did not attend the wedding, giving as an excuse that he had urgent business elsewhere, but he wrote Rebecca a letter, which troubled her and increased her foreboding mental quirks. She soon went with her husband to England. Her presentiments were realized, for her husband deserted her as soon as they arrived, and left her penniless. She learned at the same time that not only was he traveling under a spurious name as the nephew of the great Hale, but that he had a wife whom also he had deserted, and from whom he had never been divorced. To add to her misery, there was also a mistress in the offing. Rebecca fainted as she learned of her inextricable entanglement in the fabric of her husband's villainies. But she did not absolve herself from blame, attributing her suffering to a righteous judgment on her for her pride and vanity in discarding a worthy man. Rebecca's subsequent trials and her final drowning in an earthquake in Jamaica constitute one of the celebrated legends of New England. The poet found in the fate that befell a girl who married for position instead of for love the dream wish of his unconscious, for his own rejection by Mary Emerson Smith.

Margaret herself, being a noble person, suffered with Rebecca in her difficulties in deciding between Robert Pike and her spurious knight whom she did not cherish.

The book is a thing of beauty, a work of art. It is, above all, a plea for tolerance, the voice of all persecuted minorities, and is steeped in doctrines characteristic of the poet and his sect. Again and again, as he does in his poetry, he reiterates the moral that human beings ought not constitute themselves God's avengers. Repeatedly does he scourge the Puritans for their persecutions. He does not condemn them unreservedly, but depicts them as human beings with a proneness to err like all of us, prompted by a desire to act righteously. He decries their religious fanaticism and explains by natural causes events to which they gave a supernatural significance. Nor does he always condone the doings of the Quakers, though undoubtedly he sympathizes more with them.

Whittier errs, as usual, in taking for granted certain religious dogmas. He pertinaciously attributes the utmost importance to prayer in directing the course of nature and everlastingly puts God in the rôle of special caretaker of every human being.

Whittier next collected in 'Old Portraits and Modern

Sketches' ten biographical sketches. Three of his subjects were contemporaries — Nathaniel P. Rogers and William Leggett, fellow workers in the cause of antislavery, and his old poet friend Robert Dinsmore. The other sketches dealt with old poets, theologians, and Quaker martyrs.

In the sketches of his two abolitionist friends, he was able to draw on his own experiences, in detailing the difficulties they suffered in the early days of the movement. When both editors died, admirers collected their editorials in book form. Though Whittier had attacked both men in former days, Leggett in a poem and Rogers in the controversy he had with him, he now made amends by sympathetic notices of their writings. William Leggett and Nathaniel P. Rogers are undeservedly forgotten today in the glow of Garrison's fame, though one is the subject of a poem by Bryant and the other of an essay by Thoreau. Leggett had worked on the New York 'Evening Post' with Bryant, and, while not yet converted to abolitionism, had defended its adherents against New York editors, resented the riots led by mobs, and deplored the action against them of the Southern postmasters in destroying their literature. He finally devoted himself to the cause, sacrificing a brilliant political future for it. He died young, and Whittier commemorated his death in a poem as well as in the essay.

The obscurity of most of the persons dealt with in the book has been responsible for its neglect by the public. In the essay on Samuel Hopkins, an American theologian of the eighteenth century, Whittier riddles his theological views, but commends him for his abolitionism at that early date. He devotes essays to James Nayler and John Roberts, two now forgotten English Quakers of the seventeenth century who suffered imprisonment for their views. But alas, the general public was not interested in persecuted Quakers, and it has allowed the dust to gather on Whittier's apotheoses of those worthy men.

In his essay on Richard Baxter, the longest in the book,

Whittier enlivens a dull and tedious theme, by attacking the famous Puritan English divine for not being a champion of civil or religious liberty. In the essay on Bunyan he contributes something new to our conception of him, by showing him a champion for liberty, as one who translated into action the impulse to liberty that Penn, Milton, and Locke defended.

The two best of the 'Old Portraits' in the book are those of Andrew Marvell and Thomas Ellwood. Marvell, who was in many respects like Whittier — a bachelor of spotless integrity, a poet, a wit, a republican — was all the more endeared to him because he was the friend and admirer of Milton. Thomas Ellwood, also a friend of Milton, was a minor poet whose poem 'Davideis' Whittier read as a boy. Ellwood's celebrated autobiography afforded Whittier an opportunity for discoursing on autobiographical writing.

Whittier's final prose volume, called 'Literary Recreations and Miscellanies,' appearing in 1854, was made up of a heterogeneous mass of his writings. Recognizing that they bore no relation to one another, he apologized for selecting them on the ground that they were nearest at hand. The book consisted of thirty-five papers, of which fifteen were the sketches he cared to preserve out of his two earliest books in prose, 'The Stranger in Lowell' and 'Supernaturalism in New England.' Fortunately he preserved 'Yankee Gypsies,' 'The Scottish Reformers,' and 'The Training,' from the Lowell work.

The rest of the book is undoubtedly a strange medley — book-reviews of poems by Bayard Taylor and by Oliver Wendell Holmes, which led to permanent friendships with these poets; a review of 'Evangeline,' which contains a good defense of the Puritans; an account of various Utopian schemes; Indian tales and episodes in Colonial history; a splendid defense of Charles Sumner for his pacific views; a well-aimed and justly deserved attack upon Carlyle for his proslavery stand; a criticism of Macaulay's 'History of England' for unjust criticism of Quakers and lack of toleration towards Catholics.

One of the most unusual and original sketches in the volume is 'The Doctor's Match-making,' a story that is imbedded in a fragmentary work of fiction called 'My Summer with Dr. Singletary.' It is one of the most singular productions that the Quaker-Puritan ever wrote, for it is a tale in which the writer accords liberal treatment to the 'fallen woman.' Whittier himself plays a passive rôle, for he is the sole audience of Dr. Singletary, who narrates a tale of a love-match he once undertook and successfully carried out. A young lady of the doctor's acquaintance, who had discarded her sailor lover, had yielded to the seductive wiles of a more eligible suitor. He betrayed her and abandoned her before she gave birth to a child. The death of her baby then unfortunately followed; this, together with the whole train of tragic events, in which she was involved, had a softening effect upon her entire nature, making her kind and tender. By a strange turn of circumstances, she became the means of saving the life of her former sailor lover. As he was not forgetful of the wrong she had inflicted upon him by discarding him, and as he knew of her illegitimate child, he was not ready to reward her for saving his life by marrying her. It was at this stage that Dr. Singletary stepped in. He persuaded the sailor to forego conventional notions of morality and to brave public opinion and marry the girl. The marriage proved very happy, as marriages do in all of Whittier's tales, especially where the couples defy public opinion. In this tale Whittier praised those who refused to be bound by conventions; through the medium of the doctor he delivered a tirade against public opinion. Ibsen might have written this story. One feels, however, that the poet's revolt against puritanism here was in theory only, for he himself never defied public opinion in matters relating to sex. While, as he showed in a few poems which he wrote later, he was willing to condone unconventional conduct or misconduct by others, he was himself never ready to enter upon a course not sanctioned by society.

CHAPTER XVIII

THE MALE COQUET AND ELIZABETH LLOYD

IT WILL be recalled that Whittier terminated his love affair with Lucy Hooper in the summer of 1839 when he took a walk with her on the bank of the Merrimac River. He had made new acquaintances among women, who supplanted Lucy in his affections. When he had returned to live in Philadelphia in the early part of 1838, he had renewed his friendship with Elizabeth Lloyd.

Elizabeth at the time Whittier came to live in Philadelphia was about twenty-seven years old, four years younger than he. She was both beautiful and brilliant, and at the same time a Quakeress, an abolitionist, and a poet — all of which made her an ideal companion for him. Unfortunately we know very little of the details of their friendship during the poet's residence in the city. If he wrote her letters in his frequent absences from the city, they have never been found.

After Whittier relinquished his position on the 'Freeman,' he revisited Philadelphia in the following spring and called on Elizabeth Lloyd. Then for a year silence reigned between them.

In the summer of 1841 he began corresponding with her by asking her to copy for him, with her friend Elizabeth Nicholson's help, some of the poems that he had published in the city, which he wanted for the English edition of his poems. She sent the package of copied poems, but he neglected to take it out of the mails, thinking it was a bundle of newspapers. Not hearing from him, she wrote to him and sent him her 'Thoughts on Jerusalem.'[1] She flattered him by urging him to issue a collection of his poems, and thanked him for some verses from which she was going to paint scenes.

---

[1] Manuscript letter of Elizabeth Lloyd to Whittier, dated Jan. 28, 1842, in Essex Institute.

In replying to her he explained the delay and wrote, 'I long to be in Philadelphia mainly to see you all — but partly to escape these bitter blue northeasters.'[1] He forwarded the letter, perhaps tactlessly, through Harriet Maitland Winslow, of Portland, who was going to Philadelphia with her sister Mrs. Louisa M. Sewall, wife of Samuel E. Sewall.

The next summer Whittier wrote to Miss Lloyd that their common friend William J. Allinson, of Burlington, New Jersey, was staying with him, and he went on to compliment her: 'And *thy* letters and poetical sketches which I have, I estimate highly. They are unlike others — *unique* — the poetry of Quakerdom — graceful yet with a solemn beauty and reverence which reminds one of the Quaker gallery, with its fine selection from the Oriental richness of the Scriptures.' Praising the effusions of poetesses was his favorite method of fanning the affections of a girl he admired. Allinson left him after a short stay, bringing for Elizabeth a copy of verses that Whittier had written to a Western young 'lady of much intelligence' to whom he had presented 'Woolman's Journal.'

For some reason or other Whittier soon stopped writing. One day he received from her a letter from Dover, New Hampshire, in which she disguised her real purpose, which was to chide him for his neglect and to inform him that a gifted poetess — no other than she herself — was longing for his company. She did not say that she was in love with him, but she did plead with him pathetically to visit her at Dover. She wrote:[2]

'Spirit, silent, dumb and cold! What hath possessed thee? A fit of perverseness or a fit of sickness? despair or dyspepsia? Art thou suffering in a snowdrift becoming a positive petrification, the state to which, all things Northern naturally arrive? or by way of overcoming the "freeze up" tendency, hast

[1] All quotations in this chapter from Whittier's letters to Elizabeth Lloyd are from Denervaud: *Whittier's Unknown Romance.*

[2] Manuscript letter of Elizabeth Lloyd to Whittier, undated, in Essex Institute. It was a folded letter sealed with wax. It was therefore written before the year 184c when envelopes came into use.

thou taken to matrimony or my dearing? Or hath burning, unprofitable, restless, tormenting soul-wearing, heart soiling spirit of Politics eaten thee up? If this is so, I warn thee that E. L. for one, will not (bear in mind thee promised her a life estate in thy kind regard) be crowded out of thy remembrance by any such ignoble foe.'

After summoning him in a jesting manner to answer charges of various high crimes, such as neglect, indifference and so forth, she became pathetically earnest and begged him to visit her:

'Do come, Greenleaf! I am almost forgetting how thee looks and seems. And we will have many a nice long talk in our parlor about the past, and present, and to come. I sometime ask myself, if I ever did really see thee face to face, if my intercourse with thee was not altogether imagining a dream, if I am not indebted to my imagination alone for thy friendship.'

What the answer to this letter was we do not know, but there was then no more correspondence.

They rarely met, if ever, for the next fifteen years, and they interchanged only two or three letters. Elizabeth married in the mean while, and in a short time became a widow. In 1858 the old romance between her and the poet was revived on a more intense note. Before adverting to it, let us briefly give an account of what we know of his friendships with other women during the intervening years.

Whittier was in the prime of life during this period, which extends from his thirty-fifth to his fiftieth year. His interest in women had not subsided completely, phlegmatic as he had grown, for during these years he began some of his closest friendships with various women. When he was in Lowell during the latter part of 1844, he made several woman friends, the most important of whom was Lucy Larcom, the poet. She soon went West, but returned in later years to the East, and became one of his protégées. Other woman writers with whom he became acquainted in these years were contributors to the 'National Era' — Grace Greenwood (Mrs. Sarah Lippincott) and the Cary sisters, Alice and Phœbe. Both poet sisters called upon him at Amesbury in 1850 in compliance with an indirect invitation that he sent through Griswold. His friendship with them deepened in later years, after his second affair with Miss Lloyd was over. Grace Greenwood also became a lifelong friend. In 1854, a year after her marriage, she wrote to him, 'Your influence has been the strongest which has wrought for good both on my literary and my private life.' [1] We see that Whittier's interest in women did not die out.

When Whittier was verging on the age of forty, he became friendly with a girl named Ida Russell, a protégée of Mrs. Sarah Helen Whitman, the poet, and one of her closest friends. As she was interested in poetry, Mrs. Whitman discussed Poe with her before she herself met the author of 'The Raven,' to engage in the now celebrated love-affair. Miss Russell once at an antislavery convention pointed Whittier out — no doubt proudly — to George W. Curtis, then a young man, a friend of hers and an admirer of Mrs. Whitman. Curtis heard that during this period — the summer of 1846 — Miss Russell and Whittier were engaged. In fact, they really were engaged at some time or other. At least, Mrs. Whitman said shortly after she met Whittier in 1860 that the poet had once been engaged to her dear friend Miss Russell. Mrs. Whitman has also given us the reason why the two did not marry. 'She was a beautiful splendid creature,' she wrote, 'but lymphatic and impeded by worldly cares and solicitudes and ambitions. His Quaker simplicity and her bumptious tastes did not readily harmonize and so they grew to be strangers.'

Here we have the keynote to the cause of several misadventures that Whittier had in love, including that with Elizabeth Lloyd. Owing to the perversity of fate, he was always being attracted towards types of women different from him in

[1] Manuscript of Grace Greenwood's letter dated Sept. 24, 1854, in Essex Institute.

most characteristics. He, the shy, idealistic, and unpractical dreamer was always being jolted as he awoke to the realization that his sweethearts were invariably of a worldly and practical nature. He was himself compelled to break off several affairs, but if he had not done so, there is no doubt the women would have terminated the friendships. Whether Ida Russell ever inspired him to write poetry we do not know.

In the late forties and in the fifties of the century, his affections were centered on one or more women named Mary. Women called Mary figure in Whittier's life very frequently. As in the cases of Byron and Poe, the very name fascinated him. We have seen that the chief love of his youth was Mary Emerson Smith, and that a girl named Mary, in Hartford, also attracted him. He wrote several album poems to girls called Mary, among them Mary Pillsbury of West Newbury, and Mary, sister of Anna Bagley, to whose album he contributed in 1847 the lines I quoted in a previous chapter.

Before he resumed his relations with Elizabeth Lloyd, he was on very close terms of friendship with a girl named Mary E. Carter, an intimate friend of his sister.

To this girl Whittier wrote in an album:[1]

> 'Long have I sought and vainly have I yearned
>   To meet some spirit that could answer mine;
> Then chide me not that I so soon have learned
>   To talk with thine.
>
> 'Oh, thou wilt cherish what some hearts would spurn;
>   So gentle and so full of soul thou art,
> And shrine my feelings in that holy urn
>   Thine own true heart.'

The friendship, as usual with Whittier and the women he flattered, lingered. Mary Carter at last thought it best to hint to him by a letter in how high a regard she held him.

---

[1] Album poem to Mary, 1849, in Sparhawk, pp. 73–74. Miss Sparhawk gives only the initials of her name. The manuscript of the poem is in the Amesbury house and it is addressed to Mary E. Carter. Miss Caroline Carter of Boston, a niece of Mary, has given me permission to use her aunt's name.

Pretending (also as usual) not to understand her, he wrote to her in November, 1857:

'I cannot but feel that thou hast greatly over-rated the benefits derived from my society and friendship. In fact, I feel very much as a debtor in these hard times might be supposed to feel if his creditor should take occasion to thank him for his indebtedness. The obligation is on my side rather than on thine. To me and mine thou hast been an ever kind and sympathetic friend over whom we never met without pleasure or parted without regret. For myself, as for them, *my heart* thanks thee. Thou hast cheered us and helped us in many ways by example as well as words. We have read, thought, hoped, feared, enjoyed, and suffered together and ties of affection and sympathy so woven from the very tissues of our lives are not easily severed. We miss thee greatly in our little circle; we shall often speak of thee in the dark winter days and long to see thy familiar face in the light of our evening fires.' [1]

He was very diplomatic, and Mary probably understood. They kept up their friendship for the rest of their lives, and Whittier bequeathed her five hundred dollars in his will.[2]

In the early part of 1857 — the year he politely rejected the advances of Mary Carter — he published a poem called 'The First Flowers,' which we see from internal evidence was also written to a girl called Mary. This poem conceals a romance. The identity of this lady has hitherto been unrevealed.[3] I have been enabled to suggest a clue to the identity of the heroine through the circumstance of noting, in one of the volumes of 'Book Prices Current,' the sale at auction of an unpublished letter written by Whittier in the spring of

[1] Letter to Mary, 1849, in Sparhawk, pp. 71-72.

[2] There is an unidentified Mary, to whom Whittier wrote 'To Mary,' *Century Magazine*, May, 1902. The date of the poem is unknown.

[3] L. G. Swett believed the poem referred to Mary Emerson Smith. This is not the case, for it refers to a woman with whom he had been taking walks recently on the banks of the Merrimac. At this time Mary Smith was married and living in the South.

1857 to Mary L. Shepherd, thanking her for presenting him with some flowers.¹ I have not seen the letter, which contains some verses, but unless we assume that Mary Carter also sent him flowers in the spring of 1857, and that he also wrote a poem to her, thanking her for them, we must conclude from the existence of this letter that he addressed the poem 'The First Flowers' to Mary L. Shepherd.²

We know nothing about her except what the poem tells us. It is significant that he does not disclose her name, for it was his custom to wrap himself in obscurity when he was really interested in a woman. In his poems he often took a sly pleasure in puzzling his readers. He dwelt on the possibility that the idle verses in which he blended Mary and her gift of flowers might leave some trace by the Merrimac. The 'savants' of future times would be bewildered, trying to unravel the secret of these 'vagrant tracks.'

> 'And maidens in the far-off twilights,
> Singing my words to breeze and stream,
> Shall wonder if the old time Mary
> Were real, or the rhymer's dream!'

Whittier was reserved and secretive, never wanting to reveal to the world his personal relations with women. Moreover, as he was proud, he was in fear that the public might be amused by an affront to his dignity. 'The First Flowers' is an exquisite love poem, though lacking in deep passion; the affair recorded was apparently not a stormy one. Tempestuousness was to be reserved for his love affair with Elizabeth Lloyd, which was resumed shortly after the poem 'The First Flowers' was written.

During the last fifteen years Elizabeth Lloyd had acquired a poetic reputation, though she was less gifted as a

---

¹ The letter to Mary L. Shepherd about the gift of flowers is dated April, 1857, with a poem in sixteen lines, and was sold April 12, 1917, at the auction of Scott & O'Shaughnessy, Inc. *American Book-Prices Current*, 1917, p. 1074.

² For this reason I believe the possibility that Mary E. Carter may be the heroine of the poem should be given strong consideration.

poet than Lucy Hooper. Her most-copied poem, 'Milton's Prayer of Patience,' was published anonymously by Allinson, editor of the 'Friend's Review,' in January, 1848. It was frequently reprinted in periodicals, with the title 'Milton on his Loss of Sight.'

She was advancing in years. She heard from Whittier only indirectly through their common friend W. J. Allinson. When her father died, Whittier wrote her a letter of condolence.

In 1853 Elizabeth was married to Robert Howell, and since he was not a Quaker, she was read out of meeting. She was, however, soon reinstated. She asked Whittier to visit them, but he was apparently not very anxious to do so. He answered that he would like to meet her husband, who, he was glad to know, was interested in the freedom cause in Kansas, but he doubted if he could go to Philadelphia. In his letter he discussed literary matters, praised Lowell's lectures on poetry, mentioned a visit from Emerson, and expressed the hope that she would write more poetry like her 'Philadelphia Quakeress.'

In 1856 Elizabeth's husband died. Her misfortune sent her into mourning longer than the customary period. Whittier learned of her sad state of mind from her sister, Mrs. Hannah Lloyd Neall, of San Francisco, with whom he was corresponding. In answer to a letter of his asking about Elizabeth she wrote January 4, 1858, no doubt seeking to awaken his compassion: [1]

'Ah! Greenleaf, she is changed. Sorrow has wrecked her beauty, they tell me. But a friend writes that "The influence of grief had only made the character softer."... Does it seem vain in me to praise this loved one? *I* only know her through others now for her eyes have been so blind with weeping that for two years I have only had one letter from her.... I wish thee could go to Philadelphia.'

During the course of the year Whittier was in Philadelphia

---

[1] Manuscript letter of Hannah Lloyd Neall to Whittier, dated Jan. 4, 1858, in Essex Institute.

visiting Elizabeth. Here they saw each other daily; they went out calling on friends. They became more attached to each other, and he fell, or thought he fell, in love with her. They found pretexts for fondling each other's hair and brows with the object of curing each other's headaches, as they both believed in faith healing. She succeeded in curing his headaches (naturally), but he did not cure hers, because, as he suggested, her faith was not as strong as his. He used to return ecstatic to his lodgings at 528 Spruce Street, three blocks from where she lived. In one of these blissful moments he wrote to her for her 'counterfeit presentment' — her picture. He assured her that it was worth more to him 'than a whole gallery of Old World Madonnas and saints.' He looked with sadness upon the prospect of returning to Amesbury. 'Ah me! these days glide on, and I shall soon have to set my face towards the sunrise. I shall carry with me many regrets, but many sweet and precious memories also.' He went back home, but longed to see her again.

He revisited her in the spring of 1859, and on this occasion he proposed marriage to her. But, to his surprise and dismay, she told him that she wanted only his friendship, implying that no one could replace her husband; she was, however, willing to correspond with him, and Whittier was temporarily satisfied. He thought his suit would progress favorably, on the theory that when a woman wants to correspond with a man who has proposed to her, she only wants to take time to consider the proposal. He, therefore, meekly, somewhat humiliated, accepted the situation. True, the marriage, if it came, would come late — he was past fifty and she forty-two. When he returned home, he let her know how much he had been thinking of her, and he sent his sister's love, adding 'of mine, thee needs no assurance.' The very paper she had folded with her hand would be dearer to him for her sake, he said.

In a letter dated May 18, 1859, he wrote:

'Elizabeth, I have been happy — far more so than I ever

expected in this life. The sweet memory of the past few weeks make me rich forever. What Providence has in store for the future I know not, — I dare not hope scarcely, — but the past is mine — may I not say ours — sacred and beautiful, a joy forever. Asking nothing of thee, and with tenderest regard for thy grief and memories, I have given thee what was thine by right — the love of an honest heart — not as a restraint or burden upon thee, imposing no obligation and calling for no solicitude on thy part as respects myself. Nobody is a loser by loving or being beloved.'

Three days later, on his journey homeward, he wrote to their friend Allinson, but with his usual reticence said nothing of the proposal.[1]

Elizabeth, after declining the poet's invitation to come to Amesbury, had gone to Elmira, New York, for the summer. Whittier, having a premonition that she was not well, wrote of his fears. At the same time he sent her a portrait of himself. Learning that his foreboding was correct, he regretted that he was not present to take her hand in her illness. He said, 'I can understand thy feeling for I have known sorrow and trial, and loss, and I have a temperament very much like thy own, keenly sensitive and alive in every move.'

He was at the time in Newport, Rhode Island, where he met Elizabeth Nicholson and learned from her that she and Elizabeth had quarreled and were no longer friends. Trying to effect a reconciliation between them, he incurred Elizabeth Lloyd's displeasure for his meddling. To add to the complicated situation, she fell out of his good graces, because, prompted by some unpleasant personal experiences she had had with a number of Friends, she wrote in critical vein about the entire sect.

Even though he was courting her and despite her illness, Whittier would not let a charge against his own people pass unchallenged. In his letter dated June 24, 1859, after he returned home, he wrote:

[1] A copy of the letter to Mr. Allinson was sent to me by his late daughter-in-law.

'What does thee mean by talking as thee does about Friends? Does thee really think there are no good and worthy and interesting and refined people in the Quaker fold? Thee has surely too much good sense and conscience, and too delicate a sense of justice to be swayed by prejudice. Why, dear E., thou art a Quaker, and those who love thee best have learned to love thee as such. Thee owes too much to thy Quaker training and culture, to disown and deny us at this late day. I, as thee knows, am no sectarian, but I am a Quaker, nevertheless, and I regard the philosophy underlying Quakerism as the truest and purest the world has ever known. I care little for some of our peculiarities: but I love the principles of our Society, and I know that it, with all its faults and follies, is, at the moment in the very van of Christendom: that among its members, at this very hour, are the best specimens of Christians to be found in the wide world. My reason, my conscience, my taste, my love of the beautiful and the harmonious, combine to make me love the society. I cannot understand thy feeling: I am only very sorry for it.'

In extenuation of his blunder in trying to patch up an irreparable disagreement, he wrote apologetically a few days later: 'It is a feeling — weakness perhaps — of mine that I must be on good terms personally with everybody, good or bad, pleasant or indifferent, and I want those I love to have the good will of every one too. It comes of my intense longing for harmony, and a strong need of approbation, which extends to my friends, who are a part of myself.'

Nevertheless, he wrote that though he wanted to see her before the summer was over, he could not go to Elmira on account of his ill health. He was anxious, however, to know whether she would be in Philadelphia in the fall.

Next month (July), while she was still at Elmira, matters reached a crisis. As she would not withdraw her charges against the Quakers, he burst out, grandly even if unchivalrously: 'I see we cannot think alike about Friends. I am sorry, but it cannot be helped. Heart and soul, I am a Quaker and, as respects forms, rituals, priests, and churches, an iconoclast, unsparing as Milton or John Knox. But I am not going to discuss the endless subject. I shall not make a red republican of thee, nor will thee convert me to a belief in Bishops, reverend fathers, and apostolic succession. I don't see any saving virtue in candles, surplices, altars, and prayer books.'

At this time he was concerned about his brother's affairs and his sister Elizabeth's depression, while he suffered himself from severe headaches. Since Elizabeth Lloyd had complained of the food at Elmira, Whittier in his next letter refused to sympathize with her, but said, flippantly and petulantly, that *he* could eat anything, even live on the black broth of Sparta, if necessary.

From now on his letters were cold and trivial. Elizabeth was irritated, wounded in her pride, but she overlooked the injury to her vanity and complained at the change of tone in his letters. She saw that her Episcopalian leanings had sent him scurrying to shelter. He now resolutely stated the situation between them, clearly and unequivocally, thus virtually rejecting her. Using her own weapons as part of his offensive, he maintained that, after all, she was originally right when she said that he could not really be to her what her husband had been. He even commended her more than ever for the great love she bore for the late Mr. Howell. He apologized for his conduct, pleading that illness and vacillation interfered with his making a woman happy. But he mentally noted that his friendship with Elizabeth was a repetition of the old story with Evelina Bray, Lucy Hooper, and the others; he was again a male coquet, though against his own will. It seemed that fate was more spiteful to him now; Elizabeth who was a Friend, was on the point of giving up her Quaker beliefs, at a time when he most wanted her to retain them. Besides, he was over fifty years old now, and it was apparent that if he did not marry her, he was doomed to be single. So from his home in Amesbury on August 3, 1859, the poet penned a long letter to Elizabeth — one of the most characteristic he ever wrote:

'If there has been any change in the letters, I am sure there is no change in the feeling which dictated them, so far as *thou* art concerned. But I ought to confess to thee that the old feeling of self-distrust, and painful consciousness of all I would be, and of all I am not, and of my inability to make those I love happy, come back to me, the stronger, perhaps, that for a time it was held in abeyance. I have grown old in a round of duties and responsibilities which still govern me and urge me: my notions of life and daily habits are old-fashioned and homely: I could not for any length of time endure the restraints of fashion and society: art, refinement, and cultivated taste please me as something apart from myself. Constantly baffled by illness and weakness, and every way reminded of my frailty and limitation, I can scarcely hope anything, but live in the present: enduring what I must and enjoying what I can, thankful, I trust, for the many blessings which our Father has vouchsafed, and comforting myself with the faith that my trials and crosses are blessings also, in another form. But I cannot, dear E., be blind to the fact that thee lives in a different sphere — that thy sense of the fitting and beautiful demand accessories and surroundings very different from those that have become familiar and habitual to me. I am sure thy fine artist-nature would pine and die under the hard and uncongenial influences which make me what I am, and from which I cannot escape without feeling that I have abandoned the post of duty, without losing my self-respect, and forfeiting all right to be loved in return by those I love. These considerations, and the discouraging influence of illness, may have affected the tone and spirit of my letters.

'But above all — and I know thou wilt pardon me if I touch, with all tenderness, upon a subject which should be sacred — I feel that thy instincts were right as respects that very happy and beautiful episode in thy life — that sweet, calm sufficiency and fullness of love graciously offered thee for a season, which, brief as it was, had the length of years in its completeness, and which still blesses thee with the richest legacies of memory, and with hopes that outreach time and take hold upon eternity. Knowing myself, I have never felt that I could ever have been to thee what *he* was, whom the Great Goodness gave thee. And, if, in the great happiness of meeting thee I seemed at any time to forget this, I am sure thee understood me, and knew instinctively that I would not designedly thrust myself between thee and the memory of such a life and such love, nor intrude, otherwise than as a loving and sympathizing friend, upon thy sanctities of sorrow. It was no more than thy due to know how much thy unconscious influence had been to me, and how happy I was to meet thee again. I am sure, in the end, it cannot harm thee or me, to know that years and cares and sorrows have not estranged us, nor blunted our mutual sympathies. What the world suffers from is the *want* of love, not the excess of it. There cannot be too much of kindness and affection — of that large charity which will think no evil of its object, but good and good only.'

It was apparent that he was making a graceful and strategic, but cruel retreat. It was also apparent that the gap could not be bridged. He tried to make amends for his wrong by offers to dedicate his poems to her. In his letters during the next year he was friendly, though often cold. He wrote about his reading, he discussed literary matters, he retailed trivial facts, he commented on the weather, and he dwelt on his illness. She stopped writing for two months and a half, and now his conscience troubled him for his treatment of her. He apologized, and explained that his complicated nervous affection had made him an invalid. It is true he had thought last year that he was better, but he had done wrong in yielding to his feelings, in giving pain where he most desired to give happiness. She now asked him to return her her letters, but he replied that he would do so only reluctantly. Thus, unknowingly, by his effort to appease her, he hurt her all the more. What he said about his invalid state was tantamount to regretting the proposal of marriage that he had made; he had tried to make his poor health a reason for retreating. He, nevertheless, sought to retain her esteem and he reiterated his desire to publish the dedicatory poem to her, of which he sent her a copy. Even the use of her initials would satisfy him. The poem, dated March 20, 1860, was as follows:

> To thee, dear friend, who, when the popular frown
> Darkens around a toiler, faint and worn,
> In fields which since have Freedom's harvest borne,
> Where they who bind the sheaves of party, now,
> Have scarce forgiven the rugged breaking plough
> And early sowers whom they laughed to scorn,
> Wert of the few in all the scoffing town
> Who, as his vouchers, spake the words of cheer
> Which linger longest on a grateful ear —
> Count it not strange, if even now I bring
> My tardy gift — no garlands of the Spring,
> Woven of tender maple leaves and set
> With wind-flower, apple-bloom, and violet,
> But Summer's latest flowers and leaves full grown,
> And seeded grass, and roses over blown.
> Thou, who hast sung for Milton, blind and old,
> A song of faith the bard himself might own,
> Wilt pardon words of Freedom over bold:
> And, not unmindful of the grave discourse
> We sometimes dared with reverent lips to hold,
> Take up the burden of my serious verse,
> And lend thy ear to its low thoughtful tone.

Since Whittier never published this poem in his works, it is apparent that Elizabeth declined the honor of the dedication.

Their friendship, meanwhile, straggled on. In the following summer they were together in Massachusetts and climbed Mount Wachusett. Here again the same tale as of old spun itself out. There was a last walk with a sweetheart to be dropped — a repetition of the final episode in the affairs with Evelina Bray and Lucy Hooper. He even celebrated the walk in a poem as he had done on the occasion of his last walks with them. His poem 'Monadnock from Wachuset' in the series 'Mountain Pictures' is not really a love poem, but a picture of the country scenery and the rustic house that he and Elizabeth visited. The only reference to Elizabeth, and this not by name, is in the beginning where he speaks of 'her who led, Fittest of guides, with light but reverent tread.' In a later version, he changed the line to 'A fitting guide, with reverential tread.' The poem itself is Wordsworthian, drawing a moral from a trivial remark made by the farmer, that he loved the place for the sake of his mother, who had lived and died there. Whittier wrote that he and his companion were in unison about the lesson they learned, that man was more than his abode, and that the inward life was more than nature's raiment. Elizabeth could not now inspire him to write a love poem.

Meanwhile Elizabeth wrote to Whittier about his volume 'The Home Ballads' and pleased him by saying that she liked 'My Playmate' — his own favorite poem. He intended visiting her again at Mount Wachusett in company with Emerson, but for some reason did not. Something must have happened to make such a visit impossible, for we find him writing shortly afterwards to Elizabeth's sister Hannah (November 8, 1860), who had come East: 'E., I fear, was not made for a Quaker, and I cannot find it in my heart to blame her for living out her nature with its love of all beauty and harmony: and I hope and believe she has self-poise enough to sustain her in her newly found freedom. She has a deeply religious nature, but it seeks expression in other forms and symbols than those of her early faith; and circumstances have made her a little uncharitable towards the " plain Friends."'

Two years later Elizabeth tried to renew the friendship by sending him a sermon against slavery by an Episcopalian clergyman. Whittier thanked her, but at the same time complained of the pain in his head and of his lung trouble. She understood. She wrote again saying that she was going to Europe for several years and asked him for letters of introduction.[1] We do not know whether he sent them; most likely he did. But the romance had ended.

In later years Elizabeth, who had meanwhile become an Episcopalian, felt bitter towards him, and she used to criticize him as a rustic, untraveled, and without various experience. Thomas Wentworth Higginson, who met her, said she was not quite loyal to the poet's memory.

That she was no ordinary woman is attested by Hawthorne's favorable comment upon her in his journal, after she called upon him at the height of his fame, shortly before she married. He said that he found her visit the only pleasant one he received as an author. He spoke of her agreeable smile, of her eyes that responded to one's thoughts, and of the absence of affectation about her. He dwelt on her conversation and her remarks about Whittier, Lowell, Henry James, the Swedenborgian (father of the novelist), and Herman Melville.

In spite of Elizabeth's disappointment in Whittier, he remained an admirer of her work as a poet. As late as 1881 he recommended her to some Philadelphians who sought a poem from him for some occasion.[2] He wrote that she was the author of two other poems of great merit besides her famous Milton poem, which the editor of the Oxford Edition of Milton included by mistake as his.

There is no doubt that though she and Whittier had many tastes in common, they were temperamentally incompatible. A marriage between them would not have been happy. He was too steeped in Quakerism to marry one who was not loyal to its principles. He would always have felt that he had betrayed his ideals if he had married her. He could not

[1] Manuscript letter of Elizabeth's about going to Europe, undated, 252 S. 3rd St., Philadelphia, in Essex Institute.

[2] Manuscript letter dated June 4, 1881, in Pennsylvania Historical Society, contains Whittier's references to Elizabeth.

change his temperament. He was willing to continue under the burden of his unsatisfied passions rather than marry her. The affair was the end of all his hopes to marry a Quakeress, or, indeed, to marry at all. In his earlier years he was willing to marry out of meeting in the cases of Mary Smith and Cordelia Russ, but he was then not as set in his views. The Quaker creed had since become too great a part of him; he was too old to change, he had become too orthodox.[1]

[1] Elizabeth Lloyd Howell died in Wernersville, Pa., 1896.

CHAPTER XIX

THE PINNACLE OF FAME: 'SNOW-BOUND'

THE decade between the years 1860 and 1869, between 'Home Ballads' and 'Among the Hills,' represents the crest of Whittier's literary activity. Most of his better-known poems belong to this period, during which he reached the zenith of his poetic powers. Poems like 'Barbara Frietchie,' 'Laus Deo,' 'The Eternal Goodness,' and 'Snow-Bound,' raised him in the opinion of many critics to the position of America's supreme poet. Although 'Skipper Ireson's Ride' and 'Telling the Bees' first saw light in the 'Atlantic Monthly' in the late fifties, their appearance in book form in 'Home Ballads' in 1860 reawakened public interest in them.

In 'Skipper Ireson's Ride' Whittier, astounding even his admirers, made great technical strides by the sweep of the verse and the effectiveness of the refrain. He impressed the public by the humane lesson that the pangs of remorse suffered by the skipper for not rescuing a ship in distress were a greater punishment than the tar and feathers administered to him by the women of Marblehead. Whittier showed his artistic dexterity in pretending at first to applaud the hostile action of the mob, but he enhanced the moral lesson of the poem by making the women release the skipper when they saw what mental torture he was undergoing. This ballad, which may be favorably compared with any of the old English ballads, will always remain a powerful poetic protest against cruelty and revenge.

The touching Wordsworthian poem 'Telling the Bees' is another poetical triumph. The background of the poem is an old superstitious custom of telling the bees of a death in the household, and covering their hive with mourning to prevent them from deserting it. Pictures of rural scenery add greatly to the realistic effect of the poem, but the touch of genius lies in the subtle and impressive manner in which a sad story is related. The poet — or speaker — for some reason parted with his sweetheart — whose name in the poem is the favorite one of Mary. A month later he passed by the farmhouse, no doubt hoping she would see him, but he caught sight of the chore-girl covering the hives. He was struck with mortal anxiety, for he now realized that someone in the family had just died. But of course it could not be Mary; it must be her aged grandfather. As the lover drew near, he saw the old man sitting on the doorway sill. Then, as he came still closer, he was struck as with palsy when he heard the chore-girl sing:

> 'Stay at home, pretty bees, fly not hence!
> Mistress Mary is dead and gone.'

The poet conveyed so effectively the poignancy of the loss of a loved one, because he drew on his own memories of a great grief he had undergone. He put into the poem all the sorrow that he had felt when he lost his Mary — Mary Emerson Smith. Though he depicted an episode that was fictitious, he was enabled to reinforce its artistic merit and human appeal by personal recollections. He had often observed in the locality chore-girls covering bee-hives on account of deaths in the family.

The most tender and touching poem 'My Playmate,' in this volume, was also inspired by Mary. It may be ranked with Poe's lyrics in memory of lost loves — with 'To One in Paradise,' 'To Helen,' and 'Annabel Lee.' Tennyson thought it a perfect poem. It may also have inspired another famous poem in the same meter and on the same theme — the softening effects upon an individual life of the memories of a lost love — Francis Thompson's 'Daisy.'

What man, no matter how lacking in sentiment he may be, does not find himself moved by stanzas like these?

> O playmate in the golden time!
> Our mossy seat is green,

Its fringe of violets blossom yet,
    The old trees o'er it lean.

The winds so sweet with birch and fern
    A sweeter memory blow;
And there in spring the veeries sing
    The song of long ago.

And still the pines of Ramoth wood
    Are moaning like the sea, —
The moaning of the sea of change
    Between myself and thee!'

There were other spirited ballads in the volume — 'The Garrison of Cape Ann' and 'The Swan Song of Parson Avery.' Unfortunately the poet tried to make these stories prove the efficacy of prayer, as usual, by false analogy. Such poems fail to awaken a sympathetic appeal in those who do not hold Whittier's theological doctrines. Even Lowell, by no means an infidel, in reviewing the volume said that Whittier now seemed a 'Berseker turned Carthusian,' and criticized him for permitting his religious tendencies to approach morbidity. 'To put a moral to the end of a ballad,' wrote Lowell, 'is like sticking a cork on the point of a sword.' These two last ballads, familiar to many readers because of their frequent appearance in anthologies, do not give altogether a fair impression of Whittier's lyrical gifts. For in some ballads, as 'The Witch's Daughter,' his moral deductions are beyond cavil, and sometimes, as in 'The Sycamores,' which he himself thought his best ballad, he has no moral at all.

In the fall of 1860, when Lincoln was a candidate for election, Whittier again turned his pen to the service of the cause. He expressed his joy that Pennsylvania had gone Republican, by writing the campaign song 'The Quakers Are Out.' He himself was chosen one of the Presidential Electors to vote for Lincoln. When the Southern States seceded one by one, Whittier was opposed to coercing them

— a not uncommon position taken by many Northerners before the firing upon Fort Sumter. In his poem 'A Word For the Hour' he versified his view that coercion or war was madness and folly. Yet he did not approve of too much compromise by the Northern commissioners, and wrote to one of them begging him not to yield an inch of territory.

The war itself did not stimulate his muse. Being a Friend and opposed to war, he was in a strange dilemma, since he had unintentionally done his share in bringing the war about. He once said that if he could have foreseen the dreadful bloodshed from the great conflict, he would have hesitated and restrained his ardor for a more peaceful solution of the problem. But, little as he sympathized with war, he wrote some of the most widely known poems growing out of that struggle. While he never wrote a poem urging or celebrating slaughter or revenge, he did compose some of the most influential and patriotic poems, now part of the heritage of American history.

Whittier was never on the field of battle nor did he ever see a regiment, except the colored one led by Colonel Shaw. Singing indirectly of the war that he deprecated, he produced no really great war poetry, like Whitman's 'Drum Taps.' The witty poetess Gail Hamilton satirically showed him the anomalous position he occupied, by sending him slippers embroidered with belligerent eagles in Quaker drab. Still he saw with real insight that slavery, and not State rights, was the cause of the war. In his famous song, '"Ein Feste Burg ist unser Gott,"' he stated without mincing words, exactly what the South was fighting for — the maintenance of slavery. He further insisted that there could be no proper ending of the war unless slavery were abolished.

> In vain the bells of war shall ring
>   Of triumphs and revenges,
> While still is spared the evil thing
>   That severs and estranges.
>   But blest the ear
>   That yet shall hear

The jubilant bell
That rings the knell
Of Slavery forever!' [1]

When the Hutchinson singers, in the spring of 1862, sang this song to the army of the Potomac, they were driven out of the lines by Northern officers, one of whom said he thought as much of an abolitionist as of a Rebel. The singers finally appealed to the White House for permission to continue singing it. Lincoln read the poem, which made a deep impression upon him, and concluded that it was just the kind of song that the soldier should hear. He took to heart its call for abolition, for a few months later, he spoke to the Cabinet about his intention of issuing his celebrated Emancipation Proclamation. He later informed Charles Carleton Coffin, the war-correspondent, that this song had brought him to a final decision in the matter.[2] Thus our humble poet, who was not only an agent in the founding of the Republican Party, was instrumental in unshackling the bonds of the slave. He was indirectly responsible for the issuing of the greatest document in American history since the Constitution.

The most popular of his war poems was 'Barbara Frietchie,' the story of which he received from Mrs. Southworth. We know now that the main episode, as well as the details, was pure fiction, for the Confederate troops, on the evening of September 6, 1862, did not pass Barbara's house in Frederickstown, but marched through another street, Hill Alley, three hundred yards away. General Jackson was not in command of his division at the time, which was then under General Starke. He had been injured by a horse on the previous day and did not join his troops till the 10th, when he started for Harper's Ferry. Barbara was bedridden, too, and in-

---

[1] '"Ein Feste Burg ist unser Gott,"' *The Independent*, June 13, 1861. In *Poems*.

[2] Lincoln said to Coffin: 'The singing of that song by the Hutchinsons stirred me to the writing of the Emancipation Proclamation.' From letter to me dated Feb. 26, 1932, from the Hon. Albert L. Bartlett. Mr. Bartlett told me he heard Coffin tell the Whittier Society of the influence of Whittier's poem upon Lincoln's proclamation.

capable of getting up on the day the troops marched through the town. The literary merits of the poem, however, are not lessened because the story has no basis in reality. It did not become obsolete after the war ended; it still stirs us by its appeal to our sense of the heroic; essentially it is a patriotic poem based on the idea of Union, a passionate protest against secession.

Whittier included both of these poems in the volume 'In War Time and Other Poems,' as well as other war poems, like 'The Battle Autumn of 1862,' with its false analogy that nature, unlike man, is not at war, and 'At Port Royal' with its weak imitation of negro folk-song. He included other poems superior to these — exquisite ballads in his new vein, like 'Amy Wentworth' and 'The Countess'; poems descriptive of natural scenery, like 'Mountain Pictures'; prophetic outbursts in behalf of liberty for Italy, like 'Naples' and 'Italy.' The religious poems, as 'The Waiting' and 'The River Path,' had no extraordinary merit.

In the midst of the war, while his reputation as a poet was growing, he suffered the second great tragic loss of his life in the death of his sister Elizabeth. Her encouragement and sympathy had been of marked influence upon him, for the bachelor and the spinster each had what modern psychologists call a brother-and-sister complex. She replaced the affection of a wife, gave him the guidance of a critic, consoled him and cared for him. In some respects like him — in her gentleness, soulfulness, moral fervor, and wit — she was his complement in natural disposition. She was more sociable and eloquent; she was a genial hostess and a good conversationalist.

Her invalidism was aggravated a year before her death by a fall upon the rocks at Appledore, in which she injured her spine. After that she was confined to a dark room, and she suffered great pain. He was lonely and inconsolable after her death. When he wrote his poem 'The Vanishers,' he felt lost because she was not there to hear him read his latest composition. He now turned to Lucy Larcom for consolation, since she was Elizabeth's best friend. In 'Snow-Bound' he paid his sister a noble tribute, though he there dwelt more on the helpless and sentimental mood to which her death transported him.

In the following winter the most important event of the war took place. Congress passed the Thirteenth Amendment, abolishing slavery. Whittier, seeing his life's work accomplished, wrote 'Laus Deo,' a poem which composed itself as if he were in a trance, while he sat listening to the peal of the bells in the Friends' Meeting House in Amesbury. Though it is one of his most ecstatic efforts, its spirit is more to be commended than its logic. He was ensnared in the same theological meshes in which Lincoln himself became entangled in his second inaugural, by assuming that a personal God directly intervened to abolish slavery by bringing about a bloody war to punish those guilty of perpetuating the institution. To praise the Lord for directly and consciously intervening to undo injustice by wreaking a bloody vengeance is tantamount to blaming him for being doubly guilty Himself, first for not having intervened sooner, nay for having allowed slavery to be introduced at all, and secondly for bungling matters cruelly or at least deliberately making man guilty of doing so. Yet at that very time slavery flourished in Brazil. And slavery still exists today — chattel slavery in Africa, wage slavery in America. But let us not question the poet's or the statesman's logic; let us join in the hope or exultation that justice finally triumphs. The hymn is a psalm of joy on the victory of a noble cause; it almost carries conviction that injustice can never endure permanently; it is the very incarnation of fervent gratitude.

In April, 1865, the close of the war was followed by the assassination of Lincoln. As the cry for vengeance upon the South rose to hysterical heights, Whittier, in an article for the Amesbury 'Villager,' 'The Lesson and Our Duty,' called on the North to exercise no unnecessary severity, take no further life, except in the case of the criminal guilty of the murder. 'Rabbinical writers,' he said, 'tell us that evil spirits who are once baffled in a contest with human beings lose from thenceforth all powers of further mischief. The defeated rebels are in the precise condition of those Jewish demons. Deprived of slavery, they are like wasps that have lost their sting.' Here was something analogous to Lincoln's own method of pointing a lesson by homely and familiar illustration.

On April 20, 1865, Whittier wrote to Allinson:[1]

'I believe that President Johnson will be found a true man — and that his lapse on the 4th ult. was *exceptional*, as I cannot learn that he has ever before been charged with excess. What I most fear is, that, like Southern Unionists generally, he will go too far in what he calls *justice*. It would be sad now to have our good cause stained with cruelty and revenge.'

His work as reformer, agitator, propagandist was now over; he had seen the triumph of the principles he fought for; he could now with clear conscience turn to the favorite diversions of his youth — write about Colonial folk-lore and New England country life.

In this mood of deliverance, and with the purpose of beguiling some hours of illness, he set to work and, curiously enough, wrote during the summer a poem on winter, 'Snow-Bound.' Published in the following year, it both pleased the critics and won the public as no other poem of his had done. It also earned for him, to his surprise, ten thousand dollars in royalties. He began to flourish from now on; he profited by his new course in life in writing popular poems. A poem presenting beautiful Flemish verbal pictures and voicing no unpalatable ideas was more remunerative than unpopular strains in favor of liberty.

The literary value of 'Snow-Bound' is in its artistic descriptions of the snow-covered landscape and in its charac-

[1] Manuscript letter to Allinson furnished by his late daughter-in-law, Mrs. Allinson.

terization of the persons of a country household shut in by
the storm. We become almost snow-blind by the whiteness
of the outdoor scenes. We look on and take part in the talk
around the warm fireside, while the winds roar about the
house. We listen to the tales, and join in the various tasks
of the inmates to escape boredom. We even find ourselves
reading, with the family, the country newspaper, or thumb-
ing the pages of the yearly almanac.

American critics have exhausted the vocabulary of critical
eulogy in extolling the poet's pictures of a country winter.
Whittier deserves the praise, for he stands out more conspicuously as a painter of snow landscape than does any other
American poet. But he also ranks high as an etcher of portraits of rural characters — of his father, mother, uncle, aunt,
his two sisters, the country schoolmaster, and Harriet Livermore. The portraits remind us of those fine cameos in the
'Prologue' of the 'Canterbury Tales.' The types are individual and, with the exception of Harriet Livermore, are drawn
with love and sympathy. They will live as pictures of New
England folk in the early part of the nineteenth century as
do Chaucer's of Englishmen in the latter part of the four-
teenth century.

Critics have pointed out the merits of 'Snow-Bound' so
often, however, as to have caused the public to overlook its
blemishes. Unfortunately the poem has failings; in fact,
about half of it is artistically defective and even altogether
superfluous. It is, except for some passages, inferior to his
collection of songs of freedom and even to his personal poems
and ballads.

The poet naturally could not avoid the temptation of
sermonizing twice on the validity of a belief in, or at least
a hope of, immortality, when reflecting that no member of the
household except his brother and himself was alive, and when
speaking of the recent death of his sister. He also could not
help unnecessarily becoming a propagandist and introducing
his views on a speedy Reconstruction.

He blundered hopelessly when he tried to philosophize on the sex question. Some of his portrayals are not altogether true to life. His aunt, who spoke of her girlhood games, was the sweetest woman perverse Fate had ever denied a household mate, and had always held the virgin fancies of her heart apart unprofaned.

> 'Be shame to him of women born
> Who hath for such but thought of scorn.'

There you have the Puritan unreasonably condemning the social critic for suggesting that fulfilment might under some circumstances be wiser than repression. Though the poet described his aunt from boyhood memory, yet he introduced his mature reflections on her state. It is these observations that cannot pass muster.

In commenting upon the eccentricities of the most interesting person in the household, the half-welcome and half-mad guest, Harriet Livermore, Whittier again shows his superficiality and inability to explain a personality correctly. In trying to pass judgment upon her bold and passionate nature, upon her intense thoughts and acts, he solves the problem by saying we cannot know the hidden springs of her outward life, since fate and heredity had made her what she was. It was not ours, he thought, to separate 'the tangled skein of will and fate,' and to divide the circle of events 'between choice and Providence.' Of course, just that is what psychologists are successfully doing today; they overcome the work of nature and environment by remedies based on experiment, study, and nature herself. They no longer are content to say that it is the will of the Lord and then refrain from curing remediable evils due to human ignorance. We know the cause of Harriet's eccentricities; they were the result of a neurosis brought on by being very cruelly abandoned by an army doctor to whom she had been engaged. A psychoanalyst might have made her a normal person.

The reception of 'Snow-Bound' placed Whittier for the

time being above Longfellow in popular esteem. Probably no
poem written in America was so much beloved by both public and critics. Correspondents, old friends and strangers,
heaped upon him an avalanche of letters telling him what
the poem meant to them. The reviews were enthusiastic,
in fact too effusive — and new editions of his books were
called for.

In the next two years he issued two small collections that
increased his fame more than ever. He returned to ballad-
writing, to rural pictures, to New England legend. In both
'The Tent on the Beach' and 'Among the Hills' he gave
America superb poetry. He had now found himself after
straying from the path on which he delighted to travel; he returned in his fifties and sixties to the themes that he had abandoned in his twenties. When he thus went back to the ideals
of his youth, he showed his limitations — the chief of which
was that he had very little new to say. But he versified his
tales so magnificently that he made one forget their paucity
of intellectual content, or their preoccupation with ideas of
no great import. He retold these tales with great vigor and
exquisite art. He was again haunted by the old themes —
witches, Quakers, specter ships, and so forth — themes that
he had dismissed with contempt when he set out on the path
of reform. He was really happy to return to his old loves —
moral poetry, historical poetry, religious poetry, rural poetry.
He had regretted his departure from the haunts of the muses
to battle for liberty; he had done so only at the call of duty.
Writing abolition poems had, however, been of service to him
artistically, for it made him proficient in infusing his poetic
work with fervor. Even though he had mellowed he still
wrote with frenzy and animation. Above all, he was privi-
leged now to write without thinking constantly about slavery or the war; he no longer felt twinges of conscience when
writing his pleasing ballads, as he had done before and during the war.

During this decade he wrote a number of ballads with

a social purpose in the vein of 'Maud Muller.' They dealt with love-affairs between people of unequal stations in life. Judging by the frequency with which he harped on the subject of marriage between people of unequal rank, we cannot avoid coming to the conclusion that these poems had their origin in a personal grievance. Knowing as we do now the facts of his love-affairs, we are fully justified in the view that these impersonal tales have a decidedly personal bias. He was always ready to use for artistic purposes true stories of happy marriages between persons of different rank, as he did in his youth when he wrote 'The Vestal.' He found such material in an old tale, which he developed in his beautiful lyric 'The Countess.'

In 'Amy Wentworth' we have a plot centering around a girl of ancient and proud lineage living in a Colonial mansion in Jaffrey Street, who had spurned a rich suitor for the humble jerkin-clad skipper of a fishing-smack. Amy was not ashamed of him. Her love for him made her feel that the wooden masts of his boat were beaten gold. Whittier in this poem for once moralized nobly and infectiously. He speaks fully and powerfully to the point:

> 'The stream is brightest at its spring
> And blood is not like wine;
> Nor honored less than he who heirs
> Is he who founds a line.
>
> .   .   .   .
>
> 'Oh, rank is good and gold is fair,
> And high and low mate ill;
> But love has never known a law
> Beyond its own sweet will!'

In 'Among the Hills,' an imaginary tale, Whittier drew an idyllic picture of the happy wedded life of a cultured city girl who married an unlettered farmer. Though the descriptions of nature and rustic life in it rank among his best work, the story is unconvincing. The tale of the absurd courting of the cultured city girl by the rude farmer is related for the purposes of defending a thesis. A girl who had once, during a summer vacation, in a condescending tone urged a farmer to marry a country housewife is surprised by a proposal from him and marries him herself. Of course, they lived happily ever after. The poet, in company with his hostess, visited this strange blissful couple. In the poem the farmer, the hostess, and the poet all moralize respectively, in a more convincing way, it must be confessed, than the probability of the facts of the tale warrant. The poet concludes:

> 'And, musing on the tale I heard,
>   'Twere well, thought I, if often
> To rugged farm-life came the gift
>   To harmonize and soften;
>
> 'If more and more we found the troth
>   Of fact and fancy plighted,
> And culture's charm and labor's strength
>   In rural homes united.'

We now see the effect of Whittier's chief love mishap upon his poetry. Rejected in marriage because of his poverty, he wrote ballads of happy married life in which he depicted men and women in straitened circumstances accepted in marriage by their social superiors and both living happily. In these ballads he rebukes Mary Emerson Smith, who had discarded him because he was a poor boy. In youth he remonstrated with her in his poems, in vain, on her love of worldly things. Now he addressed her as one erring in following a social convention.

In the four volumes he issued during this decade he wrote with a freshness and artistry unusual in elderly poets. In spite of Lowell's charge that Whittier showed signs of age, he was perennially young. He had made a conscious attempt to recapture the spirit of his youth, and to perfect and master the poetic medium for transmitting it, and he was successful in doing so. He became one of the few poets who are known more by the productions of their old age than by those of their prime.

CHAPTER XX

LUCY LARCOM AND GAIL HAMILTON SUCCUMB

THE story of Whittier's relations with women, particularly poetesses, in the years between his sixtieth and eightieth year is almost without parallel in the history of literature. Though he was an invalid, past the age when men fall violently in love, he attracted a host of woman admirers. Being extremely vain, he sought their admiration and bestowed subtly flattering compliments upon them for their literary work. This habit, as well as the glamour of his reputation, then at its height, and the rectitude of his personal life, made many women a prey to his charms. He allowed a number of them to become infatuated with him, and though he occasionally discouraged them, he kept up most of his friendships and continued his correspondence with them. In some instances the platonic emotions, even on his side, bordered dangerously on the amorous. It is singular how many poetesses sought his company and wrote to him, how many found consolation in his poems, how many poured out their sorrows and confidences to him. Some addressed verses to him; others consulted him about their love-affairs, even parading their lovers before him. At times he became so apprehensive about the impetuosity and persistence of some of his admirers that he refused to be left alone in a room with them. To Amesbury and to Danvers, where he made his home after 1876 with some cousins, the women came in hordes. 'The Pilgrims are coming,' he used to say to his cousin's adopted young daughter, Phœbe, when they trooped down. The whole thing would have been almost a merry farce, had it not been disastrous to the pride of some of them. The women — mostly writers — were usually sentimental, proper, and religious like Whittier himself, and the mingling of religion and love often increased the ludicrousness of the situation. He consoled himself that he never gave them anything tangible 'to hang a hat on,' as he put it, but he often did encourage them. There were novelists older than he who doted on him, and youthful poetesses in their twenties who gushed before him. To marry John Greenleaf Whittier in spite of his age and invalidism was the ambition of a number of the woman writers of the day. Endowed with the fascinating powers of a Don Juan and practicing the chastity of a Sir Galahad, he was to a certain degree dangerous to the women, for he neither gave aught of himself nor accepted anything from them.

His numerous friendships and vast correspondence with woman writers in the last thirty years of his life are more baffling and incomprehensible than his early love-affairs. It is now known that there were several cases here like that of Mrs. Gilchrist and Whitman, in which the lady's admiration of the poet's talents got the better of her reserve, and led her to believe that worship of his poetry would win him as a husband. On one occasion, about March, 1867, his friendships led to a report in the newspapers that he was to be married. This apparently concerned Lucy Larcom, one of the woman friends most devoted to him. He set her mind at ease by writing to her, 'Credulity, thy name is woman! So thee almost believed that report, almost.'

Lucy Larcom,[1] author of the popular poem 'Hannah Binding Shoes,' was really a martyr to love for Whittier. Known practically throughout her life as Whittier's protégée, she helped him edit three books, which he published under his name though she did most of the work on them.

She met him when she was a mill girl in Lowell in 1844 when he was thirty-seven and she twenty years old. She considered the day she met him 'a white mark among the memories' of her lonely life. For many years after they did not meet, since she moved West. On her return to the East she became a close friend of Whittier's sister.

[1] Lucy Larcom was born on March 5, 1824, and died April 17, 1893.

When Whittier became contributing editor of the 'National Era,' he told his readers how he had met Lucy Larcom, and he praised her literary work. He continued referring to her at opportune times. She became infatuated with him, and in 1853, when she was verging on her thirtieth year, she sent him a very flattering letter. To this he diplomatically replied that her high-flown compliments originated in a sad misconception and over-estimate of him; in short, that her fancy draped him. Still he wanted her to correspond with him and submit her work to him for criticism. But his friendship with Elizabeth Lloyd was resumed in the late fifties, and Lucy was forgotten. When that was drawing to its conclusion, he renewed his relations with Lucy.

They made a visit together to the Whitefield Church at Newburyport, where they discussed the preacher's life. He recalled this walk in the introductory part of his poem on Whitefield, 'The Preacher,' which appeared in 'The Independent' for December 29, 1859, and in 'Home Ballads' in 1860. In it he described the sunset in the Merrimac Valley, which they both witnessed from Whittier Hill, in Amesbury, overlooking the steeples of Newburyport, but he scarcely alluded to his friendship for her.

She mentioned that walk with him in her diary for Christmas, 1860. Whittier had not presented her with a copy of 'Home Ballads,' though he had sent her presentation copies of earlier volumes. She was hurt; she wrote in her diary that she did not like the new book, because he had not sent it to her.

'I wonder,' she reflected, 'if that is what makes me like the songs in the "Panorama," — some of them — better than anything in this new volume, although I know that this is more perfect as poetry. I doubt if he will ever write anything that I shall like so well as the "Summer by the Lakeside," in that volume; it is so full of my first acquaintance with the mountains, and the ripening of my acquaintance with him, my poet-friend. How many blessings that friendship has brought me!—among them, a glimpse into a true home, a realizing of such brotherly and sisterly love as is seldom seen outside of books,—and best of all, the friendship of dear Lizzie, his sole home-flower, the meek lily blossom that cheers and beautifies his life. Heaven spare them long to each other, and their friendship to me!'

On an occasion when he failed to keep an appointment with her she wrote to him: 'Why is it that I always miss thy visits? Why of all things should I have lost sight of thee at the mountains? and when I was so near thee too! I cannot think why so pleasant a thing should be withheld from me, unless because I enjoy thee too much. I have no other such friends as thee and Elizabeth, and when anything like this happens it is a great disappointment. But I said all the time that seeing the hills with you could only be a beautiful dream.

'I felt the beauty of those mountains around the Lake, as I floated among them, but I wished for thee all the while; because I have always associated thee with my first glimpse of them, and somehow it seems as if they belonged to thee or thee to them, or both. They would not speak to me much; I needed an interpreter; and when they grew so dim and spectral in the moon haze, they gave me a strange almost shuddering feeling of distance and loneliness.'

He wrote to Lucy after his sister's death, in the fall of 1864, that since he knew her before Elizabeth did he now held her, as well as others who were loved by his sister, nearer and dearer to him than ever. He wanted her to feel that the old homestead was always open to her. There was even a rumor that she was going to live at his house as housekeeper. Lucy at the time worked in Boston, where she edited 'Our Young Folks,' the famous juvenile magazine, to which Whittier contributed poems like 'The Common Question,' celebrating the death of his parrot Charlie, and the famous 'In School Days.' He sent her his books, penned rhymed epistles to her, and wrote to her all the gossip and small talk in the Whittier family as if she were a member of it. She bestowed various gifts upon him. For one of these, a box of roses, he thanked her gracefully in some doggerel verses.[1]

Matters between them drifted aimlessly along. Soon came a quarrel, of which we do not know the details. She must have been losing patience with him, as for years he was subtly winning her affections without any intention of fully reciprocating. Finally he wrote to her to effect a reconciliation:[2]

'Thee art right in thinking that I don't know much about what was said on the evening thee refer to.... If I remember rightly thee was unreasonably persistent in thy contention. When one is unreasonable himself, he is in no mood for tolerating the same thing in others. I dare say that I was a fool, but that is no reason thee should make thyself one, by dwelling on it. Lay it all to dyspepsia, Ben Butler, or anything else than intentional wrong on the part of thy old friend. We have known each other too long, and done each other too many kind offices, to let it disturb us.'

She helped Whittier compile several books, the first of which was the anthology of children's poems called 'Child Life' — a book he liked so well that he published it, with her permission, under his own name. She assisted him in bringing out a companion volume of selections from prose for children, a book which also appeared without her name. She almost ruined her health by research in editing with him another book, 'Songs of Three Centuries.' This time he graciously consented to mention her name, but in the preface only. After his death, however, he bequeathed to her the royalties of the three books she had edited with him — a belated, though insufficient, acknowledgment of her services.

Lucy never publicly showed any bitterness towards Whit-

---

[1] Manuscript of these unpublished rhymed verses, year not given, in the Morgan Library. Pickard has reprinted two other doggerel poems to her.

[2] Pickard, Vol. II, p. 552. Pickard in the text does not say the letter was to Lucy, but in the index he assigns it to her. It is undated.

tier because he did not marry her. She accepted his friendship for the prestige it brought her. She worshiped him always. After one of his visits, she wrote in her diary:

'I have more reverence and admiration for such a man, from having found a higher standard in life for myself from which to look across and up to him.' [1]

In later years she became saddened, and seeking new religious comfort, joined the church of Phillips Brooks.

Her death followed not long after Whittier's. Her published letters showed that, though she regarded him highly, she had been hurt because he did not allow her to have her name on the books they edited. She was especially incensed because he had asked her not to write about him. Thinking that he did not want her to parade her friendship, she complied with his request, even refusing to write her reminiscences of him. She was also in such financial distress that even a rival of hers in Whittier's affections, Gail Hamilton, said that the poet might have left her more in his will than the royalties on her own books. But Lucy continued to love him even after his death. 'One of my best friends,' she wrote, 'is out of sight now, but I do not feel that he is far away. Life is one in all the worlds and it is life in us all that united us all.'

More aggressive in her love than Lucy Larcom was the brilliant essayist and poet Mary Abigail Dodge,[2] who wrote under the pseudonym 'Gail Hamilton.' One of her poems in the 'National Era' attracting Whittier's attention, he wrote to Bailey, the editor, asking who Gail Hamilton was.[3] The inquiry ultimately led to a correspondence between them. In the next year, 1859, she visited him — a dashing woman in her middle twenties; she fascinated him, and was in

---

[1] There are manuscript letters of Whittier to Lucy Larcom in the Yale University Library, the Huntington Library, the Morgan Library, and the American Antiquarian Society.

[2] Mary Abigail Dodge (Gail Hamilton) was born March 31, 1833, and died August 17, 1896.

[3] Whittier first inquired about Gail Hamilton in the latter part of 1858. 'Terra Incognita' was the piece that interested him.

turn fascinated, finding him 'irresistible and sweet.' She was amused and pleased at the devotion that existed between Whittier and his sister, regarding 'their Charles and Mary *Lambness* a perpetual poem.' [1] Describing another visit she paid them during the period of the Civil War to discuss a proposed biography of the late editor, Gamaliel Bailey, she wrote: 'We all three walked into Paradise, shut the gate, and threw away the key.' The two authors talked and jocularly parried lances with each other, and she thought him the king of men. During the course of her conversation she complained that she was not allowed to write anonymously. 'It is a great deal better as it is,' he replied, 'it puts thee on thy good behavior.' 'You don't trust me,' she said. 'Yes, I do trust thee, but thee has a great audacity — great audacity.' They discussed various topics, among them theology. He flattered her on her gifts. He twitted her on her delight in repartee. She said that she was amused at the parrot Charlie, that object of interest to all of Whittier's visitors. He told her that he liked her because she was not literary, adding that some good angel must have sent her, for her visit had rid him of a headache.

The friendship between the two deepened from now on. He praised her book 'Stumbling Blocks,' asking her how her young head came to have so much wisdom and promising to introduce the book to the clergy. She at times addressed him in her letters as 'My Dear Sheik,' in allusion to a comparison of Whittier's head to that of a Saracen, made by Wasson in an article in the 'Atlantic Monthly.' She again visited him, but, as she said in a letter to him later, she did not venture to demolish all his wrong opinions, because he needed some badnesses to set off his goodnesses. She was now beginning to feel that he was encouraging her affections. In reply to some remonstrance of his she wrote: 'If you had

---

[1] Most of the quotations from Gail Hamilton's letters to and about Whittier are from Dodge's *Gail Hamilton's Life in Letters* and Pickard's 'A Merry Woman's Letters to a Quiet Poet' in the *Ladies' Home Journal*, Dec., 1899, and January, 1900.

GAIL HAMILTON
1866

anything like the affection for me and respect for my character which you are so lavish in professing you would know I
should and could make no ill use of them [some album verses]
— only perhaps put them into your "Life and Letters,"
which, out of revenge, I shall either write myself or put ——
up to writing.'

When Gail Hamilton published her book 'A New Atmosphere,' Whittier wrote the poem 'Lines on a Fly-Leaf,'
which referred to her, as critics recognized, though he did not
mention her name. The poem was a defense of her peculiar
temperament — a temperament he at heart feared.

To his poem she replied in some doggerel verses.

> 'Come now in good sooth,
> Little friend, speak the truth —
> Thy love for me such is
> Thee put in those touches
> Of rebuke and restriction
> To quiet thy conscience, not speak thy conviction,
> For thee know, heart and hand
> I'm as good as thee can stand!
> Am I not sweet as maple molasses
> When thee scold me for fingering thy brasses?
> And did not the poet say of yore,
> Angels could do no more?
> Ah, would not angels pity her
> To be scolded by the "Saintly Whittier"?'

In a note which she added, she gave an interesting side-
light on the spirit of comradeship that existed between them:
'Imagine Whittier and me sitting one whole day and two
evenings, talking all the time. One of the brass knobs on the
Franklin stove was loose and came off on my hand. I turned
it over and remarked upon its brightness. He said, "Now
doesn't thee know that thee is making work?" 'How?'
I asked. "Why, destroying the brightness by handling it."
I rubbed it with my handkerchief and asked the housekeeper
if I had made her any work, "Oh," she said, "you made me
no work. Mr. Whittier takes care of the brasses himself."...

He told some company in the evening that I had talked so much it made him hoarse.'

Gail Hamilton now wanted to see Whittier oftener, for he kept her at a distance. Resenting his making love to her in a half-hearted way, she wrote to him that she did not like an occasional looking in upon him at his home, but that she wished to 'pop in' at all times; in fact, to come so often that he would have to set up a spring-trap to warn him that she was coming, so that he could slip out of the back door if he so desired. She had incurred his displeasure by some of her views, for she had noticed on her last visit that he had signalized his disapproval of her ideas by getting up and deliberately interrupting her conversation by going to the closet for wood to feed the stove, or for some other unnecessary object — a practice he indulged in when a conversation annoyed him.

A slight quarrel now broke out between them because he believed she had violated a confidence in a publication, and he wrote that he was sure her doing so really gave her no satisfaction. Amazed that a Quaker should lose his temper on little provocation, she humorously accused him of telling a 'fib,' because he said that the matter caused her no satisfaction, when he knew that it did. She then told him she could not have violated his confidence for the reason that he never gave her any; in fact, she reminded him of his manner of breaking off a conversation on a pretext. Jestingly she begged him to confide more in her, in fact to tell her the story of his life. 'I like thee scolding and I like thee smiling, and I hurl defiance at thee,' she added. The slight quarrel was soon mended. She met Whittier at the Laurels on the Merrimac in June, 1865, where he read his poem 'Revisited.'

Meanwhile Gail Hamilton had become, with John T. Trowbridge and Lucy Larcom, one of the editors of 'Our Young Folks.' She held this position for three years, till her memorable quarrel with her publishers on a matter of royalties — an episode she commemorated in her volume 'The Battle of the Books.'

Her affection for Whittier now increased. He was to some degree responsible for this, for he pleaded with her often to call upon him, sent her his poems, and praised her books.

Speaking of Gail Hamilton in a rhymed letter to Lucy Larcom, March 25, 1866, he wrote:

'For months I've scarce seen womankind; their welcome share: — except
　　when at the city,
Gail Hamilton came up, beside my lonely hearth to sit,
And make the winter evenings glad with wisdom and with wit
And fancy, feeling but the spur and not the curbing bit,
Lending a womanly charm to what before was bachelor rudeness; —
The Lord reward her for an act of disinterested goodness.'

Gail Hamilton was indifferent to the fact that Whittier was more than twenty-five years older than she. Writing to her sister about an inscribed copy of 'Among the Hills,' in which the poem to her was published, she tried to conceal her love under the garb of friendship:

'I have not read it [the book], but I know the best part of it is what he has written on the fly-leaf. I suppose the great mass of persons in the world are really incapable of friendship. No otherwise can I account for the clouds that seem to hang over so many. I am as far as possible from believing that friendship should, or can, encroach upon love. It seems to me they may run in parallel lines forever, since parallels never meet. I have a very great scorn for the notion you often find afloat that propinquity is the — what do the theologians call it? — predisposing cause of love? It may be a sufficient cause for that bread-and-butter sentiment which keeps the pot boiling, and, of course, if two substances have the natural affinity the coming together is all that is necessary, but the natural affinity is the very thing in question.'

When she visited him in the summer of 1868, she found him at the station waiting for her. They had intended going for a walk in the woods, but, as it was cold and stormy, they went to a Quaker meeting instead. She remained in Amesbury at his request for some time. 'The man himself I like better than ever, if that were possible,' she wrote in a letter describing her visit. 'He is so thoroughly sweet and simple, with such a child-like manliness.... He likes my dress much — for once in his life admired it without flaunting it in my face.... He seemed in good spirits and we had a real good time.'

On March 4, 1869, on the day Grant was inaugurated President, she wrote to him, in a letter that begins with the ominous words 'Dearly Beloved': 'Mr. Whittier, do you remember that I went to see you this winter, and added another Sunday to my immortal days? My pen scratches or I should at this point write you an epic poem on "Yourself" but I mean to bring it over and repeat it to you yet — in summer.'

During the year Gail Hamilton brooded over some grievance that she felt she had against her publishers. She thought she should have received more royalties than she did, and she started the quarrel which led to her writing 'The Battle of the Books.' She was victorious in her demands, and could now take the matter goodnaturedly. As she had the same publishers that Whittier had, she thought she might possibly offend him by the publication of her book. She wrote to him asking him to pay her his last visit, as she was going to do something disagreeable. She told him not to say that he had a cold as he usually did. In fact, she needed a man at Hamilton, as a burglar had been there recently. 'Now do for once be good and civil, and do as I bid you. You would be one of the nicest men that ever was if you were not so set and obstinate, and stiff-necked, and think you cannot sleep out of your house.'

The book duly appeared in 1870, but its publication did not interrupt the friendship between Gail Hamilton and Whittier.

In January, 1871, she moved to Washington, but did not inform Whittier of her change in residence. A longing to see her, meanwhile, overcame him and he wrote to her at her usual address inviting her to visit him. 'The dear!' she wrote in reply, 'Why, I am way down here in Washington! What a wound it is to my self-love to think you don't know it. I took a sudden start... and you never missed me. Was it not too bad? And I was so comfortable at home.... Dearly beloved, how I should like to see thee.... So now good morning to you, and call me cross, if you dare, when I love you so.'

He replied: 'I trusted to my impression as a Quaker should, or rather, as I wanted to see thee in Amesbury, "the wish is father to the thought," — that thee was at home. Had thee been, I dare say thee wouldn't have heeded my invitation, and so it is just as well thee are in Washington enjoying thyself.'

In the following summer she returned home. She wrote Whittier that she could not go to Amesbury, as she was busy superintending the carpenters and painters who were repairing her house. 'But what I do want — what I have set my heart on,' she added, 'what I will not be refused is to have you come over to Asantee and spend Sunday with me. You have no excuse for not coming, because you show by asking me that you have no engagement, and if you will come, I will certainly go over in a week or two and make you a visit — if you want me to.'

She was now insistent that he call on her. But he wrote that he was sorry she could not come, and refused to visit her, giving the heat as an excuse for his inability to do so, but adding: 'I wonder whether thee really expected me or wished me to come last week. I was not sure whether it was earnest or play of words. But if I had been able, I think I should have taken thee at thy word. I have many things to talk about, many things to show thee, and I live in the hope of seeing thee under thy roof before long. I want to talk with thee on thy articles in the "Independent," and on the subject of women's rights, labor, etc. I like thy views, generally, but I fear we should quarrel a little on some points. I regard thee as about the wisest of women, but nevertheless venture to dissent now and then, perhaps rather to the manner of saying

an unpalatable truth, than to the truth itself, which of course
is right.'

For the next two years matters drifted aimlessly along.
Gail Hamilton sent him a new volume of hers, which he
praised, though he dissented from her unfavorable opinions of
women. When she became ill, he wrote to her, very solicitous
about her welfare. She exacted the promise of a visit to her
— a promise he made in spite of his neuralgia. Then came
the news that she would return to Washington. He had been
somewhat cold to her, but when he saw that she would not
be within visiting distance, he wrote, almost grieved: 'Somehow, what with thy Congressional career and thy summer
flittings, I miss thee more and more when I need thee most.
Well, I must resign myself to it, but it is hard to let some
things drop out of one's life.'

It must have been at this time that Gail Hamilton was
puzzled by his conduct. Either his intentions were serious, or
he was a selfish bachelor who wanted her all to himself, and
yet refused to propose to her. She was then past forty years
old. He could not be trifling with her at the most crucial
period of her life. No, he must have realized what he was
doing, she thought. She became buoyant at the hope and
belief that he was in love with her. His recent letter indicated it.

On February 3, 1874, she wrote in a confident vein from
Washington: 'Dearly Beloved: Mr. Gillette was here Saturday and engaged me to lure you to Hartford, but I said
I would not. I have lured you to Hamilton, and the result
was that you were always running in upon me at odd hours,
breaking up my time, consuming all the eggs intended for
breakfast, interfering with my visitors, and being generally
disagreeable.... I have your last living picture transferred
from Hamilton, and standing before me on my mantel-
piece, — a thing of beauty and joy forever. You know, you
know, you are handsome; that is what spoils you and makes
you take on airs and stay on at home all the time, because

no one else's house is good enough for you... and O my dear, Washington is just full of stacks of people, any one of whom would drive Amesbury and Hamilton wild! There is no place like it, and nobody like you, only yours always, M. A. D.'

In the latter part of the year, after she had paid him a visit, she wrote to him addressing him thus: 'Blessed and beloved apostle. Sweetest saint in all the calendar. Worthy successor of that disciple whom Jesus loved.' Then, apologizing for speaking in this tone, she added that she would not have classed him with such holy men had she not recently heard him greatly praised by some children. He replied that he was very human, that in fact he had recently lost his temper over some fellow church-member and had also disputed a bill with an Irishman. 'I have been hoping to see thee again before it is too late for the season. Thy visit here was a most welcome one, but too short. I don't believe thee knows how glad I am to see thee. God bless thee always.'

About this time, when her niece was to be married, Gail Hamilton jokingly sent Whittier an invitation to her own wedding, but at the end of the letter she wrote that she had made a mistake — that she meant her niece's wedding. He sent her a poem in which he celebrated Gail Hamilton's wedding, but then, after pretending to have returned to her letter and learned it was her niece who was being married, he nevertheless paid tribute to the wisdom of the 'wisest aunt' that ever gave away a niece in marriage.

In 1877, after Whittier moved to Oak Knoll in Danvers, he again invited Gail Hamilton to visit him: 'I wish thee would sometimes look in upon me at Oak Knoll, where I shall be for the next six weeks. When thee are in Salem, the cars will take thee to within a short mile of us, and the coach is ready to take thee to our door. At any rate, here or there, staying or coming, politician, novelist or theologian, God bless thee!' In response to his invitation she called on him at Oak Knoll, but was frightened away by the dogs. He replied, making a joke of the matter. It seems that Gail Hamilton never felt at home in Oak Knoll; she had preferred visiting him in Amesbury to calling on him at Oak Knoll. By this time she was somewhat angered at him, yet she could not stifle her affection for him. She was also disappointed because of his reactionary attitude in labor problems, and his obsession with immortality. She voiced both her displeasure and her affection in a grand outburst:

'Dearly Beloved: I never would have believed it possible that the pomp of this world and the deceitfulness of riches would have so hardened your heart and blinded your mind to the poor workingmen and women of your own country. Why don't you write to me? Why don't you come to see me? Why don't you say you love and admire me? Because you have perched on Oak Knoll, and are lapped in luxury, and petted to death by your cousins, and are nothing in the world but a sleeping beauty! When you were in Amesbury, you seemed definite and local, but now I have lost you out of Amesbury and don't find you anywhere else. And here is your pretty book with your 'Witch of Wenham.'... I have dipped in it enough to see that it is you, and that you are stout in the faith that we shall be enjoying better Octobers when we have handed ours over to our successors.... Gay deceiver, fickle and purse-proud, do you know that I have been building a barn?'

Whittier from now on saw Gail Hamilton less frequently and rarely corresponded with her. The reason for this was that she had proposed marriage to him.[1] He feared to go to her house because she told him she had specially built it for both of them. She was at first angry when he diplomatically rejected her, but in her cooler moments she realized that he had made her no promises. She decided to make the best of the situation and to retain his friendship.

---

[1] My authority for saying that Gail Hamilton proposed marriage to Whittier, that he feared her, and that she built a house for him, is Mrs. Phœbe Grantham, who lived at Oak Knoll with her adopted mother, Mrs. Woodman, Whittier's cousin.

In 1884, when he had attained his seventy-seventh birth-day, she wrote to him a note full of affection, calling him now playfully by such endearing terms as 'dear angel,' 'sweet-heart,' and 'dearest of dears.' Several unimportant letters passed between them from this date until that of his death. Part of the time she was in Europe. She survived him by several years.

Gail Hamilton's passion for the poet, though concealed from the outside world, was known to the poet's cousins at Oak Knoll. Even the growing child, Phœbe Woodman John-son, the adopted daughter of the poet's cousin, soon learned for herself that her 'uncle' Greenleaf came to fear Gail Hamilton.

CHAPTER XXI

HE IS FASCINATED BY CELIA THAXTER AND EDNA DEAN PROCTOR

THERE were other women writers who made a deep impression upon Whittier during the years he philandered with Lucy Larcom and Gail Hamilton. Celia Thaxter and Edna Dean Proctor stand out conspicuously among them, because their personal charms impressed him more favorably than did those of many of his other woman friends and because their literary work attracted him more than that of other woman contemporaries.

The friendship between Whittier and Mrs. Celia Thaxter [1] began in the early sixties when he and his sister spent a vacation at her residence in the Isles of Shoals. She had already achieved a reputation as a poet, for Lowell had published her poem 'Landlocked' in the 'Atlantic Monthly.' She was unhappily married to Levi Lincoln Thaxter, the Browning scholar, who was much older than she. They were temperamentally incompatible, since she was worldly, while her husband preferred his study. 'Life became difficult and full of problems to them both,' according to her friend, Mrs. Fields; 'their natures were strongly contrasted but could not complement each other because he fell in love with her as a "child."' Even though Mrs. Thaxter was a married woman she fascinated Whittier, but he was too cautious to allow himself to become completely carried away by her charms. Lucy Larcom, who envied Mrs. Thaxter for her hold upon Whittier, wrote to her (in 1867): 'You *are* an enchantress. It is a great gift to *hold* and attract as you can, and rare even among women.'

Whittier liked to sit in her parlor hour by hour, and watch

[1] Celia Thaxter was born June, 1835, and died August, 1894.

her paint; under her benign influence he would lose his shyness and discourse eloquently, usually on religious topics. She would humor him, and read to him when he asked her to do so. When he returned home, he would write her enthusiastic letters recalling his pleasant times at Appledore. He would throw in such compliments as he heard about her from personages like Horace Greeley and Dickens; he would repeat to her any favorable comment about her that reached him, such as that she was the best-dressed woman in the world. He would pay tribute to her cultural gifts by sending one of his own poems for emendations. He exchanged books with her. When he sent her 'Mabel Martin,' she wrote to Mrs. Fields: 'Mr. Whittier has sent me a dear letter and *Mabel Martin*, with a poem written on the fly-leaf, — a little dear sweet poem all for poor ungrateful, undeserving me.'

Mrs. Thaxter survived both her husband (he died in 1884), and Whittier. The friendship between the bachelor poet and the unhappily married poetess, in modern Puritanical New England, was of course within the strictest limits of propriety. One is amazed that they had the courage to visit and write to each other as often as they did. She considered him New England's greatest lyric poet, one whose work comforted the old and inspired the young. 'His very name is a symbol of truth and unflinching integrity,' she once wrote.

She was not without influence upon his literary work. She inspired a sonnet when he left the Shoals for home the second summer of his stay there in the mid-sixties. He, on the other hand, persuaded her to write the prose poems that she collected in book form about the Shoals. To her he owed his poem 'The Wreck of Rivermouth,' which was prompted by the thought of her and of her sea stories and pictures. When writing it he wondered whether she would like it, for, as he wrote her he made her serve as a sort of tenth muse, since as a Quaker he could not have anything to do with the 'heathen nine.'

More attractive than even Mrs. Thaxter, and single besides, was the young poet Edna Dean Proctor,[1] whom Whittier greatly admired. Her friend Kate Sanborn wrote thus of her beauty:

'When I first met her at the home of Mrs. Storrs, I thought her one of the most beautiful women I had ever seen — of the Andalusian type — dark hair and lustrous starry eyes, beautiful features, perfect teeth, a slender willowy figure and a voice so unusual that it would lure a bird from the bough.... With those dark and glowing eyes looking into mine, I have listened until I forgot everything about me and was simply spellbound.'

Whittier was not only bewitched by her ravishing beauty but sincerely impressed by her poetic talents. 'I consider Miss Proctor one of the best women poets of the day,' he said to a friend, and then added, 'But why do I say *one* of the best? why not the best?'

After reading her poem 'The White Slaves' in the 'Independent' in 1860, he wrote to Theodore Tilton, the editor, that he greatly admired it. He was soon corresponding with the author. For a number of years they were merely two sympathetic literary persons discussing their art with each other. In the latter part of the sixties she was traveling in Europe, Asia, Africa, and again on the Pacific Coast. Ten years after they had begun their correspondence she asked him for either an autograph or an album verse, and he answered that there was nothing he would not gladly do for her asking. He angled for an invitation to visit her, which she finally sent. When he got a glimpse of the dark-haired beauty now past forty — either in Brooklyn or New England, it is not certain where — he became young again and felt his old passions awake. Later she paid him a return visit to Amesbury, and set him tingling with more ardor than ever.

'I wish I could see thee,' he wrote her after her visit, 'under my roof again! There is no dragon now to meet thee

---

[1] Edna Dean Proctor was born in 1828 and died Dec. 18, 1923. She lived first with the Storrs in Brooklyn and then in Framingham, Mass., after 1885.

on the threshold, and I should not mistake thee for an interviewer making like Capt. Cuttle "a note of it." Why can't thee come? It would be an act of discretion and Christian benevolence on thy part.' [1]

He soon again met her at the Claflins' in Boston. She entertained him with accounts of her travels in Russia, and interested him with discourses on Oriental literature. Impressed by her tales of travel in Egypt, her monologues about the Mohammedan religion, her descriptions of the ceremonies of the Greek Church, he told her that she brought the universe vividly before him.

'I had been for months literally starved for social and intellectual refreshment and communion,' he wrote her in 1873, 'and it was very pleasant to meet thee and others in Mrs. Claflin's parlors, amidst greenery and flowers, and before the cheerful woodfires. I ought to thank thee for much of the pleasure of that visit.' That same summer, anxious to see her and not hearing from her, he wrote her a letter in care of the 'Independent' 'to remind thee of thy promise last winter to make thy appearance in New England this summer. I should be very sorry to miss seeing thee, as I shall be away from home more or less. Will thee drop me a word and let me know something of thy prospects?' He heard from her that she was going either to the Isles of Shoals or to some lake; he replied that he hoped she would come to Amesbury as he was not sure whether his health would permit him to go to those resorts. In another letter the sly flatterer told her that a lady had recently spoken to him of that 'charming Miss Proctor whom she met at Hampton, who, she said, was the delight of everybody there. All which it was very pleasant to me to hear.' In the early winter of 1874, he wrote to her that he was suffering from sleeplessness, but added, 'All thy friends here wish thee could be with us again.' In November, 1875, he wrote,

---

[1] All excerpts from letters of Whittier to Miss Proctor are from the collection of fifty-four manuscript letters to her in the New Hampshire Historical Society, Concord, N.H., presented by her nephew Mr. David Proctor, of New York.

'I was greatly disappointed in not seeing thee when thee was in New England.' In the winter he wanted to go to New York — 'I do look forward to it, and as one of its strong inducements, a visit to thee and thy friends.' After he moved to Danvers in 1876, he begged her to visit him — to discuss Ann Putnam and other witches! 'Are thee not of Danvers origin? Proctor is a Danvers name of witch memories.... I wish thee could come here, when I am here this summer, and, in the twilight, we will let our fancies "materialize" her [Ann Putnam] and her weird companions.'

That summer, from Mrs. Celia Thaxter's Appledore house in the Isles of Shoals, he wrote, to Miss Proctor: 'I heartily wish thee could be here this beautiful morning. May I not hope to see thee this summer? My niece is keeping house very pleasantly in Portland, but I have two cousins in my house in Amesbury and I shall be glad to see thee there.'

Later in the year, on his sixty-ninth birthday, she sent him a beautiful scarf, which he highly appreciated. She continued sending him scarfs for years on his birthday. He took her into his confidence, wrote of his aches and pains, of his brother's illness, of the Moody-and-Sankey religious revival in Boston (of which he only partly approved), of General Gordon whom he held in great esteem, for which Bright rebuked him. Even when he was eighty years old he wrote to her expressing his anxiety to see her. She continued sending him gifts and books.

Charming Miss Proctor! Did he want her, or did she want him? Or did they want each other? And if so why did they not marry? Who knows?

CHAPTER XXII

THE PROBLEM OF THE PHILANDERING CELIBATE

WHITTIER numbered among his friends women, both old and young, who felt only a purely intellectual sympathy for him. But it is singular that some of his so-called Platonic woman friends also doted on him and even fell in love with him. When women in their seventies older than he, or budding poets nearly half a century younger than he, courted him, he was perplexed how to treat them, for he wanted to preserve their own dignity for them. He must have pondered Goethe's famous maxim that Heaven gives us in abundance in old age what we have vainly sought in youth. He had craved feminine adoration as a young man; now he had a surfeit of it as an old man. The 'Pilgrims,' as he always referred to his woman admirers, were ever pursuing him; many of them had no claim upon him, yet he could not be discourteous to them. In one of the last letters he wrote in illness from Hampton Falls he said, 'The Pilgrims and reporters have found me out, and I am still annoyed by them.' [1]

As an example of how some of his Platonic woman friends wrote to him, even when he was past eighty years of age, take the following portion of a letter from an old friend, Harriet McEwen Kimball, a religious poet who herself was at the time not young, being fifty-six years old:

'It seems especially fitting, dear Mr. Whittier, that I should tell thee to-day once more how much thy affectionate interest has been to me since the gracious bestowal of it so many years ago. There is more, much more, in my heart that I would say, but "no words outworn suffice on lips or scroll."' [2]

---

[1] Whittier's remark about the woman pilgrims visiting him was written Aug. 28, 1892. In Albree.

[2] Manuscript letter of Miss Kimball in the Essex Institute, Dec. 17, 1890.

Whittier was not always free from blame for the love some of these women bore him, since he continued to correspond with them and encourage them when he knew they were in love with him.

As he never, so far as we know, had had physical relations with a woman in his life, although he was of a passionate temperament, he developed a neurosis, and thus he offers a problem to the psychologist. It becomes a little more complicated because, being the type of man who could not satisfy his passions in any other manner than through marriage, he refused to marry though he had many opportunities to do so. He also deliberately refused to give poetic expression to any phases of sexual life — a refusal that had an anæmic effect on his art. The story that he threw Whitman's 'Leaves of Grass' into the fire may well be believed, and the incident speaks for itself. The reaction was that of a patient who becomes angry at the doctor for telling him the truth about an ailment which he himself suspects he has. In short, Whittier thus confessed that he could not conceal his own inner thoughts and desires from Whitman; he resented his brother bard's speaking the truth so plainly for him. We know that he had his moments when he cried out under the tortures of the flesh and wanted them eased, and in one of his few rare moments of frankness he spoke out, in his poem 'My Namesake,' when he gave a picture of himself in his fiftieth year:

> 'His eye was beauty's powerless slave,
> And his the ear which discord pains;
> Few guessed beneath his aspect grave
> What passions strove in chains.'

He at least conceded the existence of sexual and moral conflicts, and he half-heartedly condoned the sins of others committed in the heat of passion. He was inconsistent, but in this respect he resembled Hawthorne, who, while attempting to be liberal, condemned his heroine Hester Prynne in the same breath with which he attacked the Puritans for punishing her as they did. Whittier's attitude toward the sex question was puritanical, but yet it had a tinge of modern radicalism. When he tried to be liberal he was merely taking refuge from his own narrow Puritanism; he never personally put any unconventional views of sex into practice.

We have several poems defining his liberal attitude toward sexual sinners. In 'John Underhill' (1873) he defended the repentant hero of the Pequot War, who had been guilty of illicit relations with another man's wife, for two reasons — because Underhill wiped out his sin by repentance and because he later redeemed himself by performing some noble exploits. He saw no reason why the Bay State should not count him with her worthy sons.

Similarly, in 'The Two Rabbins,' Whittier pleaded for charity toward sexual sinners. This last poem — a favorite of his, written when he was past sixty — was based on a Talmudic story. It was the tale of Rabbi Nathan, who, meeting a strong temptation at the age of fifty, 'sinned miserably.' Having determined to lay his sins before the righteous and wise Rabbi Ben Isaac, he journeyed to meet him — and almost came near to succumbing to temptation on the way. When he met Rabbi Ben Isaac, he told him of his sorrows and sin. But Rabbi Isaac, disclosing a hair shirt, confessed he was coming to *him* for help, since he himself had greatly transgressed in thought. Each then prayed for the other, and in this manner induced heaven to forgive them their sins! Without disputing the value of the doctrinal lesson of the poem, that sin, not being completely eradicable till the self is dead, must be forgotten in the service of love, we may at least ask whether unchaste thoughts are sin, and whether a normal sex life is not a more effective cure for them than prayer.

Yet we are led to wonder why Whittier ever wrote poems like 'John Underhill' and 'The Two Rabbins.' He himself was a man of spotless virtue who never yielded to temptation, and never trespassed upon the rights of others; he never even indulged in those sexual misdemeanors which those who believe in the double standard do not seriously condemn. Whittier never forgot that one of his most distinguished ancestors, the Reverend Stephen Bachelir, had been guilty of sexual lapses. He was not, as he showed in his poem 'The Wreck of Rivermouth,' ready to condemn him outright. But there were other reasons for his liberality. He had relatives and personal friends who had deviated, through the promptings of love or passion, from conventional conduct. While he was not ready to overlook their behavior, he did not abandon his friendly relations with them because of their irregularities. He saw that it was possible for many people momentarily to stray from the path of virtue.

He also tried to condone the sexual conduct of his idol Burns, but he solved the problem by evading it. If he found a matter unpleasant, he merely tried to dismiss it from his mind. This method of evasion is a common attitude taken by superficial critics of literature and life, but it is not the modern method of dealing with any evils, real or imaginary. Whittier, being a Puritan and a Quaker, but neither a sociologist nor a psychiatrist, did not probe deeply into the human heart. He understood his weakness in that respect when he wrote of himself in his 'Proem':

'Nor mine the seer-like power to show
The secrets of the heart and mind;
To drop the plummet-line below
Our common world of joy and woe,
A more intense despair or brighter hope to find.'

We understand now why in his beautiful poem 'Burns' he charitably ignored the poet's weaknesses. He believed that he disposed of the character of Burns by overlooking his frailties and forgiving him. No doubt, Whittier would have wanted the biography of Burns rewritten without any reference to his many indiscreet loves and his several illegitimate children. The artistic qualities of Burns's poems are not unconnected, however, with his moral deficiencies. Merely to dismiss these with a plea for forgiveness, without studying them to explain them, showed Whittier's artistic and moral limitations. He was not justified in concluding that the reader of Burns's poems need not listen to the evil strain that appeals to lawless love. While Whittier as a boy was deaf to this strain, as a grown man he was bound to investigate it. He left in old age the problem of the evil strain in Burns exactly where he found it as a boy:

> 'It died upon the eye and ear,
>   No inward answer gaining;
> No heart had I to see or hear
>   The discord and the staining.'

But what did Whittier the man think of Burns's life when he reread the poems?

Even though irregular conduct was out of the question so far as he himself was concerned, he used to apologize for his chastity. He gave a very curious reason for it, enigmatically summed up in a remark of his that he remained sexually virtuous because 'there must be one good Injun in the tribe.' By this he meant that he thought he should lead a conventional life all the more because some of his relatives did not. He would often repeat a story he once heard his father tell, about a tradition among the Indians that when an entire tribe went on a drunken spree, one Indian must remain sober to prevent any disaster to the rest of the tribe.

It was natural that, being a bachelor, he should often be asked by people why he never married. To those who had no right to question him he would give an evasive answer. To the relatives with whom he stayed in the latter part of his life he said that financial difficulties did not allow him to marry, but he admitted that he had been disposed to marry some Quaker woman whom he first met at the Friends' yearly meeting. In later life, according to his cousin Mrs. Abby J. Woodman, he was not deeply enough in love to marry any of the women he knew. Once he said that he had never married because matrimony was not a success in his family, and that while he agreed with Paul that those who marry do well, he agreed with him also that those who do not marry do better.

But his happiness in life was not complete. He was not as a celibate leading a life according to nature. He occasionally betrayed this fact in verses he composed for personal friends. To a girl who was being married he wrote: [1]

> 'Go, rest thy head upon a heart
> And life with life ally,
> Thy joy unshared is scarcely joy;
> Who better knows than I?'

One effect of his bachelor life was to make him curious about the love-affairs of others. He took an interest, not only in the love problems of the young, but in all stories of married life, whether happy or unhappy. He used to give suggestions and advice to young people; those who followed it usually profited by it. He prided himself on his belief that he could make better matches for the young people than they could themselves.

His numerous friendships with women at times aroused comment. In the summer of 1868 — the year when he was probably most occupied with visits from women — a plain-spoken woman neighbor of his called upon him on some matter of business. He told her that he could not, at the time, give her his undivided attention since two women were in the parlor waiting for him. She remarked: 'What? more of them? Was ever a man so beset? But it's good enough for you. You should have married a woman long ago, and she would have kept all the rest off.'

Undoubtedly his prolonged virginity had some relation to his nervous condition. One need not even be a Freudian to realize that. Surely a life not lived fully according to the dictates of nature was a greater factor in ruining his health, fraying his nerves and bringing on insomnia than was his eyestrain which Dr. George M. Gould held responsible for

[1] In poem 'Epithalamium' in Claflin, pp. 69–70.

Whittier's troubles. The fact remains, however, that the poet used to bemoan the youthful peaceful sleep he had once known, would lie awake and look forward with eagerness to the coming of the dawn. In the early morning he would come downstairs worn and haggard.

His bachelorhood and virginity also had a ruinous effect artistically upon his poems. He rarely introduced the note of passion; he did not write of the ecstasy of love; he depicted few situations in which intense sex emotion disturbed people, as he once did in his uncollected poem 'The Vestal.' He laid emphasis exclusively upon purity and tenderness in his love poetry. He dared not praise any form of sex life, for he would be aggravating his own suffering by painting in glowing terms a life he had missed. The Puritan could not sing approvingly about that of which he was deprived. He was thus unconsciously employing a defense mechanism.

But he did re-introduce a note in love poetry. He re-advanced the view, that dwelling on the memory of a past love renews the youth of man and effects his moral reformation. This note of harping on memories of a past love, a note characteristic of his latest and best poems, had already appeared in some of his early poems. It was part of the influence of the sentimental poems of Felicia Hemans, L. E. L., and Lydia H. Sigourney, which he never altogether outgrew.

No doubt Whittier's conception of love as a tender memory of the past carrying in its wake inspiration to higher things savors of mediæval romantic devotion, and old-fashioned Platonic love. It tends to encourage a morbid psychic life. To linger tenderly upon the thought of a loved one of the past, especially of one who had shown herself cruel and deceitful, is not altogether a healthy state. But Whittier was not morbid in his brooding.[1] Those who gather from his sentimental poems that he was a sad, lonely old bachelor bemoaning everlastingly the lost love of his youth

[1] Mrs. Grantham informed me that Whittier was not of a brooding nature and that he said that his love poems were poetic licenses.

have not read him aright. He was following, however, an unconscious trait in human nature that urges one to look back with tenderness upon past events which might have had a happy conclusion. In the halo of distant time he naturally conjured up mental pictures of his old loves. On a few occasions he consciously gave them poetic expression, but he regarded them as products of a poetic license.

'Memories,' 'My Playmate,' and 'A Sea Dream' are sure of immortal life, for they strike a universal note; they are uttered with ecstasy and art, and they appeal to man and to child, to the worldly and to the unsophisticated.

Though the love poems of Whittier's later life showed far greater art than those of his youth, they were less spontaneous. The paramount note was forced tenderness and uncalled-for sacrifice, rather than warm passion or healthy indignation. In fact, he was more sentimental in old age than he was in youth; then he was more bitter and more human. He now forgot how he had raged against Mary Emerson Smith and had even had murderous thoughts when she married someone else. Overlooking her selfishness, he sang tender songs about her. Though as a result of his experience with her he wrote poems condemning mercenary marriages, he nevertheless inconsistently enough celebrated in hymns of tenderness a woman who had caused the great tragedy of his life.

Why did Whittier write poems of tenderness and sacrifice? Why did he remain a celibate? (And a virgin? the sophisticates would ask.) What made him play the philanderer? These are questions that have never been completely answered. It is very easy to dispose of them in the usual way, by saying that he was now too old or invalided to marry, that he was afraid of marriage because of unhappy experiences in his own family, that he really never cared for any of his hundred woman friends. It is also apparently easy to explain his virginity by attributing it to his Quaker training, to the religious views and moral tendencies he had imbibed from childhood. It is natural, too, to account for his philandering by his desire for intellectual communion, by his undoubted vanity, by his craving for feminine society, especially after his mother and sister died.

No doubt these explanations help in some degree to shed light on the mysteries. Modern psychologists could offer other reasons to unravel the problems. They would probably show that Whittier suffered from an unconscious over-attachment for his mother, as well as from a sister complex, because he had never broken completely away from their unconscious influences, and, therefore, never found any other woman to replace them; for it is true that both his mother and his sister dominated him. The psychologists could point out that his brother Matthew, not suffering from mother- and sister-complexes, did marry.

Since psychoanalytical critics will no doubt in the future deal with Whittier, we may as well anticipate, though not necessarily accept, their findings. The obvious interpretation of Whittier that the psychoanalysts will give, though they will never have the complete evidence to support their views, will be that he suffered from psychic impotence. They will no doubt succeed in building up a general case to support this view, but they will find complete evidence and the necessary details to sustain them lacking. Whittier's case at first glance appears to fit into Freud's explanation of psychic impotence. For, according to Freud, psychic impotence results whenever the sentiments of tenderness and sexuality do not harmoniously fuse. Their inability to blend is due to the man's having fixed his tenderness too strongly, from early childhood, upon a mother or sisters, and to his having clung to them unconsciously at puberty, but with fear because of the horror of incest. The impotence is aggravated by disappointment in love and by virginity. We have seen that Whittier felt an over-attachment for both his mother and his sister, that he was rejected by Mary Emerson Smith and Cordelia Russ, and that he never engaged in illicit sexual relations. We have seen that he decided not to marry Elizabeth Lloyd, though he had proposed to her and been accepted; that while he gave difference of religion as the barrier between them, he admitted to her that his old fears of not being able to make a woman happy came back to him. He also continued making love to women the rest of his life without proposing marriage. Finally he deliberately avoided introducing passion into his poetry, but infused tenderness into it instead. All these characteristics on the surface lend plausibility to the psychoanalytic view as to his impotence. We cannot definitely accept the theory, however, for lack of evidence regarding the secret details of the poet's life. We can never say with certainty that he was impotent; very likely, had he married, he would have achieved a normal life.

Whittier's love life was the very reverse of the traditional one of the dissipated and irresponsible poet, different from that of Baudelaire and Verlaine, from that of Byron and that of Heine. We have pointed out the weakening effects upon his physical health of his ascetic views and life. Noble as he was, he also serves as a warning that an unnatural education, unreasonable asceticism, and the ignoring of psychological factors in one's life may be deleterious.[1]

---

[1] No attempt has ever been made to enumerate all of Whittier's woman friends. We now know more about some of them from their letters recently deposited in the Essex Institute. This collection contains many unpublished letters, some important like those from the novelist Catherine Sedgwick and the Cary sisters. Women came to him for favors. Alice Cary, in a manuscript letter, Sept. 22, 1866, asked him to write about her poems. Julia C. R. Dorr in 1865 asked him to use his influence to have her poems accepted by the *Atlantic Monthly*.

CHAPTER XXIII

THE POETICAL WORK OF HIS LATER YEARS

THE year 1869, when Whittier published 'Among the Hills,' represents the high-water mark of his poetic career. From that time on he expressed few new ideas and rarely indulged in any variations from his established style. Though poems on Oriental or Teutonic subjects came from his pen, the sentiments in them were of a Puritanical stamp and the characters were pure Quakers with foreign names. Yet some of the later poems, like 'In School Days' and 'The Three Bells,' became as popular as some of the poems of his middle period. His last books were sufficiently meritorious to make the reputation of a new poet, but they were, like Tennyson's new volumes of the same period, repetitions of his old self. His art, however, remained on a fairly high level, although the old poetic fire burned with a dull glow.

He did not grow intellectually, though his scholarship widened. He frequently reiterated platitudinous preachments and he often descended to downright triteness. He wearied the reader with constant harping on the generosity of providence, the salubrity of prayer, and the infallible supremacy of the Inner Light. His recurrence to New England legends, while edifying, showed that he had exhausted his originality. His preoccupation with religious themes and hymns proved that his intellectual faculties were atrophied. His later poems were characterized almost uniformly by purity and piety, but, while not great, were not inferior to the poems that many new poets were writing at the time.

Whittier's literary decline began with 'Miriam, and other Poems,' in 1871, continued in the 'Pennsylvania Pilgrim,' issued the next year, and reached a low ebb four years later in 'Hazel Blossoms' — a volume that he padded with poems by his sister. There was a flaring up of poetic fire in 'The Vision of Echard' (1878) to burn, however, with diminished glow in the four final volumes of his poetic career, 'The King's Missive' (1881), 'The Bay of Seven Islands' (1883), 'Saint Gregory's Guest' (1886), and 'At Sundown' (1892); yet by these eight volumes he won anew his way into the public heart.

In 'The Vision of Echard' the aged poet succeeded for once in recapturing some of the poetic glow of his youth. In fact, some of the poems are more dexterously finished than anything else that he ever wrote. The ballad 'The Witch of Wenham,' which Howells selected in his review in the 'Atlantic Monthly' as the finest poem of the book, is one of the glories of American legendary and regional literature. In 'Sunset on the Bearcamp' Whittier does not desecrate his descriptions of nature with a sermon. Unfortunately, in 'The Seeking of the Waterfall,' in comformity with his Puritanical temperament, he does combine scenery and morality.

The book fired the enthusiasm of a young editorial writer on the New Orleans 'Item,' Lafcadio Hearn. Although he was a pantheist and a devotee of Gautier, he found himself surprisingly moved by the poems in which theology and morality were wedded to art. In a glow of enthusiasm he wrote in his review: [1]

'No volume of American authorship has this year appeared which ranks so high, or merits so warm a welcome as this collection of charming poems. Never has the Quaker poet sung more sweetly; never has he uttered prayers more beautiful than these. That wonderful gift of melody — that song with never a discordant note — that rhythmic flow, limpid and pure and strong, in which Whittier is unsurpassed, seems to mellow with years like good wine. It is not less enchanting in its sweet solemnity to-day than in the year when

[1] *New Orleans Item*, Dec. 4, 1878. Collected in *Essays on American Literature*, by Lafcadio Hearn, with an introduction by Albert Mordell, edited by Professor Sanki Ichikawa, The Hokuseido Press, Tokyo, Japan, 1929.

"Maud Muller" touched the heart of all the English speaking world.'

Hearn quoted the two narrative poems, 'The Witch of Wenham' and 'Solomon and the Ants,' and praised also two of the religious poems, 'The Vision of Echard' and the 'Two Angels.'

The eight volumes of new poetry that Whittier wrote in the last twenty years of his life are not significant historically in our letters. They even had a pernicious influence in moulding American literary taste, for they led to the prevailing view that the paramount requisites of great poetry were purity and piety. But as evidence that an aged poet may wield the magic wand with greater powers of enchantment than he commanded in his youth they are unique in our literature.

The most important literary work that he undertook in the last years of his life was a revision and a rearrangement of his poetry and prose for the seven-volume Riverside Edition of his works issued in 1888 and 1889. By assembling his poems under headings of common themes, Whittier himself did much to bring about a misconception of his work, for he cast out of historical perspective and chronological sequence many of his poems, the understanding of which depends upon a knowledge of the circumstance of their origin. He tried unsuccessfully to overcome the difficulty by a series of notes, as Wordsworth did in a similar rearrangement of his poems in a definitive edition. Though there is no doubt that he was right in putting into separate groups many of the poems, like the legendary, religious, and antislavery poems, he inserted poems that did not fit into these classifications, and he placed in close proximity to one another poems that were composed many years apart. It is often difficult to see why a particular poem was assigned to a particular one of the sections 'Poems of Nature,' 'Personal Poems,' 'Occasional Poems,' and 'Poems Subjective and Reminiscent'; when it might with equal propriety have been placed in any other of these divisions. He was especially prone to include religious poems among the 'Narrative and Legendary Poems.' In making his classifications he forced poems into divisions where they did not fit. In the chronological list of his poems at the end of the collection he occasionally made errors, especially in the early dates.[1] To this edition, however, he added an appendix, in very small type, containing twenty-three early and uncollected poems, including two poems from the 'Legends of New England,' and his long poem 'Mogg Megone.'

The four volumes of collected poetry received a favorable reception from the critics. One of the most intelligent of the notices was an unsigned one in the New York 'Tribune' in which the reviewer laid emphasis on the importance and value of the antislavery poems in the collection.

[1] It is said that Horace Scudder helped in compiling the list.

CHAPTER XXIV

REACTIONARY

WHITTIER was a member of the Republican Party and always supported its candidate for President. To the end of his life he was consulted by politicians for his opinions of local and State candidates for office. While he insisted on personal integrity in the character of officials, once opposing a personal friend for a high office because of some 'affair' in his private life, he always adopted the platform and policies of his party. He was even in favor of the impeachment of Johnson, whom historians in our day have fully exonerated. In a letter dated May 16, 1868, to Horace Greeley,[1] Whittier wrote:

'Impeachment I see has failed. Well — it is unfortunate; but let us not lament over it, nor quarrel about it, more than we can help. Our business now is to elect Grant, and in his election impeachment is not an issue at all; — and whoever goes for the Republican candidate, must be recognized as a Republican whatever his views may have been of the propriety of impeachment.'

He was gratified by Grant's victory and wrote a poem 'After Election' expressing his satisfaction. In 1872 he supported Grant for a second term instead of Greeley, who was running for President on the Liberal Republican and Democratic tickets.

In October 21, 1872, he wrote to Dr. Joseph G. Holland:[2]

'I am glad the election is close at hand; its personalities and bitterness vex me. I shall vote for Grant though I like Greeley personally, so well that I should be sorry to see him

[1] Manuscript letter dated May 16, 1868, to Greeley in Ford Collection, New York Public Library.

[2] Manuscript letter to Joseph G. Holland, who gave it to Rodney A. Mercur, Esq., of Towanda, Pa., its present owner.

President under the circumstances. The bad antecedents of the bulk of his supporters and the honorable prestige of the Republican Party in the past are against him. But all through I have defended him as a good and great man, when I heard him personally assailed.'

After the close of the Civil War Whittier's reforming instincts became quiescent, and his interest in radical movements practically ceased. Having witnessed the triumph of the cause he fought for, he settled down to a serene old age. It never occurred to him that 'emancipation' had not really freed the slaves; nor did he realize that in many respects the slave was now in a worse position than before, because of a caste system. He disapproved of any efforts at making former rebellious Southerners give superfluous parts of their land to the colored people — property which they had created and increased in value by the sweat of their brow. He forgot the clause in the Declaration of Sentiments that read: 'If compensation is to be given at all, it should be given to the outraged and guiltless slaves, and not to those who have plundered and abused them.' He failed to recognize the one great blunder in the emancipation of slavery — a blunder which historians are still not willing to admit — the government's neglect to help the freedmen economically.

He never dreamed that we might have followed Russia who not only emancipated her serfs but gave them land on easy terms of redemption. In his now patently naïve verses 'To the Thirty-Ninth Congress,' the first of his reactionary poems, he sought mercy for the recent 'rebels,' but left labor, both black and white, to the mercy of our lawmakers.

> 'Give black and white an equal vote.

> 'Keep all your forfeit lives and lands,
> But give the common law's redress
> To labor's utter nakedness.'

Like many others in the North, Whittier held in horror Thaddeus Stevens's 'communistic' idea of confiscating both the land owned by rebellious States and the portions of private estates that exceeded two hundred acres for the benefit chiefly of the freed blacks.

Labor problems at no time vitally concerned him, any more than they did most of the other abolitionists. None of the financial panics he lived through had ever called forth any verse from him. The chief social problems that occupied him in middle life were pacifism, prohibition, repeal of the laws for imprisonment for debt, and the abolition of capital punishment; on these questions he never changed his mind, and even late in life he wrote a poem, 'Disarmament,' in the cause of pacifism. He saw some of the reforms, for which he had fought in early years, adopted by various States.

While theoretically he sympathized with the laboring classes, he did not believe that strikes would redress their grievances. Though he did not disapprove of shorter hours and better wages for the workingmen, he wanted them to wait patiently till legislative bodies, in spite of their imperviousness to the demands of labor, should finally decide to comply with them by adequate legislation.

It is true that Whittier could not very well agitate for the rights of labor because of his age and invalidism. There was, however, another reason. Having become wealthy, he unconsciously identified his interests with the middle class to which he belonged. His friends now numbered well-to-do merchants and conservative public statesmen, corporation officers and men in high political positions. He became intellectually atrophied; he sank more and more into recreancy; he became a less militant and striking figure than of old.

On labor questions, and economic problems, he was profoundly ignorant. He once said, 'I do not know enough of this particular movement to feel authorized in expressing a decided opinion.'

In the late seventies, not many years after the sixty-hour-a-week work law went into effect in Massachusetts, he published that naïve and discreditable poem called 'The Problem,' in which he virtually deserted the cause of liberty. He assailed those idealists who fought for labor reforms as 'demagogues' proffering their vain and evil counsels; he assured the workingmen that they would find 'no answer in the catchwords of the blind leaders of the blind.' Believing he found in the Golden Rule of Christ the sole remedy to solve economic questions, he denied that there was a class struggle and asserted that the interests of the rich and poor were one and the same, inseparable. Even if the poor suffered, he found that suffering taught valuable lessons:

> 'Yea, even self-wrought misery and shame
> Test well the charity suffering long and kind.'

He tried to justify the present system by showing that the laborer derived benefits from his poverty, and that the employer had his moral sensitiveness deepened by his responsibilities for the welfare of many subordinates! He used the same arguments in defense of wage slavery that the Southern slaveholders had in behalf of their 'peculiar' institution. He considered every millionaire a Christlike, thin-skinned, gentle Friend like himself.

Yet in this very year we find him contributing to a monument for Ferdinand Freiligrath, the foremost liberal German poet of the age, mistakenly believing himself in sympathy with him. But he was thinking of Freiligrath only as one whose work had cheered the American abolitionists in the early days. Yet at the time, Whittier was rejoicing in the inauguration of President Hayes because he was safer than Tilden. Whittier surely knew that Freiligrath was a close friend of Karl Marx — indeed, one of the few men with whom Marx did not quarrel — and that he was in sympathy with socialism. Whittier knew that Freiligrath approved of those very demagogues that he himself had attacked in 'The Problem.' In short, he remained under the illusion that he was still a great liberal, and akin to the German poet who had sacrificed a pension and courted exile, and written the most revolutionary poetry of the time.

Since 'The Problem' was published in 1877 when the great railroad strikes in America broke out, the year in which the Socialist Labor Party was founded, it was particularly injurious and offensive to the cause of labor. Even though Whittier was right in condemning the strikers for their violent measures, he remained silent on the just grievances they had. Nor did he utter a syllable against the State or Federal authorities for shedding the blood of the workingmen. Although the men lost the strike, public sentiment in his own State began stirring itself in behalf of the laboring classes. Massachusetts passed the Factory Acts to protect their health and lives, showing that she recognized them as human beings.

Whittier cannot, because of his age, be altogether blamed for not entering into any new battle. 'Against all my natural inclinations,' he wrote to Elizabeth Stuart Phelps in 1878, 'I have been fighting for the "causes" half my life. I suppose I am growing old, and am disposed to ask for peace in my day.' About the same time he wrote to Gail Hamilton, 'I have had enough of fighting in the old days.' If, however, we do not expect an invalid who had done his reform work in his youth to enlist in his old age with the advance guard in liberal movements, we do not expect him to ally himself against the class from which he rose. Yet that is what he did. Thinking that the Civil War had solved all the problems of the country, when it really raised more complicated ones than ever, he applauded the feeble efforts of the employers to patronize the poor. When Winthrop sent him a copy of his Centennial Oration on the surrender of Yorktown, in which he uttered the most absurd platitudes on the question of solving all ills of the day, by such remedies as teaching religion, keeping the workingman in his place, stamping out any innovations offered by political theorists, and ignoring mod-

ern philosophers and scientists, Whittier highly praised the
unsound curatives offered by a man — noble as he was —
whose deviation from the cause of liberty Emerson noted
thirty years previously.

'To me the noblest and most striking feature of the Oration is the eloquent word lesson of its concluding pages — a
timely and needed lesson, solemn and earnest as the utterances of Hebrew prophecy and warning, clothed in fitly-
chosen words of beauty. In a literary point of view there is
nothing in American eloquence superior to it.' [1]

While the telegraph operators were getting ready to strike
for increased wages, extra pay for Sunday work and an eight-
hour day, Whittier, on Independence Day of 1883, wrote
'Our Country,' a Fourth-of-July oration in verse, in which he
virtually assumed that officials in a republic can do no wrong.
Forty-five years before he had written in an editorial in the
'Era' that tyranny may exist even under republics. Now the
gist of his contention was that we hear only complaints about
the evils of our time, but little comment upon the good. He
solves all problems by saying that we must leave everything
to hope, for eventually the country would make Labor full
requital. In the abolition days he vigorously resorted to political action to exterminate the evils of slavery.

A poem with such sentiments naturally pleased the political party in power. In fact, a politician read it at a Republican campaign meeting some years later in Philadelphia, in an
effort to defeat for governor the election of Ex-Governor
Robert E. Pattison — who was supported by one of the
foremost liberals of the state, Judge James Gay Gordon.

In the eighties, when the Knights of Labor were growing in
numbers and the working classes were combining to be the
sole judges as to what were their wrongs and to demand

[1] Manuscript of Whittier's letter to Winthrop, Nov. 25, 1881, in Massachusetts
Historical Society. The oration Whittier praised is in *Addresses and Speeches of
Various Occasions, from 1876–1886* by Robert C. Winthrop, 1886, 'The Hundredth
Anniversary of the Surrender of Lord Cornwallis.' Oration delivered at Yorktown,
Virginia, Oct. 19, 1881, pp. 296–349.

their own remedies, Whittier offered them platitudes on free
schools and taxation:

> 'Give every child his right of school,
> Merge private greed in public good,
> And spare a treasury overfull
> The tax upon a poor man's food.'

He even abandoned his concern for oppressed smaller nations, except in the case of the Indians. Toward the end of
1881, while Parnell was languishing in jail as a result of the
enforcement of the Coercion Law, Whittier, losing sight of
the grievance of the Irish in his condemnation of the atroci-
ties they committed, criticized Bright and Forster for leni-
ency — Forster whom the Irish hated for the Coercion Law:

'I see nothing for the Government to do,' he wrote, 'but
lay a heavy hand on the brutal and cowardly assassins who
think it right and proper to murder a neighbor who is honest
enough to pay his debts. It is impossible to reason with un-
reason like theirs. It seems to me that such men as Bright
and Forster have gone to extremes in their concessions to
Ireland, so far as rent is concerned.'

Where was the youthful poet who penned the songs of
liberty for Ireland and Greece? Where was the middle-aged
bard who sympathized with the struggles of France, Hun-
gary, and Italy? What had become of the man who fulminated
against Pope Pius IX and who sang of the glory of Kossuth?

Whittier does not appear in an amiable light in another
matter of national interest. The Quaker and reformer who
was opposed to capital punishment refused to intervene for
clemency in behalf of the Chicago anarchists who were unjustly under sentence of death. Howells, believing they had
not had a fair trial, revealed a more admirable figure than
Whittier, and endeavored to induce him to join in a protest
for clemency.

'I enclose a paper,' wrote Howells, November 1, 1887, in a
letter that has never been published,[1] 'on the anarchists by

[1] Manuscript of Howells letter dated Nov. 1, 1887, in Essex Institute.

a very good and very able young minister of Chicago. The conclusions reached there I reached many weeks and even months ago. The fact is that those men were sentenced for murder when they ought to have been indicted for conspiracy.

'I believe the mind of the Governor of Illinois is turning towards clemency; several things indicate this. A letter from you would have great weight with him. I beseech you to write it, and do what one great and blameless man may do to arrest the greatest wrong that ever threatened our fame as a nation. Even if these men had done the crime which our barbarous laws punish with enormitude, should a plea for mercy be wanting from *you*?'

He asserted that the press was absolutely wrong in the matter, and all the more guiltily so because ignorantly; and he pleaded with the poet to write and sign his honored and beloved name immediately, since the time was short.

Whittier flatly refused. Instead of complying with Howells's request, he virtually told him to write the letter himself, giving as an excuse for his refusal, that Howells could do it better. He added that though he did not believe in capital punishment, he was not disposed to interfere with these criminals, because they were more dangerous than other murderers. Howells did write the letter, sending a copy of it to the New York 'Tribune.' He forwarded the original to Illinois, but it only found its way to the State archives, then kept by a young man who was very much in sympathy with its purpose — Brand Whitlock. A reporter, who, meanwhile, had talked to Whittier on the subject, published an interview with him in the New York 'Tribune,' making some misrepresentations which almost brought the friendship of both famous writers to an end.

Howells protested to Whittier about some facts in the 'Tribune' article, and Whittier replied:[1]

'I think thee states that thee thought they had not had a

[1] Letter dated Dec. 19, 1888. Pickard, Vol. II, pp. 735–736.

fair trial, and that this induced thee to urge the petition. In conversing with the writer of the letter, I think I said that I supposed thee thought that the extreme penalty of death might cause the victims to be regarded as martyrs; and I mentioned that thy interest in Count Tolstoi's non-resistance views, with which I have much sympathy myself, may have influenced thee in this case. The writer of the 'Tribune' letter is a truthful and honorable gentleman, and if his version of the matter is incorrect it is doubtless owing to a lack of explicitness on my part, in a desultory conversation.... I would be the last person to believe that the crime charged upon the accused persons is less detestable and awful to thee than to myself.'

Some of the anarchists were executed and others were imprisoned. A few years later Governor Atgeld exercised clemency to those still in jail, on the ground that the jurymen were not fairly chosen, and that it was never shown that the unknown man who threw the bomb had ever read any of the writings of the anarchists. Atgeld believed that society, eager to avenge the blood of the murdered policemen, unjustly made the unpopular anarchists scapegoats for the crime. Many members of the laboring classes themselves thought that the executions were instigated as a lesson to them to compel them to renounce their appeals for economic justice. Even Whittier's belief in the guilt of the men does not excuse his negligence in doing nothing to save them. Since he had always opposed capital punishment, he should have helped Howells, even if he did not agree with him that the men had not had a fair trial. The courageous action of Howells, who hated violence and crime as much as Whittier did, will always be remembered in contrast.

Whittier's turning away from the cause of liberty in his old age paralleled the case of Wordsworth. But no Shelley nor Browning to condemn him in blasting verse for his apostasy appeared in America. He was immune from danger of attacks, even upon his dignity. The elder New England poets had already become sacrosanct. Mark Twain almost lost his reputation because at the seventieth-birthday dinner to Whittier he read a fictitious sketch in which he merely familiarly handled men like Longfellow and Emerson.

But other former fellow-workers of Whittier kept more abreast of the times. Wendell Phillips took an interest in the cause of labor, and Samuel E. Sewall, the former antislavery lawyer, when past eighty left the Republican Party because he believed it was no longer operated on its early ideals. Whittier, at the age of seventy-eight, after Cleveland's election, wrote a letter that reads like a stump speech, saying that he felt proud of the noble record of the Republican Party and that he believed it would virtually bring in the millennium.

A fortune of over a hundred thousand dollars, no doubt, helped make Whittier indifferent to the so-called poverty question that was stirring the country after the panic of the seventies, and to the various labor troubles in the eighties. Henry George, who was arousing the nation, had no influence upon Whittier; the spread of the Socialist movement also left him unmoved.

When Whittier did speak on the subject of labor, he betrayed utter ignorance of the economic foundations and growth of society. In a letter written in his eighty-second year he stated that the chief causes of poverty were intemperance, idleness, and refusal to save money when wages were good. He said that if every small town, and even every city, only practiced economy and sobriety, the country would solve the economic question; in support of his theory he referred to a town whose inhabitants had reduced their cost of living to three hundred dollars a family. Such views for the solution of the evils of our industrial system are too naïve to be taken seriously. Did he not realize that many wealthy people grew richer through exploitation in spite of their own idleness, intemperance, and extravagance? Did he never suspect that there was something wrong with our system of distribution of wealth? Could he not see about him that public-utility corporations were obtaining franchises on public property and yet were exorbitant in their rates? What folly it was to say that the reason the small wage-earners could not make ends meet was that they were extravagant! How could he recommend the gospel of Poor Richard's almanac to remedy our economic evils? How could he say that it was the poor man's own fault that he was poor?

'In the quiet of his country home at Danvers,' Howells wrote in 'Literary Friends and Acquaintances,' 'he apparently read all the magazines, and kept himself fully abreast of the literary movement, but I doubt if he so fully appreciated the importance of the social movement. Like some others of the great anti-slavery men, he seemed to imagine that mankind had won itself a clear field by destroying chattel slavery, and he had no sympathy with those who think that the man who may any moment be out of work is industrially a slave. This is not strange; so few men last over from one reform to another that the wonder is that any should, not that one should not.'

As Whittier could not himself face the unpleasant realities in life, he disapproved of the efforts of others to probe into social evils.

Whittier's later poems are deficient not only because they are tainted with Puritanism but because they are steeped in nineteenth-century respectability. Enslaved to the ideals of the middle class of which he was a representative, he debased his art. He virtually believed that since slavery was abolished there were no more social abuses to remedy. Either he remained silent on the subject, or offered as remedies worthless panaceas. He offered the Golden Rule of Christ as the solution of all economic problems — and yet approved of a high protective tariff. If he reread his old poem 'The Reformer,' he should have had a sensation akin to that of Robert Southey when he glanced over his early rebel poem 'Wat Tyler.'

Though Whittier inherited many of the ideas of the old Puritans and Quakers, he was, in his later phase, a Victorian middle-class author, with all the limitations, as well as the virtues, of that class. He was nearer to Tennyson than he was to Anne Bradstreet. Because he accepted without question the surroundings of his later life, he became the most popular American poet next to Longfellow. The fiery radicalism of Milton departed from his soul and the stolidity of a renegade Wordsworth entered instead.

Mr. V. F. Calverton has made the observation that our industrial environment, rather than old Puritanism, ruined some of our nineteenth-century writers. This applies especially to Whittier, whose sexual reticence, false optimism, and economic blindness, more than his technical defects, have affected the value and beauty of his work. He does not, however, lose his universal appeal to us as an artist, because he voices the emotions that we all, Puritan and Pagan, radical and conservative, rich and poor, have in common. He is not inferior to franker but less gifted modern poets; any more than is the reticent Dickens inferior to, say an able sex novelist like D. H. Lawrence, or the romantic Scott to a gifted social novelist like Upton Sinclair.

To some extent the neglect that has befallen Whittier was deserved, for, in his later phase especially, he is provincial and lacking in virility. Our generation is indifferent to the eternal ballads of New England history and legend, with their constant harping on the same theme, and their everlasting conclusion with the same obvious, trite moral. Since no one now denies that the Puritans were wrong in persecuting and executing witches and Quakers, why the almost meaningless and gratuitous repetitions of the same story? Why dwell on the griefs of witches' daughters or the early sufferings of a sect who are now universally loved? Many of us are gloriously unmindful of what went on in the communities in Massachusetts among some well-meaning bigots. Writers should protest against abuses in our day; they should look for plots in the lives about us. The wrongs of the laboring classes, the question of a new attitude toward sex matters, deficiencies in governmental rule, the evils of industrialism and standardization are also subjects for the writer; yet Whittier ignored such themes. He was a propagandist — why did he cease being one in later years? Obviously the new propaganda of the vanguard of radical leaders was not to his taste; he therefore avoided the subject altogether.

It is very singular that the same religious sect should have produced two contemporary poets so different as were Whittier and Whitman. But they have many points of resemblance; they have even attracted the same admirers.

To show wherein Whittier and Whitman resemble each other is of no mere academic interest. They had in common a number of qualities, and in some respects their lives were not alike. Both were deeply influenced by their mothers, and both remained single all their lives. They were editors and reformers in their early years, interested in the same causes — antislavery, temperance, the abolition of capital punishment and of imprisonment for debt. They adopted the same political principles, those of the Free Soil Party, and they both saw active service in politics. They had the same religious training, and were imbued with the spirit of the same Quaker writers, though Whittier was orthodox and Whitman a Hicksite. They believed American poets should write about their own country and not rely on the themes supplied by ancient Greece and Rome. They associated with the common people, Whitman with cab-drivers and conductors, Whittier with the villagers and farmers. Whitman chanted in stately rhythms a cab-driver's funeral; Whittier celebrated in light verse a washerwoman's marriage.

Whitman was more independent, more original, more masculine. He had the greater mind, and did not allow his Quaker training to confine him to one or two petty ideas, though he is at times as illogical in his optimism as Whittier.

He could not lay claim to Whittier's courage, fervor, and self-sacrifice. In short he was not heroic like Whittier.

Whitman was more honest than Whittier artistically and more profound intellectually. He freely expressed the sexual life of man. He has helped to break up a faulty system of education, and to make life and literature less hypocritical. Our age has sustained Whitman for telling the truth about sex matters; it has admitted that Whittier erred by being so reticent.

In their mutual critical estimates of each other Whitman was fairer in his judgment. Whitman always admired Whittier and placed him among the first three or four great American poets, sometimes as third and sometimes as fourth on the list, putting Bryant, Emerson, and Longfellow above him.

'In Whittier,' he said, 'with his special themes — (his outcropping love of heroism and war, for all his Quakerdom, his verses at times like the measur'd steps of Cromwell's old veterans) — lives the zeal, the moral energy, that founded New England — that splendid rectitude and ardor of Luther, Milton, George Fox — I must not, dare not, say the wilfulness and narrowness — though doubtless the world needs now, and always will need, almost above all, just such narrowness and wilfulness.' [1]

Of Whittier's poetry Whitman said:

'Whittier's poetry stands for *morality* (not its *ensemble* or in any true philosophic or Hegelian sense, but) as filter'd through the positive Puritanical and Quaker filters; is very valuable as a genuine utterance; with many capital local and Yankee and *genre* bits — all unmistakably hued with zealous partisan anti-slavery coloring. Then the *genre* bits are all precious; all help. Whittier is rather a grand figure — a pretty lean and ascetic — no Greek — also not composite and universal enough (doesn't wish to be, doesn't try to be) for ideal Americanism.' [2]

---

[1] Whitman's *Complete Prose Works*, 'Specimen Days,' April 16, 1881, 'My Tribute to Four Poets,' p. 173.

[2] Letter to Kennedy, Oct. 10, 1889. Kennedy, II, pp. 220–221.

Whittier, on the other hand, not only felt hostility to Whitman, but showed it. When he contributed money to buy Whitman a horse and buggy, he was the only contributor who gratuitously offered an adverse criticism of 'Leaves of Grass,' saying that he was pained by some portions of it.

He did worse. Fearing that his monetary contribution laid him open to the charge of being an admirer of those terrible sex poems, he wrote a letter to show his friends that he did not approve of them. He intended sending the letter to the Boston 'Transcript' but fortunately never mailed it. The original letter, found among his papers after his death, is an unconscious revelation of his own poetic and human deficiencies.

A WORD OF EXPLANATION [1]

To the Editor of the Transcript:

I suppose it is a necessary consequence of one's notoriety of any kind to have all his words and acts regarded as public property and subjected to exaggeration and misrepresentation. Ordinarily one does not find it of much use to complain of this; but there are cases where it seems a matter of duty to make an explanation. A friend recently informed me that Walt Whitman of Newark [sic!] N.J., was in straitened circumstances, disabled and paralytic, and that an effort was being made to procure for him the means of exercise in the open air. I did not know him personally, and had but very slight knowledge of his writings, which, while indicating a certain virile vigor and originality, seemed to me often indefensible from a moral point of view.

But I had heard of his assiduous labors as a nurse in Union Hospitals, and had read his tender tribute to the memory of President Lincoln, and with no idea of its being made a matter of publicity, gave my mite for the object to which my attention was called, stating at the same time my feeling in regard to some portions of Whitman's writings, and my wish for his

[1] Whittier's intended letter to the *Boston Transcript*, in Albree, pp. 242–243.

own as well as the public's sake, for their expurgation. I should be extremely sorry to have a simple act of humanity on my part towards a suffering man regarded as sanctioning or excusing anything in his writings of an evil tendency.

With no wish to sit in judgment upon others, and making all charitable allowance possible for differences of temperament, education and association, I must confess to a strong dislike to what is sometimes called the sensual school of literature and art. My friend, Dr. Holmes, who was also a contributor, wishes me to say that his gift, like my own, was solely an act of kindness to a disabled author, implying no approval whatever of his writings.

JOHN G. WHITTIER

Whitman never saw this letter, but he occasionally heard of hostile remarks Whittier made about his work. These reports did not prevent him from contributing a few lines in praise of Whittier on the occasion of the celebration of his eightieth birthday — lines which Whittier acknowledged very diplomatically, in a brief note. Whitman, irritated by Whittier's refusal to commit himself about 'Leaves of Grass' in this letter, relieved himself of his feelings to Horace Traubel by saying that Whittier thus steered clear of trouble. He said that Whittier, in fact, felt too much respect for his Puritan conscience to commit himself. 'It has been a part of his business,' Whitman went on, 'to keep me at a distance, to discredit my work.... I know from this or that quoted from Whittier about me — words not so much of censure as of regret — that he got started wrong with the "Leaves" and never recovered.'[1]

[1] In Horace Traubel's *With Walt Whitman in Camden*, Vol. II, p. 7, report of conversation, July 16 and 17, 1888.

CHAPTER XXV

THE DECLINING YEARS

WHITTIER'S life of retirement after the close of the Civil War presented a marked contrast to his previous career of intense activity and controversy. Poverty no longer harassed him, for the increased royalties on his books enabled him to lead a life of ease. Only occasionally, as in the early seventies, when the Massachusetts legislature passed a vote of censure against Sumner for his motion in the Senate that regimental flags should not bear the names of the battles in which they were carried, did Whittier exhibit the fiery spirit of old. In an effort to have the vote of censure rescinded he attended meetings, sent out letters, and wrote articles. After two years his labors were crowned with success; but it was too late for Sumner to enjoy his vindication very long, since he died shortly afterwards.

For a few years after the close of our Civil War Whittier retained his interest in the struggle for liberty still going on in Europe. Calling himself a 'Republican radical,' he said that he was desirous that men of all creeds should enjoy the civil liberty that he prized so highly for himself. Whittier had watched the war for independence in Italy, and had written several poems that marked stages in its progress. In his sympathies with the efforts of the Italians to become a united people he attacked the papacy, not for its religion but for its political meddlings and recreancy. His poem 'Garibaldi' is significant, as revealing the poet in his old garb trumpeting the cause of liberty across the seas. It is apparent that he was still capable of righteous indignation and of writing with a pen as sharp as a poniard. In 1870, when unable to attend a celebration in New York commemorating the union of the Italian people, he wrote a letter — his last

utterance of importance in behalf of any form of liberty —
in which he made a thrust at the priests in America who were
not pleased with the news of Italian Independence. The following passage reminds one of his old diatribes against the
slave-defending clergy:

'It is reserved for American ecclesiastics, loud-mouthed in
professions of democracy, to make solemn protest against
what they call an "outrage," which gives the people of Rome
the right of choosing their own government, and denies the
divine right of kings in the person of Pio Nono.

'The withdrawal of the temporal power of the Pope will
prove a blessing to the Catholic Church, as well as to the world.
Many of its most learned and devout priests and laymen
have long seen the necessity of such a change, which takes
from it a reproach and scandal that could no longer be ex-
cused or tolerated.'

Now and then an important incident or event marred the
quietude of his life. In 1868 he came perilously near death
from illness. In the spring of 1870 he went to New York and
visited the Cary sisters and his old friend William H. Burleigh. We obtain a glimpse of his state of mind in the early
seventies from a letter to Mrs. Rebecca Allinson:[1]

'I have been unable to write much this winter — brief
answers to a very large & unhappily increasing correspondence, is as much & more than I can do. I meant to have
spent the mo. in Boston, but the great prevalence of small-
pox deterred me. I do not see a great deal of company at this
season, although strangers are frequently calling. Thee refer
to the "Penn. Pilgrim." It has been much better rec'd among
all sorts of people than I had reason to expect. I wish it were
better: but I was ill when writing it, & could not do the theme
justice. I want to publish an edition of Dymond to follow
John Woolman, if I can feel strong enough to write.'

As he grew older, he frequently had recourse to moods of

[1] Manuscript letter to Rebecca Allinson, lent by her daughter-in-law, the late
Mrs. Francis Greenleaf Allinson.

reminiscence, but to no events did he revert so frequently as to those connected with the old antislavery days. Though he did not like to revive ancient controversies, he could not help recounting tales about his own activities and experiences. Now that the abolitionists had triumphed, their struggles were of historical interest.

Prominent English novelists visiting in the country whom he met, men like Charles Dickens, George MacDonald, and Charles Kingsley, were probably more attracted to him by his reputation as an abolitionist than by his fame as a poet. When Longfellow and some friends once called on him, he proudly exhibited his signature on the copy of the charter of the American Anti-Slavery Society. With old antislavery friends he would exchange reminiscences of the days before the war; when he was lionized at gatherings he would entertain the guests by relating his experiences. Annie Fields heard him in 1866 recite the entire story of the mobbing he and George Thompson underwent at Concord.

To the end of his life he remained proud that he had been one of the protagonists in the abolition fight. When E. L. Godkin, editor of the 'Nation,' erroneously concluded from Whittier's portrait of himself in the 'Tent on the Beach' that the poet had regretted his early antislavery work, Whittier wrote to him:

'In the half playful lines, if I did not feel at liberty to boast of my anti-slavery labors, I certainly did not mean to underrate them or to express the shadow of a regret that they had occupied so large a share of my time and thought.' He added that he was grateful to Providence for having early called his attention to the interests of humanity.

Historical and biographical works about the abolition movement, in nearly all of which Whittier was favorably mentioned, now came from the press.

When the Philadelphia Female Anti-Slavery Society of Philadelphia held its final meeting, Whittier's old friend Lucretia Mott asked him for a poem. He complied with her request, and the Society published it in its annual report. Since Whittier has never collected it, and since it embodies some of his post-war views on the subject that occupied so many years of his life, I reprint it: [1]

'Oh! if the spirits of the parted come,
Visiting angels, to their olden home;
If the dead fathers of the land look forth
From their far dwellings, to the things of earth —
Is it a dream that with their eyes of love,
They gaze now on us from the bowers above?
Lay's ardent soul — and Benezet the mild,
Steadfast in faith, yet gentle as a child —
Meek-hearted Woolman — and that brother band,
The sorrowing exiles from their "Fatherland,"
Leaving their homes in Krieshiem's bowers of vine
And the blue beauty of their glorious Rhine,
To seek amidst our solemn depths of wood
Freedom from man and holy peace with God;
Who first of all their testimonial gave
Against the oppressor, — for the outcast slave,
Is it a dream that such as these look down,
And with their blessing our rejoicing crown?

' — not a slave beneath his yoke shall pine,
From broad Potomac to the far Sabine;
For unto angel lips at last is given
The silver trump of jubilee in Heaven;
And from Virginia's plains — Kentucky's shades
And through the dim Floridian everglades,
Rises to meet that angel-trumpet's sound
The voice of millions from their chains unbound.'

Here shall the child of after years be taught
The work of Freedom which his fathers wrought —
Told of the trials of the present hour,
Our weary strife with prejudice and power, —
How the high errand quicken'd woman's soul,
And touched her lips as with the living coal —
How Freedom's martyrs kept their lofty faiths,
True and unwavering, unto bonds and death.

---

[1] Poem published in the *Thirty-Sixth and Final Annual Report, Philadelphia Female Anti-Slavery Society, April 1870.* Philadelphia, 1870.

He did include in a book a favorite poem, 'The Golden Wedding of Longwood,' inspired by the golden wedding of a Pennsylvania couple who had been workers on the old 'underground railroad.'

Whittier's article on the Anti-Slavery Convention of 1833, written about this time, is one of the best accounts of the first antislavery society formed in Philadelphia. When he wrote it, he could not help contrasting his position in his later days when he received the tribute of all, to that in former days when he was an object of derision. But he realized that the community looked upon him as a hero only because the cause had triumphed.

Even now he had his moments of disquietude. He felt that the abolition of slavery had not been properly accomplished, for it had been done through bloodshed. That was not the method that he and the fellow workers had sought or contemplated, as he wrote in the hymn after the War, on the celebration of the triumph of the cause at Newburyport. In a letter to Mrs. Child he expressed similar convictions to those he voiced in the poem.

'The emancipation that came by military necessity and enforced by bayonets was not the emancipation for which we worked and prayed, but, like the Apostle, I am glad the gospel of Freedom was preached, even if by strife and emulation. It cannot be said that we did it; we, indeed, had no triumph. But the work itself was a success. It made us stronger and better men and women.'

Early in 1875 he attended a gathering of a few of the old antislavery workers: 'Thee would have seen a sight which will not be likely to occur again,' he wrote to Mrs. George L. Stearns, 'Garrison, Elizur Wright, Samuel E. Sewall and myself together — four gray old abolitionists, dating back to 1832. It seemed strange as a dream to call back the scenes and emotions, the hopes and fears of forty years ago.'

From 1876 on, almost to the end of his life, Whittier lived in the beautiful mansion at Oak Knoll, Danvers, the home of

Colonel Edmund Johnson, a widower who had married a cousin of Whittier, and was the father of three charming daughters. But he always maintained his voting residence at Amesbury. When Colonel Johnson died, a few months after the poet came to Oak Knoll, Whittier wrote the following poem about him: [1]

'Within yon dimly lighted room,
    Half hid by curtain folds
Of billowy whiteness, like the clouds
    In summer skies unfurled, —
Dost thou not see a gentle light
    Behind those folds outshining,
As oft behind those summer clouds
    We see a silver lining?

'Uplift the veil from off thy sight;
    Behold, the light which shone
So gently, through the curtain's folds
    Came from a blest hearth-stone.

'What! seest thou but an empty chair?
    A moment longer gaze,
The shades of grief shall fade before
    The "light of other days."

'Beside the ruddy firelight sits
    A man of fourscore years,
Blue-eyed and radiant as a child;
    His white hair softly framing
A face as beautiful and mild
    As Raphael's matchless painting.

'What seemed at first an empty chair
    Henceforth shall never be;
A radiant throng of memories
    Is brightening there for thee,
No happier, truer, holier light
    E'er shone from heavenly zone
Than that a loving Father leaves
    To bless his children's home.'

---

[1] Manuscript copy of poem to Colonel Edmund Johnson, dated Feb., 1877, furnished by Mrs. Phœbe Grantham.

His life at Oak Knoll was diverted by a little girl named Phœbe, whom his cousin Mrs. Abby Johnson Woodman had adopted. She was about eight years old when he came to Danvers, and from that time on, at his request, always called him 'Uncle Greenleaf.' Whenever he returned to Amesbury or went away on vacations, he wrote her letters telling her of all his doings. He talked to her on all matters and virtually gave her an education; for her he wrote the poem 'Red Riding Hood.' He also composed for her album the following acrostic:[1]

'Pure and spotless as thy book is
    Handsome, pleasant as its look is,
Ever should its written pages
    By thy kind friends of all ages
    Even to the latest be,

'Joyous, tender, loving, free,
    One by one bring wishes good
Hopeful for thy maidenhood,
    Nothing idle, nothing rude.
Sacred friendship's signet be
    On the pages penned for thee,
Nothing false, or flattery.
    When thou shalt in after days
On the well-filled volume gaze
    Over naming all who there
Designed to leave their name and prayer
    May'st thou give the dead a tear,
And the living love sincere,
    None forgotten, there or here.'

While living at Danvers he wrote about a hundred poems. In the scenes of the neighborhood he found the inspiration for 'The Witch of Wenham.' In fact, on the very estate on which he lived the Rev. George Burroughs had been executed as a wizard in Colonial days. To get local color and gather material for the purpose of reinforcing his recollections of the

[1] Manuscript copy of 'An Acrostic,' dated Oak Knoll, 1881, furnished by Mrs. Grantham. Whittier spelled her name 'Phebe.'

old witch legends, he one day took a jaunt through the country with his cousins. When he arrived home, he wrote the poem, introducing some new features into the traditional story of the young witch who had been arrested and confined in a garret. Whittier made her lover rescue her and he represented some Quakers sheltering her till the witch epidemic died out. This poem made Oliver Wendell Holmes break down on reading it.

The life of the poet at Oak Knoll was comfortable and even luxurious. The estate was a large one, and the rich surroundings were in sharp contrast to the old homestead at Haverhill or the plain village house at Amesbury. He roamed the country, he played with two pet animals, a dog and a turkey; he read and wrote, he received visitors, he had the society of little Phœbe. Prosaic details of his home life from time to time appeared in the press; they show that his later life, though comparatively happy, lacked color. He read widely, but his intellectual faculties did not grow more perspicacious. Had he had a Boswell to record his judgments and comments, they would not have proved either penetrating or novel.

However, he won the admiration of younger poets like Stedman, Aldrich,[1] and Stoddard, and he gained the respect of politicians like Senator Hoar and James G. Blaine. He attracted, besides, two unusual foreign admirers, one a leading statesman and the other an emperor. He was fairly worshiped by John Bright, who, like himself, was a Quaker. He was idolized by the accomplished Emperor of Brazil, Dom Pedro II, who had translated the poet's 'The Cry of a Lost Soul.' Whittier, in turn, admired him because he had been instrumental in the gradual emancipation of slavery in Brazil, for which the poet praised him in his poem 'Freedom in

---

[1] Whittier thought highly of Stedman's poems. He was also very fond of Aldrich's poetry, especially of the poem 'Memory,' which he had read to him when he was in Hampton Falls in the year of his death. See Ferris Greenslet's *Thomas Bailey Aldrich*, p. 258 (1908).

Brazil.' When Dom Pedro visited America in 1876, he was anxious to meet Whittier. Whittier gives an account of the meeting in Boston in the following letter to Mrs. Louise Chandler Moulton:[1]

Oak Knoll
Danvers, Mass.
16th 6 mo. 1876

MY DEAR MRS. MOULTON:

It was very kind in thee to think of me amidst the pleasures and excitements of thy tour in Italy. I am grateful to know that thee have seen some of my friends — the Howitts. I have never seen [them], but they seem like old friends, for I do not remember the time when I did not know & love them. The Alexanders are very excellent people, and I have long ago assisted in the canonization of Francesca. I have a beautiful pen picture of hers of an Italian peasant girl.

I expect to see the Claflins soon, and shall be glad to welcome them back.

Don't give thyself any uneasiness about Frank Sanborn's story — to use a polite term. Nobody really believes his gossip. Mrs. Sargent did not think it worth noticing. I wrote her a line warning her of its utter falsehood & absurdity. The satire was very clear and witty — but I think the writer himself in his sober second thought must regret it.

I was in Boston yesterday & saw Dom Pedro. He is a very handsome man and learned & intellectual. He met me in the style of Brazilian friendliness, with a hug; and was exceedingly cordial & complimentary.

I am stopping a part of the season with my cousin Arthur's place — a delightful summer home. My niece who has been with me for 12 years had just married the Editor of the Portland Transcript & I am left alone. But, she is happy and that is much as the world goes. The spring weather has been very trying to me but I trust the East wind has blown itself out for this season. I have not yet visited the Centennial wonders at

[1] Manuscript letter of Whittier to Mrs. Moulton in Library of Congress.

Philadelphia & hardly think I shall at all. It costs too much fatigue & excitement.

Hoping that thee are having a pleasant time in England, I am, dear Mrs. Moulton, always thy friend,

JOHN G. WHITTIER

In these later years he was on terms of close friendship with only two of his literary contemporaries — Bayard Taylor, who died in 1878, and Oliver Wendell Holmes, who outlived him. He was drawn to Taylor because he was a Quaker as well as because he was a poet and a traveler. He drew vignettes of him in poems like 'The Last Walk in Autumn' and 'The Tent on the Beach.' In his poem 'Centennial Hymn' Whittier used, with Taylor's permission, a few lines from his poem on the same subject. Incidentally, his influence helped Taylor to become minister to Germany in 1878.

With Oliver Wendell Holmes, Whittier's relations were closer than with any of the other New England poets. They had known of each other for many years, but it was only late in life that they corresponded frequently with each other. They had in common a dislike for Calvinism and a readiness for repartee. They wrote poems to each other.

In his relations with Longfellow and Lowell, whom he did not find as sociable as Holmes, Whittier was somewhat at a disadvantage.[1] They were not only of Brahmin stock, but college graduates, and had been on the faculties of Harvard University; their lineage and scholarship added to their prestige as poets. He, on the other hand, was only the son of a farmer, whose education had been limited to two terms at an academy. True, he had received the honorary degree of Doctor of Laws from Harvard College and had served as a member of the Board of Trustees of Brown University, but he was not a college man. Knowing that Longfellow and Lowell were more cultured than he, and of higher lineage, and being

[1] Mrs. Phœbe Grantham informed me that Whittier imagined that Longfellow and Lowell considered themselves his superiors.

sensitive because of his academic shortcomings and farmer ancestry, he imagined that they patronized him. He was as famous as they, yet he believed that there was a gap between him and them. Whether he was justified in believing that they acted condescendingly toward him, or not, he saw little of them, yet he addressed poems to them on various occasions, as they did also to him. It is especially surprising how rarely he and Longfellow, the two most popular poets of the time, met or wrote to each other. One of the few letters he sent to Longfellow is the following, written for his seventy-fifth birthday: [1]

Oak Knoll
Danvers 2 *Mo.* 25, 1882

DEAR LONGFELLOW:

I would not add to the overwhelming burden of congratulation and grateful appreciation which thy birthday must bring, but I cannot let the occasion pass without expressing my gratitude for the happy hours I have spent over thy writings, & the pride which I share with all Americans in view of thy success as an author and thy character as a man. It is permitted to but few in this world to reach a position so honorable as that which thee occupy or to enjoy so widely the love of thy fellow men.

With our dear friends Emerson & Holmes, we are nearing the inevitable end of earth, & we must soon leave younger writers the places we hold. But it is a matter for thankfulness that we shall also leave them the example of the brotherly kindness and sympathy which have marked our intercourse with one another.

May God continue to bless thee, dear friend, & bless us all here & hereafter.

Ever truly thine
JOHN G. WHITTIER

Curiously enough, Whittier established in late life closer relations with Paul Hamilton Hayne, a Southern poet who

[1] Manuscript Whittier letter to Longfellow in Longfellow House, Cambridge.

had upheld slavery and secession, than he did with the New England poets. Hayne, who, after being ruined by the war, had moved from South Carolina to Georgia in 1870, sent Whittier a poem, 'The Legend of Daphles.' From that time on, an intermittent correspondence between both poets continued till Hayne's death. Hayne and the older poet now found themselves intellectually in agreement with each other. It was a curious friendship, between the old abolitionist, who had written violent poems against slavery, and the Southern fire-eater. Now they had become genteel and respectable bards who had a common ground for dislike of decadents like Swinburne and Baudelaire — poets more gifted than either of them. They both admired the talents of the late Henry Timrod, the most rabid and pugnacious of all Southern poets. After corresponding with Whittier for a number of years, Hayne, accompanied by his wife, paid Whittier a visit. Recalling it a year later, Whittier wrote to Hayne: [1]

> Oak Knoll, Danvers
> 10th Mo., 11, 1880

My dear Hayne:

It is very nearly a year ago since thee and dear Mrs. Hayne were here. I was wishing this morning that you could see our trees, which Autumn has painted more gorgeously than ever before. I think that you do not get quite such tints at the South.

How do you do? The newspapers say thy health is better, but I was pained to hear of thy illness some months ago. For myself I am feeling the effects of age, am rarely free from pain, and find all writing or serious thought very wearisome. I realize that there is little left for me but to trust and wait. I have outlived most of my relatives, and early friends, and the great world, with its strifes, trials, ambitions and gains, seems falling away from me. Yet I am very grateful for many

---

[1] Manuscript letter from Whittier to Paul Hayne in National Academy of Letters. Most of Hayne's letters are in Duke University, N.C.

blessings, for friends, for books, for the ever beautiful nature, and for the hope that, despite of many errors and shortcomings, I have not lived wholly in vain.

The poetical temperament has its trials and keen susceptibility to the hard, harsh and unlovely things of life, but, my dear friend, we have also a capacity for enjoyment which others do not know, 'the still air of delightful studies,' the glow and enthusiasm of rhythmic utterances, the rapturous love of all beauty and harmony, and, as Holmes says, it is a satisfaction 'sometimes to sit under a tree and read our own songs.'

My cousins, Abby and Caroline, have been to California and had a pleasant time. We are much as we were when you were here. Phebe does her best to keep us feeling young. The dogs and cats and cows and horses are the same, but we have now a voluble mocking bird in addition.

The election is at hand. However it goes I hope the country will not suffer. I long for peace and kindly feeling.

Our folks all send their love, with mine, to Mrs. Hayne. I am always and truly,

Thy friend,
JOHN G. WHITTIER

Hayne visited Whittier a second time in the summer of 1885, not long before his own death. Southerner that he was, Hayne was interested in early New England history and legend; Whittier entertained him with old lore as well as with tales of his youth, while Hayne set forth the tragic circumstances of his own life. What a picture of contrasts they presented! The fiery abolitionist, now mellowed, and the hot-headed slave-partisan, now subdued; one suffering from insomnia and the other from consumption. This visit was the occasion on which Whittier told Hayne about the opening of Haverhill Academy, to which he and the aged Scotch rustic bard, Robert Dinsmore, steeped in liquor, marched at the head of the procession.

Whittier's antislavery memories crowded thickly upon him in Danvers, as they had done in Amesbury. He had as neighbors two old friends who had worked with him in the antislavery days — Richard P. Waters, of Beverly, who had been a consul in several ports, and Colonel Albert G. Browne, of Salem, who had been with Sherman on the famous march. They used to call on him and saunter over the grounds, and in recalling mirthful incidents they all would burst out into explosive laughter. They enthusiastically showed their satisfaction in having done their part for the triumph of the cause.

The death of one of the old abolitionists, of Garrison, or Lydia M. Child, would call out from Whittier a poem, a reminder of the old days. He forgot that he had had differences with the members of the old organization. As a matter of fact he came under the delusion that he had never quarreled with Garrison at all, as we see by a letter to the editor of the 'Independent' accompanying his elegy on Garrison.[1]

'Something on my part,' he wrote, 'seems due to the intimate friendship of more than fifty years unbroken and undisturbed by any difference of opinion and action during the long antislavery struggle.' He did, however, dwell a little later on their differences in his introduction to Oliver Johnson's 'William Lloyd Garrison and His Times.'

Yet his old friend and benefactor William Lloyd Garrison had been a thorn in his spiritual flesh. Irrespective of whether Garrison, by word or deed, ever reminded Whittier to what extent he owed his successful career to him, Whittier realized only too well his indebtedness to the elder man. While he might maintain that he would have been a poet and an abolitionist even if he had not met Garrison, he was not pleased that he stood before the public as a product, manufactured, packed, and shipped, as it were, by the editor of the 'Liberator.' Garrison had given him the first literary recog-

[1] Manuscript letter to Editor of *Independent* dated May 30, 1879, in Huntington Library.

nition by publishing his first poem; Garrison had obtained for him his first position as editor, which prepared the way to the other editorial positions he later held; Garrison had not only converted him to abolition, but had been instrumental in getting him to come as a delegate to the Philadelphia American Anti-Slavery Convention. In short, wherever Whittier turned retrospectively, the ghost of Garrison arose before him.[1]

Invitations to various anniversaries brought before him memories of the old struggles. A request to attend the anniversary in Philadelphia of the introduction of printing in the Middle Colonies by William Bradford, who had also published a pamphlet against slavery, recalled to Whittier the days of the burning of Pennsylvania Hall. Unable to attend the celebration, he wrote:

'I never heard that Printer Bradford or his press were molested on account of so doing; but it seems now, more than it did then, a strange circumstance that a century and a half later, when I was editing the Penn. Freeman in your city, my office was broken open, sacked & burned, for doing the same thing. It surely becomes us all to thank God & rejoice that a system which denied not only personal liberty but the liberty of the Press is no longer in existence, and that an unshackled Press, South as well as North, rejoices over its downfall.'[2]

Old co-workers in their letters to him reminded him of episodes of the past. Charles C. Burleigh, in a letter, awoke Whittier's memories of the old days at Healy's boarding-house in Philadelphia. To a note from Henry B. Stanton, with whom he had traveled hundreds of miles in eight or ten States, Whittier replied:

'What times we had together when we fought the wild beasts at Ephesus. I think over the old days a great deal.

[1] Mrs. Grantham is my authority for saying that there was an unconscious resentment in Whittier against Garrison, and that Garrison felt, and showed that he felt, a certain superiority. However, there was nothing of malice on the part of either in their feeling toward each other.

[2] Manuscript letter to Charles Roberts, Esq., Dec. 4, 1885, in Haverford College.

Life is now all behind me. Most of our early friends have passed away. Sewall and a few others still remain.'

When Moncure D. Conway, visiting Whittier in the last years of his life, and finding him playing croquet against himself, spoke to him about the old abolition days, the poet dropped the mallet and talked vehemently, his eyes kindling with fire as he spoke.

As late as 1889 Whittier had an opportunity for rehearsing the old days when a veteran abolitionist, John M. Barbour, then eighty-four years of age, visited him. They went over the incidents of the lives of former workers — of Alvan Stewart, Gerrit Smith, John Pierpont, John Quincy Adams, Garrison, Wendell Phillips, Sumner, Leavitt, Cushing, Webster, and Rantoul. They talked of the English abolitionists who had done effective work long before Garrison had become converted to the cause — of Wilberforce, Clarkson, and Sturge. They related to each other their experiences in being mobbed, and dolefully recalled that only two other active workers with them of the old days were alive, Dr. Henry I. Bowditch and Samuel E. Sewall.[1] Of course there were younger men, who had entered the cause at a later date, but of the workers of the thirties they alone were left.

Nevertheless, when there was danger of reopening old wounds publicly, he was not always ready to recall the old days. On one occasion he refused to write a poem celebrating the founding of the Anti-Slavery Society.

Except for the dinners on his seventieth and eightieth birthdays, or meeting an English celebrity like Matthew Arnold, very little of importance happened to him in these later years. In 1881 he engaged in a controversy on the historical truth of his poem 'King's Missive' with the Rev. George E. Ellis. In 1883 he lost his brother Matthew by death from inflammatory rheumatism, and became thus the only surviving member of the family. Matthew also had engaged in journalism, but he had very little in common with his brother. He

---

[1] Theodore D. Weld was also still alive.

held a position in the Boston custom-house in the last years of his life.

During these later years of Whittier's life strangers wrote to him in increasing numbers. Writers sent manuscripts and books to him for his opinion, and the autograph-hunter was abroad in the land. Most of the poets of the country sent him their books, and he usually praised them. The invalid poet devoted his mornings to letter-writing, to the neglect of his own poetic composition. His correspondence finally became so burdensome that he wrote to the 'Critic' asking strangers not to write to him. There was, however, little cessation in the volume of correspondence that made its way to Oak Knoll and Amesbury.

Feeling that his life would soon be over, Whittier now arranged for his posthumous biography. He knew that biographers would write about him and he naturally preferred that somebody authorized by himself should do so. He had supervised in his lifetime a biography by Francis H. Underwood, formerly an editor on the 'Atlantic Monthly'; he not only contributed material to it, but apparently directed the eulogistic tone in which it was written.[1] He was not pleased with a book published earlier — the first written about him by W. S. Kennedy, and he would not have it in the house. Kennedy shortly before Whittier's death wrote another biography, containing probably the best account of the poet's abolition work.

Whittier was anxious to find a sympathetic biographer with literary ability. He wanted his niece's husband, Mr. Pickard, to do only the detail and research work, and to amass and classify the papers. He was anxious to have Howells

[1] In the library of Yale University is a letter dated July 8, 1882, addressed to Underwood by Whittier, sending him the pamphlet *Justice and Expediency*, the letters in reply to the attacks of a Richmond newspaper, and the poems 'Isabella of Austria' and 'Bolivar' (given by Underwood in his book), which Whittier considered the best specimens of his early writing. Whittier also sent him other published letters of his from the *Essex Transcript*, the *Anti-Slavery Standard*, and various other papers, with a promise of more when he returned to Danvers. Whittier took a part in the direction of the book.

write the biography, but Howells was unable to do so, since he had contracted to write only for Harper & Brothers and Whittier had promised his biography to Mr. B. H. Ticknor.

Whittier then tried to get Edmund Clarence Stedman to be his literary executor, but for some reason Stedman could not. He finally arranged that Thomas Chase, the President of Haverford, should, with Pickard's assistance, write the biography. (Chase died shortly after Whittier did, and Pickard finally wrote the book.)

Although Whittier was approaching the end, he continued to be gallant to the women to the last. When eighty-three years old he wrote to Mrs. Moulton: 'Hundreds of times within the last two years I have looked at thy photograph, and wished I could see or hear from the original.' [1]

Less than a year before his death he wrote to Annie Fields the widow of his former publisher: 'The best thing on my birthday was to meet thee and our dear Sarah [Orne Jewett] on the stairs, and the worst was that you went away so soon.'

The remaining events of Whittier's life, his birthday celebrations, his sojourns at mountain resorts, and other matters call for little attention. One incident is of passing interest. In 1890 he promised to write a poem on the occasion of the celebration of the two hundred and fiftieth anniversary of the founding of Haverhill. After he had obligated himself, the 'Atlantic Monthly' offered him a thousand dollars for a poem on Haverhill, provided he would not publish it in any newspaper before it appeared in the magazine.[2] Wanting the thousand dollars, he asked the committee to release him from his obligation. Thinking that he was poor and not wishing to deprive him of so large a sum, they agreed to permit him to

---

[1] From manuscript letter to Louise Chandler Moulton, dated Jan. 18, 1890, in Library of Congress.

[2] Information about the Haverhill poem based on the documents in the Haverhill Public Library. Mr. Albert L. Bartlett writes to me that Whittier consented to write the poem through the influence of his friend Colonel Jones Frankle, and that Horace Scudder, the editor of the *Atlantic Monthly*, finally overlooked the breach.

make his terms with the magazine, but they saw no reason why he should not allow his poem to be read on the occasion of the anniversary. He agreed, and on the celebration held in July, 1890, Albert L. Bartlett read the poem. Unfortunately, it did get into the newspapers. Naturally, the editor, Horace Scudder, of the 'Atlantic Monthly,' was indignant, and he exchanged a sharp correspondence with Whittier's friend Colonel Frankle, one of the committee. The poem finally appeared in the 'Atlantic Monthly' — too late to have any effect of novelty.

In January, 1892, while on a visit to his cousins the Cartlands, Whittier suffered a severe attack of the influenza, from which he fortunately recovered.

In the spring he returned to Danvers and also paid a visit to Amesbury. Planning to spend the summer in Centre Harbor in New Hampshire, but prevented from doing so by his weakness, he decided to go with his cousin Gertrude Cartland and some friends to visit Miss Sarah A. Gove at Hampton Falls, New Hampshire. Here he remained for the summer, enjoying his rest, and here he wrote his last poem, that on Holmes's birthday. Women admirers — the 'pilgrims' — intruded, much to his discomfiture. During the month of August he wrote letters to several of his women friends — one to Frances E. Willard to console her for the death of her mother, and another to his poet friend Elizabeth Jones Cavazza, to whom he sent a clipping about her book. One of the last letters he wrote was to Elizabeth Stuart Phelps Ward, to tell her how much he liked a poem of hers in the 'Atlantic.'

He had an attack of illness, but recovered. Then, on the morning of the 3d of September he had a paralytic stroke, which affected his right side and compelled him to take to his bed. He lost the use of his throat, and could take medicine or food only with great difficulty. Knowing that his end was not far off, he sent 'Love — love to the world.' He was becoming unconscious, but to show that he was not so fully, he answered his niece, when she asked him if he recognized her, 'I have known thee all the time.' Lying in bed helpless, he protested against having the shades drawn, as he wanted to see the sunrise in the morning. As the 7th day of September dawned, he died, without pain.

Three days later he was buried 'in the plain and quiet way of the Society of Friends' in the family lot of the cemetery overlooking his Amesbury home.

CHAPTER XXVI

RELIGION AND RELIGIOUS POETRY

ALTHOUGH Whittier included about seventy-five poems in his collected works under the division 'Religious,' he could have admitted here many of those that he classified as 'Personal' and 'Narrative.' As a matter of fact, he wrote religious poems all his life, scarcely publishing a volume that did not include some of them. Being an orthodox Friend, with all the virtues as well as the faults of that noble sect, he steeped his poetic work in Quaker doctrines. His appeal to allow one's conscience to be one's guide in moral matters, his passion for freedom of speech, his love of justice, his sympathy with the oppressed, his insistence upon personal integrity rather than upon conformity to religious doctrines, were all derived from his heritage. His religious beliefs exerted the greatest influence upon his work and art.

It would undoubtedly be easy to show the hollowness and falsity, philosophically speaking, of the poet's favorite doctrines. Closing his eyes to the changes brought about in the religious world by scientific discoveries, he continued to sing dogmatically of the personal immortality of the individual soul. While he discarded much religious baggage found in other creeds, he clung to a belief in a celestial paradise where one met in person one's relatives, and continued to enjoy associating with them eternally. He thought that by persistently repeating his untenable views, he would give them greater force and validity. He became obsessed on the subject and showed irritation because the intellectuals dissented from him. Rejecting any social improvements inconsistent with the doctrines of Christianity, he was unjust to reformers who did not accept his creed. Believing that the hope of humanity rested on the Christian religion, he gave

no consideration to radicals who sought to go beyond it.
He felt great annoyance because Emerson placed Jesus
merely among moral teachers; he pitied him because he had
no real faith in immortality. Although he admired William
Ellery Channing, he strongly disapproved of his Unitarian
views, his 'peculiar religious opinions,' as he called them.
Yet his own beliefs often dangerously bordered on Unitarian-
ism. He was very much perturbed because Celia Thaxter
did not pray, for he could not understand how life could go
on without daily prayers. Singularly enough, he did not himself engage in daily prayers, in the religious sense, though he
practiced silent religious meditation. He had a favorite
theory that even Nature in her own way prayed to God — a
theory that influenced the tenor of many of his religious
poems. When speaking about religion, he would become
enthusiastic, evincing the fervor of an evangelist. Once, in
the ardor of a religious discourse at Mrs. Thaxter's, he made
himself ill. His conscience even pricked him if he dissipated
his energies in discussing other matters than his religious
views.

His favorite doctrine was that of the goodness of God. He
once said that the conviction of the loving fatherhood of God
came to him after he had witnessed some kind act that his
mother performed with tenderness for some erring person
who had never anticipated such benevolence. He concluded
that God always came to the rescue of the needy, even by human agency, but he failed to mention innumerable occasions
on which the distressed clamored in vain for aid. In the psychological terminology of today, a mother complex awoke
in him the belief in the Eternal Goodness.

Yet Whittier's doctrine of eternal goodness was needed in
his time, to disintegrate the prevailing Calvinism with its
emphasis on God's vindictiveness. It had a salutary influence
upon the human mind, by liberating it from the effects of a
baneful theological conception. He once told an English
Quaker who visited him that he wrote his poem 'The Eternal

Goodness' to counteract the Calvinistic teaching of God as tormentor.[1] Yet, as he himself had a genuine conviction of sin, he was not very far removed from the tenets of Calvinistic theology.

He thought that the natural corollary of his trust in a good God was a belief in the immortality of the soul. 'I do not think that God's love for His creatures ever ceases,' he said, 'or that probation closes with the grave. This view seems to me the necessary consequences of our retaining our personality in the after life. God will not in the resurrection make us mere automata. We must have the exercise of free will, the power of choice, or we cease to be ourselves.'

Yet Whittier was not unaware of the compelling doubts that perplexed the believer. In 'Questions of Life,' written before Darwin had propounded his theory of evolution, Whittier presented the arguments of the sceptic with force and even conviction. He was familiar with the pantheistic conception of the universe, because of his studies in Oriental literature, and he had himself been in danger of yielding to its plausibility. Though he became intellectually entranced by it, he determined to reject it. He did not deny that he had his moments of uncertainty, though he never yielded to despair.

'He has found it hard to reconcile the creed he held by inheritance with the subtle logic of more modern modes of thought,' he said, speaking of himself in the third person, in a biographical article he wrote.

Sometimes, as in the poem 'Trust,' written shortly after he composed 'Questions of Life,' he admitted that he had no logical reply to many persuasive arguments. His only answer was what he learned at his mother's knee:

> 'All is of God that is, and is to be;
> And God is good.'

Whittier drew his religious inspirations from two sources —

[1] Conversation with the English Quaker Stanley Pumphrey in 1879, *Dial*, Dec. 16, 1907, 'Some Friendships of Whittier,' by Annie Russell Marble.

the Bible and the Quaker doctrine of the Inner Light. He was more familiar with the Bible than was any other great American poet; he found many themes for poems in it, and gathered many phrases and citations from it. He dwelt less on the miraculous and supernatural episodes in it than on the passages that bring comfort to the spirit.

Being strictly orthodox in his Quakerism, he would not compromise with Elias Hicks and his unitarian tendencies. Yet he had at one time preferred to associate personally with the Hicksites than with the orthodox, because the former showed more sympathy with abolition. But he remained orthodox all his life. To a woman who was under the impression that he was unitarian, he wrote, in 1871: 'I am a member of what is called the Orthodox part of our unhappily divided society. But I am not sectarian and I have fellowship with good people of all denominations, and think more highly of practical piety than of mere doctrinal soundness. I incline rather to the old standards of Quakerism than to the new lights, who I fear would hardly tolerate George Fox or John Woolman if they were now living.' [1]

A deservedly derogatory view of his religious poetry prevails in the main among the literary critics who are steeped in the scientific spirit of our age. After all, the theology of Whittier, liberal as it is, is so much chaff. He was indeed sensitive to adverse judgment on his religious poems, because he was dimly aware that they did not satisfy the intellect. He raged against Kennedy's first book about him, because it smote him on the hip for his naïve religious assumptions. Kennedy's charges pierced Whittier's armor in its vulnerable places. Whittier was a man hampered by a creed that forbade catholic sympathy with human nature; he always donned the garb of sectary, thus becoming weak and uninteresting; above all, he did not incorporate 'any of the untheological unanthropomorphic explanations of things

---

[1] Manuscript letter dated Dec. 5, 1871, to Sallie Stalker (Smith), now in possession of Medora Minchin Bybee, of Berkeley, California.

which are necessitated by science, and admitted by advanced thinkers, both in and out of churches.'[1] Kennedy was right when he said that it was disagreeable and monotonous for a poet to carry his religion to such a length that out of his five hundred poems there were only half a dozen (this is somewhat of an exaggeration) that did not contain some pious exhortation or allusion.

To a clear and independent thinker like Emerson, Whittier, with his implicit faith in prayer and immortality, was an anomaly.

When Emerson once jestingly said that he was glad some Calvinist woman was daily praying for him because of his heterodox doctrines, and that as a matter of fact he even prayed for himself, Whittier asked him what he prayed for. 'Well,' replied Emerson, 'when I first open my eyes upon the morning meadows, and look out upon the beautiful world, I thank God that I am alive and that I live so near Boston.' Just as irreverently as Emerson treated Whittier's obsession on prayer, did he hint of his own indifference to the Quaker poet's faith in personal immortality. On one occasion, when Whittier wanted to draw Emerson into a discussion on the subject, the transcendental philosopher evaded it by telling him that he was busy but to come to Concord some day, when they would dip their buckets into the well and see what they could draw up.

One may account for the constant reiteration of the religious motive, especially in the late poems, by regarding it as a product both of the mental crisis that Whittier went through during the dark days of 1840, when he was in ill health, and of the never-fading influence upon him of the mother he loved so devotedly. He did not believe that the doctrines that she taught him on her knee could be wrong — rather he did not want them to be wrong, he idolized her so. Though he did not attend church — he once said that he had heard only six sermons in his life — he always harked back to the memories

[1] See Kennedy, I, p. 187.

of his early religious associations. All that he was came from these.

Another fact, deducible with psychological aid, is that he sought religious consolation because he was always ill and had often faced death. His poems setting forth his utter fearlessness in the face of death were really the result and proof of his actual fear of it. He disguised his compulsion as courage, and unconsciously sought for consolation, to ease his suspicions that there was no after life. He once even said that his trust in God was not strong enough to overcome the natural shrinking from the law of death.

Yet he really persuaded himself to believe that he was not in terror of the grave. After recovery from his almost fatal illness in 1868, he wrote to his friend Allinson:

'I have been very sick, so much so, that I had little expectation of recovery. I was favored with a vivid sense of the infinite goodness of God, and felt no anxiety nor fear, — I was in the best of all places, in His hands whose mercy endureth forever.' [1]

The truth is that he loved life dearly and felt horror at the thought of annihilation. He grasped at any absurd analogy in an effort to assure himself of immortality, as, for example, in his poem 'The River Path.' [2] The death of his mother, the illness of his sister, and his own recent proximity to the land of shadows, all combined to make the theme of mortality absorb him at the time. If one reads between the lines of this poem breathing a bravado spirit, one will see that the poet really was frightened. Like a boy who whistles in the dark, he kept on rehearsing timeworn maxims to himself, pretending he was ready to go courageously. But he wanted the day of departure delayed a very long time. As a matter of fact, he almost suffered from thanatophobia. Just as timid poets sometimes sing of courage in the field of battle, so he reiter-

---

[1] From manuscript letter to W. J. Allinson, furnished by the late Mrs. F. G. Allinson.

[2] 'Independent,' July 19, 1860. In *Poems.*

ated constantly his firm hope as to what the future had in store for him. Modern psychology has enabled us to see through the self-consolations built up by neurotics as a defense mechanism against their phobias. Thus does Nature protect and heal her unfortunates.

In 'The River Path' he depicts himself as standing at a place where the darkness of evening had fallen and noticing that the hills across the river were lit by the glow of the setting sun. He then draws a false analogy that as sunlight illumined the natural scene before him, so the light of God would break through across the dark river that divided life from death.

The religious poems that were meant to console people at the prospect of death were especially popular with the aged and the invalid. They wrote letters telling him of the comfort his poems were to them. Decrepit women repeated the poems on their sick-beds. Miss Catherine M. Sedgwick, who had in her early days been as famous among woman writers as Cooper was among male authors, and who became an invalid in old age, poured out her grief to Whittier in reams of undecipherable letters, dwelling on the great consolation she found in his religious poems. Dorothea L. Dix wrote him that his poem 'At Last' meant more than any minister's administrations. She died with its words upon her lips and requested that a copy of the poem be buried with her. When the beneficial effect of a poem upon people is such, both science and literary criticism must assume a philosophically pragmatic stand.

Whittier was sincere in his beliefs. Religion became an obsession with him, and for years he spoke and wrote letters about it. Though he never descended to spiritualism, he became so transported by religious subjects that he was verging dangerously near religiomania. His unpublished letters [1] are full of religious disquisitions. To Louise Chandler Moulton he wrote:

[1] Take the letter of Oct. 26, 1881, in Haverford Library, to a friend:
'Have thee seen Dr. Allen's *Continuity of Religious* [*Christian*] *Thought?* It seems

'But is not this awful mystery of life, with its sorrow and sin and suffering, a sad and serious thing after all? There is a vast amount of make-believe mirth and joy in the world. The only real and permanent joy is in finding ourselves in harmony with the Divine Will, and trusting in the Divine Goodness.' [1]

His conversations on religion became tedious and puerile. 'With Elizabeth Stuart Phelps,' wrote Mrs. Claflin, 'his favorite theme was the occupations of heaven. They would sit — their two heads together — over the dying embers, at the twilight hour, and talk of what they should require to satisfy their souls in heaven.'

Yet some of Whittier's hymns and religious poems will always be read, though they have, with few exceptions, never made their appeal to the young, to the literary critics, and to the thinker. There are epigrams in his religious poems that are eternally true, that may be placed in a universal Bible.

While he may not console the readers who use their logical faculties, and while he hedges and evades and declaims, he is a healthy religious poet; he radiates the comfort that administers to grieved spirits incapable of exercising their intellects or unwilling to do so. Since his religious views were part of him, we must accept him as he is. While many of us would not exchange Emerson's 'Brahma' for all of Whittier's theology, we envy him the simplicity and sanity of his faith, wishing that it were true. Though he was scientifically and philosophically in the wrong, psychologically and morally he was right.

to me valuable in the resuscitation of the doctrine of the Divine Immanence as taught by the Greek Church in the early Christian centuries.'

[1] From manuscript letter to Mrs. Moulton, Feb. 26, 1878, Library of Congress.

CHAPTER XXVII

NOT SAINTLY BUT HEROIC

WHITTIER, modest though he was, was not exempt from one of the chief personal failings of bachelors — vanity about his personal appearance. He was much photographed in his lifetime; in fact there are almost as many portraits of him as of Walt Whitman. Most men verging on old age are not so much preoccupied with their portraits as Whittier was.

At the time of the opening of the Haverhill Library he contrived, through Charles H. Brainard, to have a bust of himself placed in it, carefully cautioning him, however, not to disclose his own wishes or part in the matter. This fact is apparent from the following letter addressed to Mr. Brainard: [1]

Amesbury 2nd 11 mo. 1875

DEAR FRIEND

The Haverhill Library has its dedication on the 11th inst. It has a splendid building the gift of Hon. E. J. M. Hale of H. & already some 20,000 volumes. It occurs to me they might purchase a 'graven image' of their townsman to place in their Hall. Who has charge of it? A letter to Jas. H. Carleton Esq., or to Mr. Hale might be of service. Or, if thee could put thyself in communication with them I am inclined to think the thing could be arranged unless Mr. P.[2] sets too high a price on the blockhead. It would be a strong inducement to have it at the dedication. Merely throw out the hint. Of course *I* do not want to be meddling with it and this note of course *confidential.*

Thy friend   J. G. W.

Dr. Jas. R. Nichols who has an office 'Journal of Chemistry,'

[1] Manuscript of letter to Brainard in the Library of Harvard University. In 1856 Brainard published on one sheet the portraits of Whittier and other antislavery workers, styling them 'Seven Champions of Freedom.'

[2] Preston Powers was the sculptor. Since Mr. Carleton and Dr. Nichols were old Haverhill boyhood friends, the poet felt safe in mentioning their names.

Boston, after all perhaps would be the best man to apply to. He is wealthy.

The proposal to get the bust in the library was successful. Yet later in the same year on the occasion of a monument to Poe, he said he did not favor ostentatious monuments to the dead, barring some exceptions. Some years later Whittier reciprocated Brainard's service by speaking in his behalf for a political position. It was one of the few occasions when he violated his rule to refuse to meddle with matters relating to office.

In personal appearance Whittier was tall, erect, proportionately built, with a frame rather spare. He walked alertly and with a firm step. In his later years, after he became bald, he kept the white hair on the back of his head uncropped. He cultivated a beard that encircled his entire face, spreading out in disordered profusion and half-concealing his large ears; he left the upper part of his chin clear of hair and he wore no moustache. Because of this mane of white hair, his black eyebrows, black eyelashes, large, luminous dark eyes, and swarthy complexion stood out in more marked contrast than when he was younger. His forehead was narrow, high, and receding; his cheek-bones were not low; his nose was prominent, and from both sides of it long, deep lines extended beyond his thin lips. When his face, always mobile and youthful, was in repose, it was rather austere, yet lit up with geniality.

With his long black coat, the only Quaker garment he wore, and with the 'stove-pipe' hat fashionable in those days, he appeared very unlike the poet of popular tradition. In fact, he was almost prosaic-looking.

Being vain of his personal appearance, he observed with sorrow his whitened hair constantly dropping out. When he had photographs made to be sent away for publication, he touched them up with a lead-pencil, adding a few hairs to his bald pate and darkening a few of the white hairs in his beard.

He was defective in some physical characteristics, for he was color-blind on red and green, seeing no difference between the red apples and the green leaves on the tree, and he was handicapped by being deaf in one ear. He suffered from neuralgic headaches and therefore went out rarely and moved little in society. He had no ear for music; he was never in a theater or circus; he attended no concerts or lectures; he indulged in no known sports except croquet, nor did he attend any games.

He had a characteristic personality. Irrespective of whether he said anything of significance, he left an indelible impression upon those who met him. He spoke not like a scholar but like a cultured New England farmer, introducing colloquialisms and rural terms, often using pronunciation smacking of the soil; but his speech flowed smoothly, and was subject to no hesitancy. He used the Quaker 'thee' at all times, even in its ungrammatical relation, and he dropped the 'g' from the 'ing' ending of participles. His language made farmers think him one of themselves. The tone of his voice was neither deep nor sonorous, neither full nor strong, and in later years he was slightly hoarse. However, when he read poetry aloud his voice became clearer, louder, and more articulate.

His well-known geniality and personal integrity, together with the oft-told tale of his noble sacrifices in the antislavery cause, helped spread the legend that he was a perfect saint. He himself protested against such a view of him, as we saw in the letter to Gail Hamilton, in which he described his loss of temper once at a fellow church-member, and another time in a dispute with an Irishman over a bill.

That he had unsaintly qualities we saw in his relations with women; a saint does not trifle with their affections, nor does he seek credit for literary work done by others, as he did for Lucy Larcom's. Yet he showed unmistakable kindnesses on many occasions to numerous persons. He wrote letters to obscure poets, unreservedly praising the books they sent him.

He often gave money, when called upon, to people whom he did not know personally. He was ever ready with pen and purse to aid some noble cause, though he doled out his charities in small sums. He educated and supported relatives.

He was, however, a typical thrifty Yankee. Since he had suffered much from poverty, he was very economical, and indulged in no luxuries. He made safe and good investments, on which he preserved a singular reticence. He allowed people to remain under the impression that he was in merely moderate circumstances. For this reason the committee for whom he wrote his poem on Haverhill permitted him to sell it to the 'Atlantic Monthly.' When he died, he left a fortune of about $125,000.

Affable as he was, he expressed his dislikes strongly, and in fact was combative with those whose opinions he did not share. He did not like Walt Whitman nor William Sloane Kennedy nor Frank Sanborn, and he did not hesitate in saying so. He was more inclined to be tolerant, always repenting when he had been too severe in his criticism of anyone. It was this trait of tolerance that made him inconsistent, even incapable of maintaining the same opinion of anybody for a long period. He amazed old abolitionists, for example, when he wrote a flattering eulogy on the occasion of the death of Edward Everett, a man he had justly attacked often in his earlier days. In numerous letters he flattered Winthrop, who showed no heroic spirit when the Republican Party was formed. When he was asked why he wrote a poem on Tilden, of whom he did not approve politically, he said he simply had to do it.

He especially reserved his wrath for those who ventured to express to him in strong terms their animosity to his favorite religious views, such as the goodness of God, the immortality of the soul, and the value of prayer. But he would grow angry, too, at those who differed with him politically. He expressed himself strongly about men in public life whose course he disapproved of. The name of General Butler was always a 'red rag' before him, and the policy of President Harrison in the Chile affair provoked him.

As he sometimes attacked people in private whom he praised in public, he came perilously near the verge of duplicity. In a letter to Lucy Larcom, he spoke disparagingly of his friend and publisher James T. Fields and his wife Annie, but he continued to call on them. While Fields was bringing out 'Snow-Bound' for him, Whittier once refused to visit him when in Boston, and sent an apology through Lucy Larcom, giving her the real reason for his neglect:

'Tell *Annie Fields* that I was sorry to miss of a visit at her home when I was in Boston. Gail Hamilton advised me not to think of going to Charles Street. The lack of domestic peace & harmony there, Mrs. F.'s brusque rough way & Mr. F.'s exacting and tyrannical behavior would, she said, make my visit anything but agreeable.' [1]

Yet in the same year he drew a genial portrait of Fields in 'The Tent on the Beach,' where he wrote of him:

> 'He loved himself the singer's art;
> Tenderly, gently, by his own
> He knew and judged an author's heart.'

But gentleness and tenderness accord very little with 'exacting and tyrannical behavior.'

After Fields gave up his career as publisher about 1870, Whittier continued his friendship with him, and he celebrated his death in an elegy in 1880. Mrs. Fields published a biographical tribute to her husband in spite of the 'lack of domestic peace and harmony.' She continued to adore the poet, and wrote one of the most winning sketches about him after his death. One wonders if she ever suspected that the poet spoke of her 'brusque, rough way.'

Gail Hamilton had also been a friend of Fields but broke

[1] Manuscript letter to Lucy Larcom, Feb. 7, 1866, in the Morgan Library. Pickard has two extracts from this letter, Vol. II, pp. 503 and 515, but had to omit the passage quoted, as Mrs. Fields was living at the time.

with him after the dispute that she recorded in 'The Battle of the Books.' She was more consistent than Whittier. Yet it was she who defended Whittier from the charge of inconsistency, when he praised Edward Everett.

Though Whittier was a mild and courteous person, we saw him, in his early stage, as a vituperative lampooner, often approaching sheer termagancy and even ribaldry. Nor was Whittier entirely modest, any more than he was always genial. He spoke deprecatingly of his own work but had a high opinion of it; nor was he averse to inflating his own reputation. He wrote the account of himself in 'Appletons' Cyclopædia of American Biography,' in a strain that was too fulsome.[1] It is possible that the editors, James Grant Wilson and John Fiske, may have supplied a few of the more laudatory lines, but if they did so, the poet was careful not to delete them. Yet this following self-adulatory gem represents the view of himself that he sought to spread broadcast:

'It is worth remark that the nobler qualities of the Puritans,' wrote Whittier, 'have nowhere found such adequate literary expressions since Milton as in this member of a sect which they did their utmost to suppress. Almost alone among American poets, he has revived the legends of his neighborhood in verse, and his "Floyd Ireson" is among the best of modern ballads, surpassed by none save Scott, if even by him. ... Whittier has done as much for the scenery of New England as Scott for that of Scotland. Many of his poems (such, for example, as "Telling the Bees"), in which description and sentiment mutually inspire each other, are as fine as any in the language.' [2]

It is also a matter for inquiry how much he contributed to

---

[1] Mrs. Phœbe Grantham informed me that Whittier wrote the account of himself in *Appletons' Cyclopædia of American Biography*. The sketch is in Vol. VI (1889).

[2] Yet he pretended to be indifferent to his literary reputation. To a relative of Schuyler Colfax who sent Whittier some complimentary remarks about him made by Colfax, Whittier wrote (May 22, 1883): 'I have reached an age when I value such words far more highly than the notoriety of a merely literary reputation.' Letter in possession of Mrs. M. W. Stevens, Stratford, Camden County, N.J.

the book about himself by Francis H. Underwood. We know he sent Underwood poems, letters, and newspaper articles, that he supervised and read the book before publication. We may safely say that some of the passages sound very much as if written by Whittier himself.

On another occasion he indulged in a publicity venture which is open to criticism. He wrote, in the guise of a newspaper reporter, an interview with himself on the subject of his dislike of being interviewed, with a view to its insertion in the village newspaper on the celebration of one of his birthdays. He stated that Whittier shifted his quarters, like Tennyson — in his own case from Amesbury to Oak Knoll — to escape the importunities of interviewers, but that the poet realized, like most famous people, he could not escape the interviewers: 'Our townsman Mr. Whittier,' Mr. Whittier, the reporter, wrote, 'is by no means an exception to the general rule. Interviewers find him out; and he has often to see impertinent descriptions of his incomings and outgoings, and facts (often mere fancies or misrepresentations) of his private life, habits and opinions paraded before the public, as if the fireside had no sanctity. To a sensitive man who has never courted notoriety and who has scrupulously avoided all occasions calculated to call attention to himself, such gratuitous advertising must be extremely annoying.' [1]

One must admit that this is a very original form of interview.

The truth is, Whittier was neither modest nor boastful. Probably he underestimated his achievements as a man and his merits as a poet.

Though Whittier wrote only serious poetry, he possessed a keen sense of humor. It was accompanied by subtlety and a propensity to joke and tease. Many stories could be collected illustrating his wit, which was more kindly than pungent, yet

[1] Manuscript of the interview by Whittier with himself is in the Morgan Library, in Whittier's handwriting. It is of course possible that it was finally not published in the village newspaper.

occasionally spiced with corrective intent. One or two such tales will suffice as examples of his wit.

A niece of his used to go out driving with a young man for whom the poet believed she did not truly care. The only reason, in her uncle's opinion, why she went out with this admirer was that he drove a pair of fine horses. Telling of his niece's love of ostentation to another person, he said he could do nothing to prevent her from riding with the youth — except to look for a man who drove *three* horses.

When called upon, to his surprise, to speak at Sumner's funeral, he told the story of the burial of a colonel on whose grave an unfriendly regiment fired a salute, when an onlooker said, 'If the Colonel could have known this, he would not have died.' 'So I feel,' he added, 'if my friend Sumner could have known that I should have been asked to speak at his funeral he would not have died.'

Though he liked to hear stories about the foibles of people, he would listen to no gossip. This trait of his was no doubt due to his natural kindness, but also illustrated his dislike of unpleasant truths. He wanted nothing to mar life for him: he was an incurable optimist.

He was neither a morbid nor a brooding person. He did not exclude himself from the company of his relatives in Danvers, but always sat with them in the evenings, took walks with them, joked and told stories. He at times sought solitude for reading, but he was not the recluse that some visitors believed him to be. He had more company than he could manage. He was dignified and reserved, and did not (at least late in life) hobnob with everybody. He loved society, mingled with young people whenever he could, and enjoyed his old age as much as his health permitted. In his optimistic outlook, despite his advanced years, and in his freedom from morbidity, he was like Walt Whitman. He did not suffer, as Miss Elizabeth Stuart Phelps believed, from loneliness or a deep inward desolation.

Whittier was a greater person than a mere saint; he was a

hero, and he himself had the noble qualities he celebrated in his poems. He sacrificed the most important years of his life for the cause. He entered into political campaigns, and allied himself with the abolitionists for the benefit of the blacks. He sought nothing for himself. Though he was shy, preferring the study of the scholar and the poet, he plunged into a life distasteful to him. He performed the work of drudgery, which he really hated, because others shirked their tasks and left the work to him. Knowing the work had to be done, he did it himself.

As an antislavery worker he made a personal sacrifice, because he shut himself off from the possibility of making connections with magazine editors and publishers. In those days 'Graham's Magazine' and Harper & Brothers refused to publish anything that savored of abolition sentiments. Whittier for many years had to circulate his work through the medium of obscure publishers in sympathy with the cause.

He also suffered ostracism socially. In 1846 he wrote to Frederick Palmer Tracy: 'I know very few Editors and Publishers.... I too am essentially tabooed in good society.' [1] His labors were so arduous that he was exhausted long before the battle was over. In 1849, when he was only forty-two years old, he wrote to Grace Greenwood: 'Over-worked and tired by the long weary years of the anti-slavery struggle, I want mental rest. I have already lived a long life, if thought and action constitute it. I have crowded into a few years what should have been given to many.' There were other unpleasant features of the abolition movement he had to encounter. Though the cause enlisted the most noble spirits in America, like all reform movements, it attracted cranks and the lunatic fringe. Contact with them was not pleasant to him, nor was he able to brook the coarseness of some of his fellow-workers. In after years he wrote to Miss Elizabeth Stuart Phelps about his early sufferings in the abolition

[1] Manuscript letter to Frederick Palmer Tracy, Jan. 18, 1846. Copy furnished by Mr. Tracy's grandson, Frank Tracy Swett, of Berkeley, California.

movement, 'I have suffered dreadfully from coarseness, self-
seeking vanity and asinine stupidity among associates, as
well as from the coldness and open hostility, and, worst, the
ridicule of the outside world.'

In later years he had the consolation of feeling that his life
had in some respects paralleled his idol Milton. Like him, he
had also early abandoned his poetical career to devote several decades of his life to the cause of liberty. Like him, in
his old age after the successful outcome of the struggle, he returned to his muse. The best portrait of Whittier, probably,
is his own in the 'Tent on the Beach,' beginning with the
stanza:

> 'And one there was, a dreamer born,
>   Who, with a mission to fulfil,
>   Had left the Muses' haunts to turn
>   The crank of an opinion-mill,
>   Making his rustic reed of song
>   A weapon in the war with wrong,
> Yoking his fancy to the breaking-plough
> That beam-deep turned the soil for truth to spring and grow.'

CHAPTER XXVIII

THE POET

WE CANNOT altogether rely on Whittier's appraisal of his own poetry, because he was often as poor a critic of himself as he was of others. His deficiencies as a literary critic were bound somewhat to affect the value of his own work. Though he read widely, he did so without discrimination, and his judgment on a book is almost worthless. His early studies of Cotton Mather and the Quaker writers were not conducive to developing his æsthetic faculties. He thought Longfellow's 'Tales of a Wayside Inn' not inferior to the masterpieces of Chaucer or Boccaccio, and he found in Bayard Taylor's 'Prince Deukalion' reminders of the solemnity and power of Æschylus and Sophocles. He regarded Oliver Wendell Holmes as a 'Montaigne and Bacon under one hat.' He wrote to Mrs. Zadel Barnes Gustafson that he could only compare her elegy on Bryant with Milton's 'Lycidas.' [1] He considered a poem of Edmund Clarence Stedman, 'Corda Concordia,' the greatest occasional poem of the last quarter of the century. He found 'Walden' 'very wicked and heathenish'; he criticized Tolstoy for being unpleasant and depressing; he was certain that the humblest and meekest follower of Christ was to be envied more than Byron, Voltaire, or Rousseau.

Though he read and enjoyed Dickens, Charles Reade,

[1] Whittier's opinion of Mrs. Gustafson got him into an amusing controversy. *The Critic* ventured to doubt that Whittier had ever said her 'Meg, a Pastoral' was unexcelled except by 'Lycidas' (*Critic*, Oct. 11, 1884). In the next issue the *Critic* said that Whittier corroborated it and wrote that he certainly never could have compared this unpretentious poem with 'Lycidas.' Then the author, who was in London, wrote to the *Critic* that Whittier compared, not 'Meg' but the elegy on Bryant, in the volume *Meg, and Other Poems* to 'Lycidas,' and she said that he had given her permission to quote his endorsement from his letter of Dec. 24, 1878. (*The Critic*, Dec. 13, 1884.) Whittier soon confirmed her story to the *Critic* even before she sent in the letter. Her book had a poem on Whittier.

Scott, Sterne, and Captain Marryat, he admired books not for their literary value, but because the authors preached some favorite doctrine of his own, such as liberty of speech or the benevolence of providence. Though he mentions Goethe and Shelley in his poems, it is doubtful if he ever properly appreciated them. The paganism and broad cultural demands of the former, and the ideas on religion, free-love, and reconstructed society of the latter were beyond his ken and even distasteful to him. Of Italian and Spanish literature he was ignorant, for the Latin temperament was not within the scope of his comprehension.

He had so large a following because he was always lucid and presented no difficulties to the reader. He used to say that no Browning societies would be necessary to explain or interpret his poems.

Though Whittier's poems are easily read, they were composed with great difficulty. He revised them so often that he made his final drafts almost entirely different from the original. Since his vocabulary in earlier days was limited, he could not find words to express himself, but he later mastered his medium. Not believing himself a finished artist, he allowed editors to make emendations, and he accepted suggestions for revision. Often, after he had finished a poem he would have some afterthought which necessitated changing the entire poem. In later life, like Whitman, he had his poems set up in type because he could correct them that way better.

Next to Whittier's simplicity, his optimism endeared him to the public. Dwelling on the pleasant side of life, he never depressed his readers. He sang of common, universal sentiments, and as he never analyzed emotions, he never came near morbidity. He touched the American soul in 1830 with the poem 'New England,' as he did in 1890 with the poem 'The Captain's Well.' All the people could not be wrong all the time in their estimate of his poems.

Do his poems satisfy the literary critic of today? Have

they withstood the onslaught of time? Is he only a minor, provincial poet?

To determine the relative merits of Whittier's poetry affords a fascinating and baffling problem to the critic of American literature. As we saw, there are several groups into which Whittier classified his poems: Narrative and Legendary, Anti-Slavery, Religious, Personal, Subjective, and Occasional, descriptive of nature and propagandic for reform. Every one of these divisions has poems of a high order with the qualities that make for literary permanency. He also wrote occasional poems in which he celebrated events of local and temporary interest. But even some of these are of enduring value, as for example his nature poems celebrating his visits to the Merrimac River.

Many critics believe that Whittier achieved his highest distinction as a poet in his ballads. Notwithstanding their narrowness of range, their superficial pictures of life, their limited social and intellectual point of view, they are often of so high an order as to challenge comparison with the best old and new English ballads. 'Cassandra Southwick,' 'Barclay of Ury,' 'Telling the Bees,' 'Skipper Ireson's Ride,' 'Mabel Martin,' and 'My Playmate' are not 'minor' poetry, for they are true lyrics, voicing, with almost technical perfection and moving ecstasy, imperishable and important ideas.

Investing his lyrics with his own noble personality, he enhanced their value; he wrote disguised autobiography in the tales of the mocked Barclay of Ury, the self-sacrificing Knight of St. John, and the persecuted Barbara Southwick. He sang of his love griefs in 'Maud Muller' and 'Telling the Bees.'

Nor did he hesitate to record more directly his spiritual difficulties and pass judgment upon his life as a man and his work as a poet in such poems as 'My Namesake,' 'An Autograph,' and 'Ego.' In the extreme personal touches in the great body of his poetry he resembles Burns. Whittier himself thought highly of some of his subjective poems — the section that contains the poems just mentioned, as well as

'Memories,' 'The Barefoot Boy,' 'In School Days,' and 'Snow-Bound.' In his estimate of the poems of this section the public has sustained him in the main.

He is also a faithful painter of rural life. His poetic creed at one time was, as we see in his essay on Dinsmore, that poetry should be rural and regional. He believed that the true American poet must describe American customs and institutions, the simple emotions of the common people centering around love, ambition, remorse, misfortune, aspiration. He wanted Yankee pastorals, songs about domestic scenes. He insisted that the poet find inspiration in the old American legends, and he himself pointed out their moral implications. He thought that the true poet was he who faithfully depicted rural life and characters.

Whittier's knowledge of Nature was gained from observation and experience, but, unlike many farmers, he was sensitive to impressions from her. He had his predilections for her in her varied phases. He was especially stirred and spiritually elevated by the sight of mountains; this fact in part accounted for his spending his vacations among the hills of New Hampshire. He was always lulled into a peculiar mood by the trickling noise of the waters of a brook or stream. He knew the fauna and flora of the Merrimac Valley. The birds flit and twitter, the trees sway and tower, and the flowers bloom and dazzle in his poems. Though he mentions more than thirty birds, he preferred the bluebird. His letters, especially those written in the late winter, often express the longing to hear the bluebird sing. He mentions thirty species of trees, the pine tree more frequently than any other. Norman Foerster has traced references to it in sixty-five poems. Other favorite trees of Whittier were the birch, the maple, and the elm.[1] But Whittier was especially fond of flowers; those

[1] Whittier was opposed to the cutting down of trees. In a manuscript letter to Mrs. Alice Freeman Palmer, dated April 8, 1891 (now in Wellesley College) he wrote: 'I hope you may persuade your former neighbor not to cut away the trees which skirt the lovely little lake in your town. If there is no other way to stop such desecration it might be best to pay the owner, what the wood is worth on the stump and leave it standing "a thing of beauty and a joy forever."'

who wanted to win his kindly feelings sent them to him quite often. He was known to prefer the wild rose and the lily of the valley. There are about forty kinds of flowers mentioned in his poetry, among them harebells, daisies, violets, laurels, asters, and pond-lilies.

While he obtained enjoyment from contemplating Nature and went to her for solace and for moral elevation, refusing to see that everything in Nature was at strife, he did not love her with a true artistic and pagan love. He even resented Wordsworth's and Bryant's overestimate of her, though they too found lessons of humanity in her. He saw Nature with squinting eyes, for he heard a sermon in every flower and saw a preacher under every tree.

Since he himself had been a country lad and had lived and worked on a farm, he felt that he was most qualified to give us the best pastoral poetry. It is apparent that he was thinking of himself, and saying 'I am the man,' when he wrote these lines in the essay on Dinsmore:

'And here let us say that the mere dilettante and the amateur ruralist may as well keep their hands off. The prize is not for them. He who would successfully strive for it must be himself what he sings, — part and parcel of that rural life of New England, — one who has grown strong amidst its healthful influences, familiar with its details, and capable of detecting whatever of beauty, humor, or pathos pertain to it, — one who has added to his book-lore the large experience of an active participation in the rugged toil, the hearty amusements, the trials and the pleasures he describes.'

In spite of this limited conception of the function of the poet, he always wrote what he had lived and seen. His life had been a preparation for the practice of his poetic art as he conceived it. Yet in one respect, and an important one, he fell short in his writing as a poet of rural life. He hated realism and naturalism and he was untrue to life in his art. For example, he avoided painting depressing scenes; if he described poverty, he only praised it; if he drew morons, he depicted them as noble and intellectual types. Once he did feel guilty that he was painting only the idyllic side of life. When writing 'Among the Hills,' he realized he was not giving a true picture of New England by dwelling only on its charming landscapes and the happiness of its tillers of the soil. He decided, therefore, to present the other side in the Prelude. Had he continued writing in this manner, he would have been a greater writer.

He falls short of Wordsworth and Crabbe because he was too greatly confined in the scope of his ballads. He ignored, as material for poems, the stories in the New England histories, palpitating with adultery, seduction, and illegitimate-child murder. He wrote few tales of struggles with temptation: if he did record such a struggle, it was one, like 'King Volmer and Elsie,' where the tempter was foiled. His stories are often flat, because they are lacking in variety of plot, and never touch the seamy side of life. He knew he was not telling the whole truth, and that he had adopted the ostrich-like policy of sticking his head into the sand in order not to see the enemy. He did not, in choice of theme, have the courage of other New England writers, like Hawthorne, who wrote about adultery.

The chief defect of Whittier as a writer, then, was that he did not depict life faithfully. He adopted the current view that he could dissolve the evils of society by treating them as if they did not exist — by remaining utterly reticent about them. He did not realize that he was adopting the same attitude that the Southerners had taken toward slavery, who blamed not themselves, but the abolitionists, for creating a slavery problem.

He had, however, a quality in his work that makes us overlook his falseness to life — his worship of the heroic character. Ostracized because of his abolition views, he portrayed men like himself, who were ready to sacrifice all comforts for the right deed or cause. He unconsciously incorporated in his work his own noble heroism. To the end of his days this militant Quaker admired heroes more than any other type of people. He was moved by any act of heroism, whether in the arena of politics or in the forum or in the field of battle, whether in private life or in the course of duty. His worship of the martyr type, which began in his boyhood, when he sang of heroic Quakers, almost became an obsession with him. He was thrilled and excited whenever he read about heroes and heroines. He found themes in newspapers; from them he derived inspiration for his early poem 'The Female Martyr,' celebrating the death of a nurse during a cholera epidemic. In them he found the story of Conductor Bradley, who gave his life in averting a wreck, and the tale of the captain of the Three Bells of Glasgow, who lay by all night to cheer another ship during a storm.

He saw heroism in the lives of the common people. When, in 1868, he was asked by Agnes A. Aubin, of Newburyport, to write something for the 'Breeze,' a paper published for the benefit of a fair for aged women, he sent in a tale of a heroine, 'Nancy Martin,' a seller of fruits and vegetables in Detroit, who gave the tract of land on which her cottage stood for a hospital for wounded soldiers.[1] One of the last prose stories he wrote was about Abigail Becker, the heroine of Longport, who rescued several men from a shipwrecked vessel. His hero-worship made him admire the courage of military men like Garibaldi and General Gordon.

His test of heroism was the willingness of a man or woman to give his or her life for a good deed or a noble act, as in the case of Barbara Frietchie. For this reason he so greatly admired Algernon Sidney and Sir Henry Vane, who were both unjustly executed for treason. He wrote many elegies to the memories of men who fought for liberty, because he believed that there were Bayards still with us, as he said in his poem 'The Hero,' wherein he celebrated the exploits of Samuel Gridley Howe in the Greek war for independence.

[1] The manuscript of the story of Nancy Martin, April, 1868, is in the Morgan Library. Whittier never collected the tale in his works.

His poems on the deaths of contemporary heroes, most of whom he personally knew, are unfortunately not well known — especially his elegies on Charles B. Storrs, S. Oliver Torrey (not to be confused with the Reverend Charles Torrey), Thomas Shipley, Charles Follen, Daniel Wheeler, Robert Rantoul, Jr., Thomas Starr King, George L. Stearns, and many others whom posterity has forgotten. No poet ever celebrated the deaths of a nobler set of men than did Whittier.

The transition from celebrating heroes in ballads, to pleading for the slave in abolition poems, was gradual and natural. If Whittier could sing of Quakers ready to die for their religion, he could just as consistently write about abolitionists ready to give up all the comforts of life for their ideals; yet the critics have placed his abolition poems under the ban as being propaganda. They have regarded them as mere landmarks connected with events no longer of timely interest. In recent years literature bearing a social message has been more liberally interpreted; propaganda has even been recognized as a requisite of a higher form of art. We may with propriety, then, dismiss the view that Whittier's poems on abolition are 'out of date.' Some critics recognize that many of his poems of freedom are just as applicable today as they were in the days of slavery. His protests against stifling free speech, his pleas against social and moral injustice, his attacks upon men who condoned institutions that supported vested interests, are still timely. In short, it is to Lowell's, and not to Whipple's, estimate of Whittier, that we should return.

Radical literary critics, with few exceptions, have rejected Whittier. Reformers who have accepted Garrison as their idol have inconsistently ignored the Whittier of the abolition period. He should be their representative, their mouthpiece, for he voices their protests against social injustice artistically and vigorously, and he was shrewder and more practical than Garrison.

We should no longer entertain the point of view about

Whittier presented a quarter of a century ago by Paul Elmer
More, who entirely dismissed all the poet's abolition poems in
favor of the poems painting the ideal home and those affording religious consolation. Mr. More saw in Whittier only the
type of poet who, like Cowper, composed hymns and sang of
the sofa in 'The Task'; he ignored the Miltonic strains that
breathe through Whittier's work. His assertion that Whittier's gifts on the altar of freedom cannot be compared with
his picture of the ideal of the home and his hymns of homely
comforts of the spirit is characteristic of the tendency of conservative critics to select only the innocuous poems in the
radical poets whom they are compelled to admire.

Misrepresentation of Whittier began in the seventies and
eighties, when a period of critical adulation and unbalanced
judgment set in that destroyed for a time any possible sane
view of his work as a whole. The public was led to look upon
Whittier as the poet of the school-children and as the con-
soler of the aged, and to ignore his early work in the anti-
slavery cause. Edwin Whipple, who was the first critic to
launch Whittier into respectability, in spite of his abolition
verse, wrote to him in later years:

'And then the singular purity of your poetry. You not
only never touch the sensual, but hardly ever touch the sen-
suous elements which enter into so much of what we still
must call good poetry. The moral atmosphere of everything
you have written is as free from taint as the breath of a new
born babe: I have always considered you one of the great
moral and purifying forces of the time.'

Piety and moral purity are more lovable qualities in a poet
than blasphemy and sedition, from the public and academic
point of view. Moreover, since Whittier never altogether outgrew his early allegiance to the ever popular Mrs. Sigourney
and Mrs. Hemans, he again attracted by his later poems
readers of ordinary mental caliber. As he never altogether
abandoned his allegiance to Cowper and Burns, he appealed
also to the critics with a timid vision of life, who were only

too glad to minimize his affinity to Milton and Shelley. Yet nothing is more apparent than that he too sang of liberty, attacked the priesthood and statesmanship of his time, and hated absolutism in government. Essentially he had Milton's spirit, but he spun it out in the texture of Burns. Yet he made a contribution to poetry that was all his own — his denunciatory, Huguenot-Quaker-Puritan soul hating the oppressor and loving the noble in character.

Whittier has had little or no influence upon our great contemporary writers who unflinchingly record the harsh realities of life, upon men like Eugene O'Neill, Edwin Arlington Robinson, and Robinson Jeffers.

'He has not influenced me in the slightest,' Eugene O'Neill assures me. 'I never could see much beyond elocution class exercises in anything he ever wrote. (But maybe my judgment was permanently warped by first making his acquaintance *via* an elocution class and being forced to memorize "Barbara Frietchie.")' [1]

'I am not conscious of any influence of Whittier in my work,' writes Edwin Arlington Robinson, 'though I may have absorbed something of him in my early career. An author never quite knows about that.'

'I am not conscious,' Robinson Jeffers informs me, 'of any influence of Whittier's work on mine. I enjoyed some of his poems when I was a boy. They were not a part of my school-work.'

His influence has, however, been great upon writers of our day who have combined propaganda with their art; upon authors like Upton Sinclair, William Ellery Leonard, and Edwin Markham.

'We who in these days are daring to challenge wage slavery,' Sinclair said in 'Mammonart,' 'and are witnessing mobbings and jailings and torturing for the cause, must not

---

[1] The comments of Eugene O'Neill, Edwin Arlington Robinson, Robinson Jeffers, William Ellery Leonard, and Edwin Markham of Whittier's influence or lack of influence upon them are from letters to me, in response to my request for information.

forget that back in the 1830's this gentle Quaker poet was stoned and nearly lynched in Massachusetts, and mobbed again and had his office burned about his head in Philadelphia.'

Edwin Markham has understood Whittier better than most of our critics, as is apparent from his poem to Whittier for the unveiling of Whittier's bust in the Hall of Fame. He declares: 'While still a young man, at a time when simpering poets are inditing sonnets to some languishing lady, our Quaker bard was facing excited and lawless crowds in Boston and Philadelphia. He was our Amos demanding justice: he was our Isaiah prophesying doom. These were the characteristics of Whittier which strongly drew my attention in my young manhood: it was this spirit which was upon me in those early mornings in 1899 when I was writing "The Man with the Hoe." These influences are still upon my life.'

'He was our most passionate poet,' insists William Ellery Leonard, 'as the man most full of fire — the old eyes reveal it still, untricked by gusts. Of course, he wrote a heap that had mainly ephemeral purpose — yet even all that is documentary of the times and has often enough, too, something in it more than the times (as "Massachusetts to Virginia"). He was a propagandist in his art — that is, he was most stirred to make verses by the urge to convince people that his vision of life should prevail — that is, an urge back of "Snow-Bound" along with the urge of reminiscence. It has been the urge back of most great literature; best art is propaganda, though not all propaganda is art (this holds, too, of J. G. W.).'

We may with justice ask: Did the poet show wisdom in his return, in old age, to the writing of tales about specter ships, Indians, and New England superstitions, instead of voicing other humanitarian causes that emerged after slavery was abolished? Was he greater as a poet and more laudable as a man when he went back to those legends than he was in the middle years of his life, when he was penning attacks upon clergymen and statesmen for their support of slavery? Should we give up 'Clerical Oppressors' and 'The Pastoral Letter' for 'The Swan Song of Parson Avery' and 'The Dead Ship of Harpswell'?

The fame of the martial ringing verses of his middle years was obliterated by the repeated reprintings of his poems of country life and of sentimental regret. The public forgot that no American poet had written more indignantly and pro-testingly against moral and political injustice, that no one had wielded a more vitriolic pen against sponsors of, and compromisers with, oppression.

Most of the school readers, naturally, had harmless se-lections. I found, after examining a score or more of school readers that their compilers chose most frequently the simplest and most innocuous of his poems, like 'The Bare-foot Boy,' 'Maud Muller,' 'The Three Bells,' 'In School Days' and 'The Corn Song.' McGuffey, however, had in his 'Fifth Reader' a poem of propaganda, 'The Prisoner for Debt.'

Unfortunately, Whittier himself was pleased by the en-thusiasm of the school-children and the epistolary effusions of woman writers. He voluntarily resigned his laurels as the champion of the oppressed and spokesman of the reformers.

He was not a minor poet, nor altogether a provincial one. In spite of his intellectual deficiencies and his trivial technical faults, he is a poet of a high order, because he effectively dealt with important themes. His intensity of emotion, his universality of appeal, and his natural gift of expression en-hance the value of his poetry. Of course, he ranks far below Milton and Shelley, but he should be placed with them among the poets of liberty. He was not a mere sectarian poet, like Bernard Barton, nor a poet of a class only, like Ebenezer El-liott. He stood out as a poet of nature, as a balladist, as a singer of the home affections, as a recorder of old legends, as a poet of reform, as a religious poet, as a composer of hymns, as a writer of elegies, but, above all, as a champion of liberty;

he takes his position on a higher plane than poets with more limited ranges and less intensity — poets like Bryant, Lowell, Holmes, Longfellow, and Poe. His messages of the antislavery days are vital for all time, because liberty always remains an ideal for which to fight, because oppression with the sanction of the law still exists, because modern capitalist is old slaveholder writ large. As long as social injustice and wage-slavery last, Whittier's poems of freedom will find responsive chords in human hearts. He is one of the great New England literary quartette — he ranks with Emerson, Hawthorne, and Thoreau. He is the one of the few prophets in American literature.

CHRONOLOGY

1806	Sept. 3	Mary, Whittier's oldest sister, born.
1807	Dec. 17	John Greenleaf Whittier born, in Haverhill.
1812	July 4	Matthew Franklin, Whittier's brother, born.
1815	Dec. 7	Elizabeth Hussey, Whittier's youngest sister, born.
1817	Summer	President Monroe visits Haverhill.
1822		Schoolmaster Joshua Coffin introduces him to the poems of Robert Burns.
		At school. Attracted to his cousin, Mary Emerson Smith.
	December	Time of the scene described in 'Snow-Bound,' at which Harriet Livermore was present.
1824		His uncle Moses Whittier killed by the fall of a tree.
1826	June 9	Whittier's first poem, 'The Exile's Departure,' published in Garrison's *Newburyport Free Press*.
		Garrison visits Whittier.
1827	*circa*	First visit to Boston.
		Begins to contribute poems to the *Haverhill Gazette*.
	April 30	Reads poem at dedication of Haverhill Academy.
	May–Sept.	Student at the Haverhill Academy.
		Meets here Evelina Bray.
1827–28	Winter	Teaches school at Birch Meadow.
1828		Contributes poems to the *Boston Statesman*.
	January	Prospectus issued for poems by Adrian (Whittier).
		Contributes introduction and poem to a book of poems by Robert Dinsmore.
	Summer	Second term at Haverhill Academy.
		Poems by Whittier appear in Garrison's *Philanthropist*, George D. Prentice's *The New England Review*, and Garrison's *Bennington Journal of the Times*.
	Sept. 26	John G. C. Brainard dies.
1829	January	Becomes editor of the *American Manufacturer* in Boston.
	April	Writes in despair to Mary Emerson Smith.
	August	Resigns from the *Manufacturer*.
	November	Publishes 'The Minstrel Girl' in *The Yankee*.
1830	January	Editor of the *Essex Gazette*.
	March	Issues proposals for *History of Haverhill*.
	June	Father dies.
	July	Editor of the *New England Review*, Hartford.
	October 18	Poem 'New England' published in *Review*.
1831	January	In New York gathering material for Prentice's *Life of Henry Clay*.
	January	Garrison founds the *Liberator*.

1831	February	*Legends of New England,* his first book.
	June 7	James Otis Rockwell dies in Providence.
	Fall	Chosen delegate from Connecticut to National Republican Convention, for Clay.
		Biography of Henry Clay by G. D. Prentice, of which Whittier wrote the last part.
	Latter part of year	Advances to Cornelia Russ rejected.
1832	January	Ill and resigns from the *Review.*
	Spring	Publishes *Moll Pitcher.*
	Summer	Edits *The Literary Remains of John G. C. Brainard.*
		Begins to contribute to the *New England Magazine.*
		Supports Caleb Cushing for Congress and then proposes to run himself.
		Garrison publishes *Thoughts on Colonization.*
1833	Spring	Garrison converts Whittier to abolitionism.
	June	Whittier publishes *Justice and Expediency.*
	Fall	Loses nomination for State Senator from Essex by one vote.
	November	First antislavery poems 'Toussaint L'Ouverture' in *New England Magazine* and 'To the Memory of Charles B. Storrs' in the *Liberator.*
	December	In Philadelphia as delegate to the first meeting of the American Anti-Slavery Convention.
1834	Spring	Helps found Haverhill Anti-Slavery Society.
	May	At convention of New England Anti-Slavery Society in Boston and helps draft *An Address to the People of the United States.*
	June	Presents resolutions at Essex County Anti-Slavery Society, of which he is corresponding secretary, for abolition of slavery in District of Columbia.
	July 4	Rioting at meeting in Chatham Street Chapel, New York, where Whittier's hymn is sung.
	September 13	Poem 'Our Fellow Countrymen in Chains' in the *Liberator.*
	Fall	Persuades Cushing to comply with demands of Essex County abolitionists, and thus brings about his election to Congress.
		Elected member of the Massachusetts legislature.
1835	Early part of year	In session of the legislature in Boston.
	September 4	Mobbed with George Thompson in Concord, N.H.
	Fall	Again elected to legislature, but does not serve.
1836	February	Letter in the *Haverhill Gazette* attacking Edward Everett for seeking to suppress free speech.
	April	Trial of Dr. Reuben Crandall in Washington for giving away Whittier's reprinted pamphlet *Justice and Expediency.*
	May	Becomes editor of the *Essex Gazette.*
	June	Publishes his poem against Pinckney's Resolutions in the *Gazette.*

1836	July	Family moves to new home in Amesbury after having sold the farm at Haverhill.
	December	Leaves the *Gazette*.
1837	January	In Philadelphia with the Thayers. Meets Elizabeth Lloyd.
	January 31st to February 3rd	At Harrisburg at the convention of the Pennsylvania Anti-Slavery Society.
	March	Lobbying in Boston against Van Buren, in behalf of abolition of slavery in District of Columbia, and succeeds in having a right-of-jury bill for fugitive slaves passed.
	June	*Poems* published in Boston.
	June to Fall	In New York in employ of the American Anti-Slavery Society.
		Meets Lucy Hooper in New York.
	October	'The Pastoral Letter.'
	November 7	Rev. Elijah P. Lovejoy, abolitionist, murdered at Alton, Illinois.
1838	January and February	In New York.
	March 15	Becomes editor of the *Pennsylvania Freeman* in Philadelphia.
	March 22	Publishes 'The Farewell of a Virginia Mother' in the *Freeman*.
	May	Attends annual meeting of the American Anti-Slavery Society in New York.
	May 17	Pennsylvania Hall in Philadelphia, office of the *Freeman*, burned to the ground by the mob.
	November	At Liberty Party Convention at Salem urging Cushing to renew his pledges for re-election.
	November	*Poems* published in Philadelphia.
1839	February	Writes poem against Governor Porter of Pennsylvania.
	April	Back in Philadelphia.
	July	Visits Harrisburg and tours central Pennsylvania for the antislavery cause.
	August	At the antislavery convention in Albany to smooth over difficulties.
	October 22	Benjamin Lundy dies.
	Fall	Back in Philadelphia.
1840	January 13	Professor Charles Follen perishes in the fire on the steamboat 'Lexington.'
	January	Visits Washington and calls on John Quincy Adams.
	February	Resigns from the *Freeman* on account of ill health.
	March and April	Back in Amesbury.
	Spring	Again in Philadelphia to attend meeting of Pennsylvania Anti-Slavery Society.
	May	Disruption of American Anti-Slavery Society and forming of the political-action party, the Foreign and American Anti-Slavery Society.
	June	Back in Amesbury.

1840	November	Supports the Liberty Party Ticket, James G. Birney and Thomas Earle.
	November and December	Controversy with Nathaniel P. Rogers in the *Freeman* and *National Anti-Slavery Standard* about the London Anti-Slavery Convention and about the Liberty Party.
1841	First half	Contributes to *Knickerbocker Magazine*.
	Spring and Summer	Tours eastern United States with Joseph Sturge, the English abolitionist.
	August 1	Lucy Hooper dies.
	September and October	Editor of *American and Foreign Anti-Slavery Reporter*, of New York, he remaining at home.
	December (1841) and January (1842)	Temporary editor of the *Emancipator* in Boston.
1842	February	Member of the State Central Committee (Mass.) of the Liberty Party.
	November	Candidate for Congress on the Liberty Party Ticket.
		Attacked by Rogers and Garrison.
1843	January	Poem 'Massachusetts to Virginia' in the *Liberator* *apropos* of the Latimer case.
		Whittier continues candidate throughout the year to keep up the deadlock.
	March	Cushing nominated by President John Tyler for Secretary of Treasury. Whittier publishes Cushing's abolition letter of 1838 and Cushing is rejected three consecutive times by the Senate.
	May	*Lays of My Home*.
		Contributes to *Democratic Review*, having begun in 1837.
1844	January	Recognition by Edwin Whipple in the *North American Review*.
	July	Becomes editor of *Middlesex Standard* and moves to Lowell.
	August 1	Hears Emerson's first antislavery speech at Concord, Massachusetts.
	September	Tries unsuccessfully to persuade Longfellow to run for Congress on the Liberty Party Ticket.
	November	Meets Lucy Larcom at Lowell.
	November	Candidate on the Liberty Party Ticket for State Legislature.
		Birney runs again for President on Liberty Party Ticket. Clay defeated by Polk.
	December	Writes in the *Standard* in behalf of Rev. Charles T. Torrey, convicted in Baltimore of aiding a fugitive slave.
		First English edition of his poems published.
1845	January	Active in trying to prevent Texas from being annexed to the United States.
	March	Texas annexed.
		Whittier leaves the *Standard*.

1845	July	Writes to Charles Sumner about his oration for peace; beginning of their friendship.
	October	Campaigning in behalf of the Liberty Party.
		The *Stranger in Lowell* published.
		Writes editorials for the *Essex Transcript*, having begun a few years previously and continuing a few years later.
	December	In Washington with Henry Wilson to carry petition against the admission of Texas as a slave State.
1846	May	Mexican War begins.
		Voices of Freedom published.
		Maiden aunt Mercy Evans Hussey, mother's sister, dies.
	May 9	Rev. Charles T. Torrey dies in jail.
		Whittier attends funeral.
	Summer	Is reputed to be engaged to Ida Russell.
	October	Accidentally shot in cheek by boy shooting at a mark.
	October 16	Nathaniel P. Rogers dies.
		John P. Hale elected United States Senator from New Hampshire.
		'The Reformer' poem in *The Fountain* for 1847.
1847	January	Becomes corresponding editor of the *National Era*, Washington, D.C.
	September	General Scott captures Mexico.
	September	Advocates Hale as presidential candidate on Liberty Party Ticket.
	October	Hale nominated in convention at Buffalo.
		Supernaturalism in New England published.
1848	February	In Washington and calls on John Quincy Adams shortly before his death.
	February 23	John Quincy Adams dies.
	February	Treaty of Peace with Mexico.
	August	Martin Van Buren nominated for President by Free Soil Party, and Hale no longer a candidate.
	November	General Taylor, Whig candidate, elected.
		Poems, 1849 edition, issued.
1849		Makes friendly overtures to Mary E. Carter.
		Leaves from Margaret Smith's Journal.
1850	March 7	Webster's Seventh of March speech in favor of Fugitive Slave Law.
	May 2	Whittier's poem 'Ichabod' in the *National Era*.
	July 1	Bayard Taylor first visits him.
	Early summer	*Songs of Labor* published.
	Summer	Persuades Charles Sumner to run for U.S. Senator on Coalition ticket.
	September	Fugitive Slave Law passed.
	October	Whittier declines nomination for State Senator by Democrats to run on a coalition ticket.
		Coalition ticket of Democrats and Free Soilers in Massachusetts wins.

1850		*Old Portraits and Modern Sketches* published. Alice and Phœbe Cary visit him.
1851	April	Thomas M. Sims, fugitive slave, ordered returned from Massachusetts to Georgia.
	April	Whittier very ill and near death.
	April	Sumner chosen Senator by the Massachusetts legislature.
	December	Kossuth comes to America.
1852		Leaflet circulated asking Whittier be indicted for treason.
		Uncle Tom's Cabin published.
	June 29	Henry Clay dies.
	August 7	Robert Rantoul, Jr., dies.
	October 24	Daniel Webster dies.
	November	John P. Hale runs for President on Free Soil Platform.
		Franklin Pierce elected.
1853		*The Chapel of the Hermits* published.
		First meets Oliver Wendell Holmes.
	September	Politely accepts Lucy Larcom's adulation.
1854		*Literary Recreations* published.
	April and June	Tries to persuade Robert C. Winthrop to become leader of the new Republican Party.
	May 23	Kansas-Nebraska Bill passed.
	May	Anthony Burns, fugitive slave, ordered to be returned.
	May 26	Meeting at Faneuil Hall. Attempted rescue of Burns by Thomas Wentworth Higginson and others fails.
	December	'Maud Muller' published in *National Era*.
1855	January	'The Barefoot Boy' in *Little Pilgrim*.
1856	May 22	Sumner assaulted by Preston S. Brooks for his speech 'The Crime against Kansas.'
		The Panorama and Other Poems published.
	July	Chairman of a Committee of Resolutions at a Fremont meeting in Amesbury.
	November	John C. Fremont, Presidential Candidate of Republican Party, defeated by James Buchanan, Democrat.
1857	November	First issue of the *Atlantic Monthly* appears, with poem by Whittier.
	November	Discourages the kindly attentions of Mary E. Carter.
	November 25	James G. Birney dies.
	December 27	Whittier's mother, Abigail Hussey, dies.
1858	February	Elected by legislature member of the Board of Overseers of Harvard College.
	November	Theodore Tilton asks Whittier to write for *The Independent*.
	November	In Philadelphia visiting Elizabeth Lloyd.
1859	May	Again in Philadelphia visiting Miss Lloyd.
	May 14	Joseph Sturge dies in Birmingham, England.

1859	June	Crisis in the affair with Elizabeth Lloyd.
	September	Gail Hamilton's first visit to Whittier.
1860	January 7	Mrs. Mary Caldwell, Whittier's oldest sister, dies.
	Spring	*The National Era* goes out of existence.
		Honorary Degree of Master of Arts from Harvard.
	November	The affair with Elizabeth Lloyd over.
	November	Lincoln elected. Whittier member of the Electoral College.
		Home Ballads published.
1861	February	Whittier opposed to coercing Southern States but also to too great a compromise.
	Summer	At Salisbury Beach.
1862	Spring	Lincoln reads Whittier's poem '"Ein feste Burg ist unser Gott."'
1863		Meets Mrs. Thaxter on visit to the Isle of Shoals.
1863	Summer	Cousin Moses A. Cartland dies.
1863	October	'Barbara Frietchie' published.
1863		*In War Time, and Other Poems* published.
1864	March	D. A. Wasson's article on Whittier in the *Atlantic Monthly*.
	May 19	Nathaniel Hawthorne dies.
	September 3	Elizabeth Hussey Whittier, his sister, dies.
	November	Lincoln re-elected. Whittier member of the electoral college.
1865	January 15	Edward Everett dies.
		Thirteenth Amendment passed.
	February	'Laus Deo' published in *Independent*.
	April 9	Peace of Appomattox.
	April 14	Lincoln assassinated.
	June	Reads his poem 'Revisited' at the Laurels on the Merrimac.
	July 23	Arthur Tappan dies.
	September	Working on *Snow-Bound*.
1866	February	*Snow-Bound* published.
		Doctor of Laws from Harvard.
	October	Collected Prose in two volumes.
1867	January	Very ill.
		The Tent on the Beach published.
	December	Meets Charles Dickens in Boston.
1868		*Among the Hills* published.
	February to May	Impeachment and acquittal of President Johnson.
		Votes for General Grant for President.
		Some Recollections of our Anti-Slavery Conflict by Samuel J. May.
1869		Member of the Board of Trustees of Brown University.
		William Claflin becomes Governor of Massachusetts.
1870	January	'In School-Days' in *Young Folks*.

1870	Spring	In New York, visiting the Cary sisters, William H. Burleigh, and others.
1871	February 12	Alice Cary dies.
	March 18	William H. Burleigh dies.
	July 1	Samuel J. May dies.
	July 31	Phœbe Cary dies.
		Miriam, and Other Poems published.
		Edits the *Journal of John Woolman.*
		Meets Bret Harte in Boston.
1872		First volume of Henry Wilson's *History of the Rise and Fall of the Slave Power in America.*
	August	Whittier's house struck by lightning.
	October 30	George MacDonald, English novelist, visits him.
		The Pennsylvania Pilgrim published.
	November	Votes for Grant against Horace Greeley.
1873	March	Explains in Boston *Daily Advertiser* his petition for rescinding resolutions of the Massachusetts legislature to censure Sumner.
	December 19	John P. Hale dies.
1874	June 13	Rev. J. Miller McKim dies.
		Contemplates publishing an edition of Dymond.
		Meets Charles Kingsley.
	August 15	Charles Sumner dies.
		Hazel Blossoms published.
1875	November	Arranges through Charles H. Brainard to have a bust of himself in Haverhill Public Library.
	November 22	Henry Wilson dies.
1876	June	Meets Dom Pedro II, Emperor of Brazil, in Boston.
		Writes Centennial Hymn.
		Niece, Elizabeth Whittier, marries Samuel T. Pickard.
	Summer	At the Bearcamp House, West Ossipee, N.H., with Lucy Larcom working on the compilation *Songs of Three Centuries.*
	Summer	Takes up his home at Danvers with his cousins the Johnsons.
	November	Votes for Hayes against Tilden.
1877		Attacks radical demagogues in his poem 'The Problem.'
	December	Seventieth Birthday Dinner in Boston.
1878	June 12	William Cullen Bryant dies.
	June 13	Charles C. Burleigh dies.
		The Vision of Echard published.
	December 19	Bayard Taylor dies while at Berlin.
1879	January 2	Caleb Cushing dies.
	May 24	William Lloyd Garrison dies.
	June	At yearly meeting of Friends in Portland.
	November	Jubilee Singers of Fisk University call on him at Amesbury.
	Latter part	Paul A. Hayne and his wife visit Whittier.

1880		Writes an introduction for Oliver Johnson's *Life of Garrison*.
	October 20	Lydia Maria Child dies.
	November 11	Lucretia Mott dies.
1881		*The King's Missive* published.
	March	Controversy with Dr. George E. Ellis about authenticity of the facts in *The King's Missive*.
	April 24	James T. Fields dies.
	July	Replica of Powers bust placed in Boston Public Library.
1882	March 24	Longfellow dies.
	April 27	Ralph Waldo Emerson dies.
	Summer	At the Asquam House, Holderness, N.H.
		General Benjamin F. Butler elected Governor of Massachusetts by the Democrats and Greenbackers.
		The first book about Whittier published by W. S. Kennedy.
1882–83		Winter in Boston at a hotel.
1883	January 7	Death of his brother, Matthew Franklin, leaving Whittier the only surviving member of the family.
	Summer	Again in New Hampshire hills.
	November 28	Goes to luncheon to meet Matthew Arnold in Boston.
		The Bay of Seven Islands published.
		Letters of Lydia Maria Child with an Introduction by Whittier.
1884	February 2	Wendell Phillips dies.
	Summer	Again at Asquam House and then near Center Harbor, N.H.
		Portrait of Whittier presented to the Friends' School at Providence, Rhode Island.
		Votes for James G. Blaine against Cleveland.
		F. H. Underwood's book on Whittier, supervised by him, published.
1885	May	Edmund Clarence Stedman's article on Whittier in the *Century Magazine*.
		Paul Hamilton Hayne again visits him.
	September 10	Reunion of students at Haverhill Academy.
	November 21	Elizur Wright dies.
		Publication of the story of Garrison's life by his children begins.
1886		*Saint Gregory's Guest*, published.
	Summer	At Center Harbor, N.H., with the Cartlands and Lucy Larcom.
1887	January 14	Henry B. Stanton dies.
		A town near Los Angeles named 'Whittier' after him.
	Summer	At Lake Asquam.
	November	Whittier banquet given in Boston by the Essex Club, with testimonials from leading statesmen of the country.

1887	November	Refuses to write a letter petitioning to have the Chicago anarchists' sentence commuted.
	December 17	Eightieth birthday celebrated throughout the country by the school-children.
	December	Writes the quatrain for the Milton Memorial Window in St. Margaret's Church, London.
1888		Appearance of the collected and reclassified Riverside Edition of his poetical works in four volumes.
1889		Ill most of the year.
	Summer	At Conway, N.H.
		Whittier's article about himself in Appletons' *Cyclopædia of American Biography*.
		Prose works published in three volumes.
	December	Birthday spent at Amesbury.
1890	Summer	On the Piscataqua River, Eliot, Maine, with his cousins Joseph and Gertrude Cartland.
		At Sundown privately printed.
		Receives $1000 for the 'Captain's Well' from the New York *Ledger*.
		Receives $1000 for the poem 'Haverhill' from the *Atlantic Monthly*. The poem read at celebration of the town.
1891	August 12	James Russell Lowell dies.
	November	At Newburyport with his cousin Joseph Cartland.
1892	January	Recovering from very severe illness at Newburyport.
	April	At Oak Knoll.
	May	At Amesbury.
	Summer	At Hampton Falls, N.H., at Sarah A. Gove's home.
	August	Writes poem on Oliver Wendell Holmes, his last poem.
		Kennedy's second book on Whittier appears.
		Corrects proofs for popular edition of his last volume *At Sundown*.
	September 3	Suffers a paralytic stroke.
	September 7	Dies.
	September 10	Buried at Amesbury.

BIBLIOGRAPHY

The following brief list contains the more important books by and about Whittier. The abbreviated form in parenthesis is that used in the notes.

Whittier, John Greenleaf: *Complete Poetical Works. Cambridge Edition*. Boston: Houghton, Mifflin & Co., 1894.

This edition follows the four-volume Riverside Edition, in which the arrangement was that finally adopted by the author. It includes an appendix of early and uncollected poems and those printed in Pickard's *Life of Whittier*, besides the final volume *At Sundown* (1892) and it has full notes and a chronological list of the poems.

Whittier, John Greenleaf: *Complete Poetical Works. Household Edition*, with one hundred and twenty-nine illustrations. Boston. Houghton, Mifflin & Co., 1904.

This edition is based on the Cambridge Edition, but the notes are not quite so complete and the chronological list is not included. (Poems)

Whittier, John Greenleaf: *Poetical Works. Household Edition*. Boston: Houghton, Mifflin & Co., 1887.

This represents Whittier's poems before he classified and revised them, and as they were known to the readers of his day. Its value to the student of Whittier is that it preserves the order of his first two collected editions, those of 1849 and 1857, and that it contains all the succeeding volumes intact and in chronological order. (*Old Household Edition*.)

Whittier, John Greenleaf: *Margaret Smith's Journal; Tales and Sketches*. Boston: Houghton, Mifflin & Co., 1889. (*Prose*, Vol. I)

Whittier, John Greenleaf: *Old Portraits and Modern Sketches; Personal Sketches and Tributes; Historical Papers*. Boston: Houghton, Mifflin & Co., 1889. (*Prose*, Vol. II)

Whittier, John Greenleaf: *The Conflict with Slavery; Politics and Reform; The Inner Life; Criticism*. Boston: Houghton, Mifflin & Co., 1889. (*Prose*, Vol. III)

The preceding three volumes are the fifth, sixth, and seventh volumes of the collected writings of 1889.

Whittier, John Greenleaf: *Prose Works*, 2 vols. 1866.

Kennedy, William Sloane: *John Greenleaf Whittier — His Life, Genius and Writings*. 1882. The first book published about Whittier. References are to the 1886 edition. (Kennedy I)

Kennedy, William Sloane: *John G. Whittier, the Poet of Freedom*, American Reformers. 1892. (Kennedy II)

Underwood, Francis H.: *John Greenleaf Whittier: A Biography*. 1884. (Underwood)

Claflin, Mary B.: *Personal Recollections of John Greenleaf Whittier.* 1893. (Claflin)

Linton, W. J.: *Life of John Greenleaf Whittier.* Great Writers, London, 1893. (Linton)

Fields, Annie: *Whittier: Notes of His Life and His Friendships.* 1893. Reprinted in *Authors and Friends.* 1896, to which volume the references apply. (Fields)

Pickard, Samuel T.: *The Life and Letters of John Greenleaf Whittier.* 2 vols. 1894. The standard life. (Pickard) The one-volume edition of 1907 has a few additions and corrections.

Pickard, Samuel T.: *Whittier-Land.* 1904. (*Whittier-Land*)

Flower, B. O.: *Whittier: Prophet, Seer and Man.* 1896. (Flower)

Higginson, Thomas Wentworth: *John Greenleaf Whittier.* English Men of Letters. 1902. (Higginson)

Carpenter, George Rice: *John Greenleaf Whittier.* American Men of Letters. 1903. (Carpenter)

Woodman, A. J.: Reminiscences of John Greenleaf Whittier's Life at Oak Knoll, Danvers. *Historical Collections of the Essex Institute,* April, 1908. Also issued separately. (Woodman)

Albree, John (Editor): *Whittier Correspondence from Oak Knoll Collections, 1830–1892.* Salem, Mass., 1911. (Albree)

Denervaud, Marie V. (Editor): *Whittier's Unknown Romance: Letters to Elizabeth Lloyd.* 1922. (Denervaud)

Sparhawk, Frances C.: *Whittier at Close Range.* 1925, The Riverside Press, Boston. (Sparhawk)

Pray, Frances Mary: *A Study of Whittier's Apprenticeship as a Poet. Dealing with Poems Written between 1825 and 1835 not available in the Poet's Collected Works.* Thesis. Pennsylvania State College. 1930. (Pray)

BIBLIOGRAPHIES

The John Greenleaf Whittier Centenary Exhibition at the Essex Institute, December 17, 1907–January 31, 1908. *The Essex Institute Historical Collections,* April, 1908. pp. 123–146.

Poole's Index, 1881, and succeeding volumes to 1906. Under 'Whittier.'

Reader's Guide to Periodical Literature, 1900 and succeeding volumes to date. Under 'Whittier.'

Anderson, John P. In W. J. Linton's *Life of John Greenleaf Whittier,* pp. i–viii.

Bierstadt, E. H. 'A Bibliography of the Original Editions of John Greenleaf Whittier,' *The Book Buyer,* May–October, 1895.

Ristine, Frank Humphrey: in *The Cambridge History of American Literature,* Vol. 2, 1918, pp. 436–451. The most complete bibliography.

The Stephen H. Wakeman Collection. 1924. (Whittier Nos. 1076–1279.)

Pray, Frances Mary: *A Study of Whittier's Apprenticeship as a Poet.* 1930. Contains a bibliography of uncollected poems from newspapers, magazines, and periodicals up to 1835, and from Annuals up to 1855.

BOOKS AND ARTICLES CONTAINING CRITICAL AND
BIOGRAPHICAL MATTER

The following select bibliography is meant to be supplementary to the items given by John P. Anderson and Frank H. Ristine, though it has a number cited by them. Manuscript sources and newspapers which Whittier edited or for which he wrote are not given, as they appear in the notes.

Adams, Alice Dana: *The Neglected Period of Anti-Slavery in America.* Radcliffe College Monographs, No. 14, 1908.

Adams, Henry: *The Education of Henry Adams.* 1918. (Contemporary History.)

Adams, Charles F.: *Memoirs of John Quincy Adams.* 12 vols., 1874–1877.

Addison, Daniel D.: *Lucy Larcom, Life, Letters and Diary.* 1894.

Allan, Elizabeth Preston: *The Life and Letters of Margaret Junkin Preston.* 1903.

American Book Prices Current.

American Monthly Magazine, The, February, 1830. The Editor's Table. (A eulogy by N. P. Willis.)

Appletons' Cyclopædia of American Biography. Edited by J. G. Wilson and John Fiske, 6 vols., 1887–1889. Articles on John P. Hale and John Greenleaf Whittier.

Barrows, Mary Minerva: 'The Love Story of Whittier's Life. Personal Reminiscences of the Poet's Sweetheart, Evelina Bray.' *New England Magazine,* April, 1905.

Bartlett, A. L., and Kelly, C. E.: *The Haverhill Academy.* 1890.

Batchelder, Charles E.: 'Rev. Stephen Bachiler,' *New England Historical and Genealogical Register,* Jan.–Oct., 1892.

Birney, Catherine H.: *The Grimké Sisters: Sarah and Angelina Grimké.* 1885.

Birney, William: *James G. Birney and His Times.* 1890.

Blackwell, Alice Stone: *Lucy Stone.* 1930.

Boston *Daily Advertiser,* Dec. 17, 1887. A valuable number devoted to Whittier on the occasion of his eightieth birthday. It includes a poem by Bliss Carman, never collected.

Boston *Pilot,* April–May, 1839: Defence of O'Connell. (A eulogy on Whittier's article.)

Boston *Quarterly Review,* January, 1838. Review of the 1837 edition of the poems.

Boutwell, George S.: *Reminiscences of Sixty Years.* 2 vols., 1902. (Contemporary History.)

Bowditch, Vincent Y.: *Life and Correspondence of Henry Ingersoll Bowditch.* 2 vols., 1902.

Bryant, William Cullen: *Selections from American Poets.* 1839.

Buck, William J.: 'John G. Whittier' in *The Cuttalossa, and its Historical, Traditional and Poetical Associations,* pp. 54–56. Privately printed at the Intelligencer Office, Doylestown, Pa., 1897.

Burleigh, William H.: *Poems.* 1871.

Burr, Anna Robeson: *Weir Mitchell.* 1929.

Burroughs, John: 'Nature and the Poets,' *Pepacton.* 1881.

Burton, Richard: *John Greenleaf Whittier.* The Beacon Biographies. 1901.

Calverton, V. F.: *The Liberation of American Literature.* 1932.

Chamberlin, Joseph E.: *The Boston Transcript.* 1930.

Channing, William E.: *A Tribute to the Abolitionists* (n.d.).

Chase, George W.: *The History of Haverhill.* 1861.

Cheever, George B.: *Commonplace Book of American Poetry.* 1831.

Christy, Arthur: 'Orientalism in New England,' *American Literature,* January, 1930.

Clarke, J. C.: *Study of English and American Poets.* 1900.

Common, John R., and Associates: *History of Labour in the United States.* 2 vols., 1918. (Contemporary History.)

Conway, Moncure D.: *Autobiography.* 2 vols., 1904.

Cowley, Charles: *Illustrated History of Lowell.* 1868.

Crawford, M. C.: 'Whittier's Lost Love' in *Romance of Old New Roof Trees,* pp. 366–381. 1903.

Crawford, Nelson Antrim, Editor: *Poems of John Greenleaf Whittier,* Little Blue Books, No. 741.

Critic, The, Oct. 11 and 18, 1884, Dec. 13, 1884. Comments and letters about Mrs. Gustafson's poem on Bryant.

Critic, The, June, 1886. Letter of Whittier on religion.

Critic, The, Jan. 22 and 29, 1887. Comments on autograph-hunters who annoyed Whittier.

Cuyler, T. L.: *Recollections of a Long Life.* An Autobiography. 1902.

Davis, Rebecca B. H.: *Bits of Gossip.* 1904.

Demarest, A. J.: *Snow-Bound — Explanatory Notes,* Classics in the Grades. 1911.

Democratic Review, August, 1845. 'Whittier in Prose.'

Descriptive Catalogue of the Gluck Collection of the Buffalo Public Library. 1899. Letter from Whittier about the death of his sister to Theodore Tilton. (Tilton.)

Desmond, M. E.: 'The Story of Whittier's "Countess,"' *Catholic World*, Jan., 1901.

Dodge, H. Augusta: *Gail Hamilton's Life in Letters.* 2 vols., 1901.

Donaldson, Thomas: *Walt Whitman.* 1896.

Dwight, John S.: Review of *Supernaturalism in England*, in *Harbinger*, March 6, 1847.

Eastburn, Iola Kay: *Whittier's Relation to German Life and Thought.* (Thesis.) University of Pennsylvania. 1915.

Emerson, Ralph Waldo: *Journals*, edited by Edward Waldo Emerson and Waldo Emerson Forbes, 10 vols., 1909–1914. (Contemporary History.)

Emerson, Ralph Waldo: *Miscellanies.* 1883. (Contemporary History.)

Everest, Charles W.: *Poets of Connecticut*, 1843. (Contemporary Literary History.)

Farley, Harriet: *Operative's Reply*, Lowell, 1850.

Felton, Charles C.: Review of *Mogg Megone*, in *North American Review*, April, 1837.

Foerster, Norman: 'Whittier as Lover.' *The Freeman* (New York), Feb. 14, 1923.

Foerster, Norman: *Nature in American Literature.* 1923.

Follen, Eliza Lee, Editor: *The Works of Charles Follen, with a Memoir of his Life.* 5 vols. 1841.

Free State Rally and Texan Chain-Breaker. Vol. I. Nos. 1 and 3. Boston, Nov. 15 and 27, 1845. 'Address by Whittier.'

Fuess, Claude M.: *The Life of Caleb Cushing.* 2 vols., 1923.

Fuess, Claude M.: 'Whittier as a Politician,' *Haverhill Evening Gazette*, Dec. 18, 1926.

Garrison, Wendell Phillips and Garrison, Francis Jackson: *William Lloyd Garrison: The Story of his Life Told by his Children.* 4 vols., 1885–1889.

Godwin, Parke: *A Biography of William Cullen Bryant.* 2 vols., 1883.

Goodrich, Samuel G. (Peter Parley): *Recollections of a Lifetime.* 2 vols. 1856. (Contemporary Literary History.)

Gould, George M.: *Biographical Clinics*, Vol. II, 1904.

Gould, Laura and George M.: *Life and Letters of Edmund Clarence Stedman.* 2 vols., 1910.

Greenleaf, James Edward: *Genealogy of the Greenleaf Family.* 1896.

Greenslet, Ferris: *Thomas Bailey Aldrich.* 1908.

Greer, Walter: Letter to New York *Herald Tribune*, Nov. 10, 1927. Disproving the authenticity of the Barbara Frietchie story.

Griswold, Rufus W.: *The Female Poets of America.* 1848.

Griswold, Rufus W.: *Poets and Poetry of America.* 1842.

Hale, Sarah J.: *Flora's Interpreter*. 1832. (Anthology, containing uncollected poems.)

Hall, Thomas Cumming: *The Religious Background of American Culture*. 1930.

Hamilton, Gail: *Chips, Fragments and Vestiges*. Collected by H. Augusta Dodge. 1902.

Hamilton, Luther, Editor: *Memoirs, Speeches and Writings of Robert Rantoul, Jr*. 1854.

Hansen-Taylor, Marie, and Scudder, Horace E.: *Life and Letters of Bayard Taylor*. 2 vols., 1884.

Hart, Albert Bushnell: *Slavery and Abolition, 1831–1841*. 1906. Vol. 16 of *The American Nation: A History*.

Hawkins, Rev. Chauncey J.: *The Mind of Whittier*. 1904.

Hawthorne, Nathaniel: 'Supernaturalism in New England' in the *Literary World*, April 17, 1847.

Hayes, John Russell: *In Memory of Whittier*, a poem. Philadelphia: 1910.

Hearn, Lafcadio: *Japanese Letters*. 1910.

Hearn, Lafcadio: *Essays in American Literature*. Introduction by Albert Mordell, Hokuseido Press. Tokyo: 1929.

Herberg, Will: 'The Civil War in New Perspective,' *Modern Quarterly*, Summer, 1932. (Contemporary History.)

Higginson, Mary Thacher, Editor: *Letters and Journals of Thomas Wentworth Higginson, 1846–1906*. 1921.

History of Pennsylvania Hall, The. 1838.

Hoar, George F.: *Autobiography of Seventy Years*. 2 vols., 1903.

Hood, Edwin Paxton, Editor: *The Master Minds of the West* (n.d.). London.

Howe, Julia Ward: *At Sunset*. 1910. (Two poems on Whittier.)

Howe, M. A. De Wolfe, Editor: *Memories of a Hostess*. Drawn chiefly from the diaries of Mrs. James T. Fields, 1922.

Howe, Will D.: 'Whittier,' in *American Writers on American Literature*. Edited by John Macy, 1931.

Howells, Mildred, Editor: *Life and Letters of William Dean Howells*. 2 vols., 1928.

Howells, William Dean: Review of *Miriam, Atlantic Monthly*, Jan., 1870.

Howells, William Dean: Review of *Hazel Blossoms, Atlantic Monthly*, Jan., 1875.

Howells, William Dean: Review of *The Vision of Echard, Atlantic Monthly*, Dec., 1878.

Howells, William Dean: *Literary Friends and Acquaintances*. 1901.

Hughes, Sarah Forbes, Editor: *Letters and Recollections of John Murray Forbes*. 2 vols., 1899.

Hurd, Harry Elmore: 'Paradoxes in the Life and Poetry of John Greenleaf Whittier,' *Poetry Review* (London), 1926.

Hutchinson, J. W.: *Story of the Huchinsons.* 1896.

Independent, Feb. 8, 1849. Review of the 1849 edition of the poems.

Independent, Sept. 15, 1892, Whittier number.

Jones, Rufus M.: *The Later Periods of Quakerism.* 2 vols., 1921.

Jones, Rufus M.: *The Trail of Life in College.* 1929.

Keese, John, Editor: *Poetical Remains of Lucy Hooper*, with a Memoir. 1842.

Kettell, Samuel: *Specimens of American Poetry.* 3 vols., 1829.

Kreymborg, Alfred: *Our Singing Strength.* 1929.

Larcom, Lucy: *A New England Girlhood.* 1889.

Leggett, William: *A Collection of Political Writings.* 2 vols., 1840. (Edited by Theodore Sedgwick.)

Lewisohn, Ludwig: *Expression in America.* 1932.

Literary World, Dec. 1, 1877. Whittier number.

Literary World, Feb. 9, 1884; March 22, 1884. Whittier's uncollected poems on the Mexican War.

Livermore, Rev. S. T.: *Harriet Livermore.* 1884.

Longfellow, Samuel: *Life of Henry W. Longfellow.* 2 vols., 1886.

Lovejoy, J. C., *Memoir of Charles T. Torrey.* 1847.

Lowell, James Russell: Review of the 1849 edition of the poems in the *National Anti-Slavery Standard*, Dec. 21, 1848.

Lowell, James Russell: *A Fable for Critics.* 1848.

Lowell, James Russell: *The Function of the Poet*, edited by Albert Mordell, 1920.

Mabbott, Thomas O., and Pleadwell, Frank L.: *The Life and the Works of Edward Coate Pinkney.* 1926.

MacDonald, Greville: *George MacDonald and His Wife.* 1924.

Manners, Motley (pseudonym): *Parnassus in Pillory.* 1851. A satire in verse.

Marble, Annie Russell: 'Some Friendships of Whittier. With Letters Hitherto Unpublished,' *Dial*, Dec. 16, 1907.

Massachusetts Register, The. 1835.

May, Samuel J.: *Some Recollections of Our Anti-Slavery Conflict.* 1869.

May, Samuel J., Life of. (A composite work.) 1874.

Merrill, Joseph: *History of Amesbury.* 1880.

Miles, Rev. Henry A.: *Lowell as it Was and as it Is.* 1845.

More, Paul Elmer: 'Whittier the Poet,' *Shelburne Essays*, Third Series, 1907.

Morley, S. G.: Letter to the *Saturday Review* (N.Y.), Sept. 26, 1931. On Whittier's religious poetry.

Morse, J. T., *Life and Letters of Oliver Wendell Holmes*. 2 vols., 1896.

Moulton, Charles W., Editor: *The Library of American Criticism*. 8 vols., 1905

Moulton, L. C.: *In the Garden of Dreams*. 1890. (Poem to Whittier.)

Nason, Elias, and Russell, Thomas: *Life of Henry Wilson*. 1876.

National Era, Feb. 1, 1849. Review of the 1849 edition of the *Poems*, by J. G. P.

National Era, Oct. 3, 1850. Review of *Songs of Labor*.

Neal, John: *Wandering Recollections of a Somewhat Busy Life*. 1869.

Nevins, Allan: *The Evening Post*. 1922.

New Englander, January, 1848. Review of *Voices of Freedom* (by D. March).

New England Magazine, May, 1832. Review of *Moll Pitcher*.

New England Magazine, Sept., 1832. Review of Whittier's edition of Brainard's poems.

New England Magazine, Feb., 1893. Whittier's 'Countess' (by L.O.M.A.).

New England Quarterly, 1930. Letters from Lucy Larcom to John Greenleaf Whittier. Edited by Grace F. Shepard. (Seven letters from 1855 to 1892.)

New York Mirror, The, March 19, 1831. A two-page review of Whittier's 'Legends of New England' by George P. Morris.

New York Review, March, 1837. Review of *Mogg Megone*.

New York *Tribune*, Oct. 21, 1874. Review of *Hazel Blossoms* by Mrs. L. C. Moulton.

New York *Tribune*, Dec. 9, 1888. Review of the final collected edition of the *Poems*.

New York *Tribune*, Dec. 16, 1888. Interview with Whittier.

North American Review, Oct., 1843. Review of *Lays of My Home*.

Oberholtzer, Ellis P.: *The Literary History of Philadelphia*. 1906.

Orians, G. H. 'New England Witchcraft in Fiction,' *American Literature*, March, 1930.

Parrington, V. F.: *Main Currents in American Thought*. 2 vols., 1927.

Payne, William Morton: 'Whittier' in *The Cambridge History of American Literature*, Vol. III, 1918.

Penn Monthly, Nov., 1872. Review of the *Pennsylvania Pilgrim* (by the editor, Robert Ellis Thompson).

Perry, Bliss: *Park Street Papers*. 1908.

Perry, Bliss: 'John Greenleaf Whittier,' in *The Early Years of the Saturday Club*, 1855–1870, by Edward Waldo Emerson. 1918.

Phelps, Elizabeth Stuart: *Chapters from a Life.* 1896.

Phelps, William Lyon: 'A Noteworthy Letter of Whittier's,' *Century,* May, 1902.

Piatt, John James, Editor: *The Poems of George D. Prentice.* 1876.

Pickard, Samuel T.: 'A Merry Woman's Letters to a Quiet Poet,' *Ladies' Home Journal,* Dec., 1899, Jan., 1900. (Letters from Gail Hamilton.)

Pickard, Samuel T.: *Whittier as a Politician,* 1900. (Letters to Elizur Wright.)

Pierce, Edward L.: *Memoir and Letters of Charles Sumner.* 4 vols., 1877–1893.

Pierce, Frederick Clifton: *Batchelder, Batcheller Genealogy.* 1898.

Poe, Edgar Allan: *The Complete Works of.* The Virginia Edition. 17 vols., edited by J. A. Harrison, 1902.

Pomeroy, Sarah Gertrude: 'Whittier in Connecticut,' *Connecticut Magazine,* 1907, pp. 569–573.

Powell, Aaron M.: *Personal Reminiscences of the Anti-Slavery and other Reformers.* 1899.

Prince, J.: *A Wreath for St. Crispin, Being Sketches of Eminent Shoemakers.* 1848.

Proceedings of the Great Convention of the Friends of Freedom in the Eastern and Middle States, held in Boston, October 1, 2, and 3, 1845. Lowell, 1845. 'Address by Whittier.'

Proceedings of the New England Anti-Slavery Society Convention, held at Boston, May 24–26, 1836.

Proceedings of the Pennsylvania Convention at Harrisburg on the 31st of January and 1st, 2nd, 3rd of February, 1837. (Pennsylvania Anti-Slavery Society.)

Proceedings at the Presentation of a Portrait of John Greenleaf Whittier to Friends' School, Providence, R.I. Tenth Month, 24th, 1884. Cambridge, 1885.

Proctor, Edna Dean: *Complete Poetical Works.* Edited by Grace Ware van Praag and David Gould Proctor. 1925.

Putnam's Monthly, July, 1856. Review of *Panorama.*

Quarterly Anti-Slavery Magazine, July, 1837. (Edited by Elizur Wright.) Review of 1837 edition of *Poems.*

Quint, Rev. Alonzo H.: 'The Hussey Ancestry of the Poet Whittier,' in *New England Historical and Genealogical Register,* July, 1896.

Rantoul, R. S.: 'Some Personal Reminiscences of the Poet Whittier,' *Historical Collections of the Essex Institute,* April, 1901.

Reports of the American Anti-Slavery Society.

Reports of the Massachusetts Anti-Slavery Society.

Reports of the New England Anti-Slavery Society. 1833–1836

Rice, S. S.: *Edgar Allan Poe: A Memorial Volume.* 1877.

Richards, Laura E., and Elliott, Maud Howe, assisted by Hall, Florence Howe: *Julia Ward Howe, 1819–1910.* 2 vols., 1916.

Richards, Laura E., Editor: *Letters and Journals of Samuel Gridley Howe.* 2 vols., 1906.

Richards, Thomas C.: 'A Crucial Year for the Quaker Poet,' in the *Boston Transcript,* Feb. 28, 1931.

Robinson, Harriet Hanson: *Loom and Spindle, or Life Among the Early Mill Girls.* 1898.

Rogers, Nathaniel P.: *The Newspaper Writings of.* 1847.

Sanborn, Frank B.: 'Whittier as Man, Poet, and Reformer,' in the *Bibliotheca Sacra.* 1907.

Sanborn, Frank B.: *Recollections of Seventy Years.* 2 vols., 1909.

Sanborn, Kate: *Memories and Anecdotes.* 1915.

Sargent, Mrs. John T. (Editor): *Sketches and Reminiscences of the Radical Club.* 1880.

Scharf, J. T., and Westcott, T.: *History of Philadelphia.* 3 vols., 1884.

Schurz, Carl: *Reminiscences of.* 3 vols., 1907.

Scudder, Horace E.: *Life of James Russell Lowell.* 2 vols., 1901.

Sears, Lorenzo: *Wendell Phillips.* 1909.

Sinclair, Upton: *Mammonart.* 1925.

Smedley, R. C.: *History of the Underground Railroad.* 1883.

Smith, Gerrit: *Constitutional Argument.* 1844.

Stanton, Henry B.: *Random Recollections.* 1887.

Stanton, Theodore, and Blatch, Harriet Stanton, Editors: *Elizabeth Stanton Cady as Revealed in her Letters, Diary and Reminiscences.* 2 vols., 1922.

Statue of John P. Hale, The, presented to the State of New Hampshire, by W. E. Chandler: Account of the unveiling ceremonies, August 3, 1892. 1892.

Stearns, Frank Preston: *The Life and Public Services of George Luther Stearns.* 1907.

Stedman, Edmund Clarence: *Poets of America.* 1885.

Stevens, James Stacy: *Whittier's Use of the Bible.* University of Maine. 1930.

Stillman, William J.: *The Autobiography of a Journalist.* 2 vols., 1901.

Stoddard, Richard H.: *Recollections Personal and Literary.* 1903.

Strong, Augustus Hopkins: *American Poets and Their Theology.* 1916.

Swett, Lucia Gray: *John Ruskin's Letters to Francesca and Memoirs of the Alexanders.* 1931.

Tapley, Harriet S.: 'John Greenleaf Whittier Manuscripts. The Oak Knoll Collection.' *Historical Collections of the Essex Institute,* April, 1931.

Tappan, Lewis: *Life of Arthur Tappan*. 1870.

Thaxter, Celia: *Letters of*. Edited by her Friends A. F. and R. L., 1895.

Thirty-Sixth and Final Annual Report, Philadelphia Female Anti-Slavery Society, April, 1870.

Thoreau, Henry D.: *Miscellanies*. 1894. (Contemporary History.)

Ticknor, Caroline: *Poe's Helen*. 1916.

Tiffany, Nina Moore: *Samuel E. Sewall*. 1898.

Traubel, Horace: *With Whitman in Camden*. 3 vols., 1906–1914.

Trent, W. P., and Erskine, John: *Great American Writers*. 1912.

Trial of Reuben Crandall, charged with publishing seditious and incendiary papers, etc. By a Member of the Bar. Washington, 1836. (There is also a pamphlet with a New York imprint.

Trumbull, J. H.: *Memorial History of Hartford County, 1633–1844*. 2 vols., 1886.

Turner, Lorenzo Dow: *Anti-Slavery Sentiment in American Literature Prior to 1865*. 1929.

Unity, Dec. 15, 1892. Chicago. Whittier Memorial Number.

Untermeyer, Louis: *American Poetry to Whitman*. 1931.

Wasson, D. A.: 'Whittier,' *Atlantic Monthly*, March, 1864.

Whiting, Lilian: *Louise Chandler Moulton*. 1910.

Whitman, Walt: *Complete Prose Works*. 1892.

Whipple, Edwin P.: *Essays and Reviews*. 1850.

Whittier, D. B.: *Genealogy of Two Branches of the Whittier Family, 1620–1873*. 1873.

Wilson, Henry: *History of the Rise and Fall of the Slave Power in America*. 3 vols., 1872–1877.

Winthrop, Robert C., Jr.: *Memoir of R. C. Winthrop*. 1897.

Woodberry, George E.: *Makers of Literature*. 1900.

INDEX